LET ME TELL YOU HOW I REALLY FEEL ... WITH A VENGEANCE

"More of the Best of Laura Wagner's Book Reviews from Classic Images."

BY LAURA WAGNER

Foreword by Eve Golden

LET ME TELL YOU HOW I REALLY FEEL...WITH A VENGEANCE

Published in the USA by:
BearManor Media
1317 Edgewater Dr #110
Orlando, FL 32804
www.bearmanormedia.com

Perfect ISBN 979-8-88771-542-1
Case ISBN 979-8-88771-543-8
BearManor Media, Orlando, Florida
Printed in the United States of America
Book design by Robbie Adkins, www.adkinsconsult.com

"If you can't annoy somebody with what you
write, I think there's little point in writing."
—Kingsley Amis

"You're a bitter little lady."
"It's a bitter little world."
—*Hollow Triumph* (1948)

To the fearless Bob King, who took a huge chance on me almost 30 years ago in the pages of *Classic Images* and *Films of the Golden Age*. He continues to inspire me and I am proud to call him my friend.

And to the wonderful Peggy Biller, one of my most trusted and cherished friends, who made it all possible.

Table of Contents

Foreword
by Eve Golden

"YOU'RE TOO SOFT. I don't think you could stand up to a writer and say, 'Your work is no good,'" veteran editor Amanda Farrow told neophyte Caroline Bender in *The Best of Everything* (1959). "I don't think you've got the guts."

Laura Wagner does have the guts, and would make Amanda Farrow proud. I am slightly terrified of Laura, though we have been friends for many years and she has always been kind to my own books. Because I know that if my work did not meet her high standards, she would give it to me with both barrels. I respect Laura and trust her opinion, as she has no patience for bad writing, bad editing, bad cover art, or even bad book titles. On the other hand, as a fan of old movies and good books, she is enthusiastic about what she does like, and a writer whose work she formerly blasted will get a rave review upon improvement.

Enclosed herein you will find great suggestions of books to buy, and books to avoid. You will also be highly entertained by Laura's writing, which I dare to compare with Dorothy Parker's book reviews (Mrs. Parker's bread-and-butter work as a theater and book reviewer has dated much better than her stories and poetry). Laura is tough, but she is also funny, knowledgeable, and fair—she is just as happy to recommend a book as she is to slice it into bits. I don't always agree with her, but I always respect her opinion. And I have thoroughly enjoyed her own books (two previous volumes of book reviews, a biography of Anne Francis, and the re-readable *Hollywood's Hard-Luck Ladies: 23 Actresses Who Suffered Early Deaths, Accidents, Missteps, Illnesses and Tragedies*—I eagerly await the male sequel).

So set aside a pad and pencil to make "buy this!" and "avoid this!" notes, and settle in for an enjoyable read.

Eve Golden

Eve Golden is the author of eight show business biographies, most recently of Jayne Mansfield and Lupe Velez.

Introduction

TWO THOUSAND TWENTY-FOUR marks my 23rd year writing book reviews for the print-only publication *Classic Images*. Twenty-three years of death threats, hate mail, near-lawsuits, some nice mail, and some headaches. It's hard to believe it's been that long, but here I am still plugging away. True, my output has slowed, but the number of books I get has dwindled considerably. Publishers who used to send me mounds of books, now only send a few. I still have more than I can handle, though. Adding to the burden, I have now become contributing editor for both *Classic Images* and *Films of the Golden Age*—a job I love.

Unlike some so-called reviewers, I actually read every book, every word, cover to cover, with a handful of exceptions. While some book reviewers pen nothing but positive critiques in order to "help" other writers, I see no point in that. Someone once told me that as an author myself, I "owe" it to other writers to give them raves; if I give a bad review, I am a traitor. How ridiculous. It's better to be honest than to write insincere flattery which will do no good for the writer or the reader. As for myself, I feel that genuine criticism of my writing helps me improve. I will always give an honest assessment of a book—and that includes the books of friends. I don't like it when I send something to a friend to critique and they immediately write back, "It's great!" Um, no, it's not. I would rather have helpful criticism than praise. Too often, people dread the consequences of honesty. Sorry, but I want honesty, even brutal honesty, about what I write. I am especially indebted to my *Killer Tomatoes: Fifteen Tough Film Dames* co-writer Ray Hagen. I remember when I first started writing book reviews. He went through one of my columns and circled all my exclamation points—there was a ton of them. He shamed me into breaking that bad habit. His sharp comments on my writing, and his influence on how I see movies and actors, have made me a better writer. Thanks, Ray!!

I've also heard that I shouldn't review bad books because doing so only gives them undeserved publicity. But if I don't point out the mistakes and gossip-reported-as-fact, who will? Too many movie fans take everything they read as gospel. A simple comment can snowball into a "fact," even if it is phony. I see this a lot on Facebook. I once saw a photo of Guy Madison with a serviceman. The comments were crude, many assuming there was something romantic going on between them. I wrote, "That's his *brother!*" Nevertheless, the comments continued and one of the people on the thread posted the photo on his Timeline and embellished the lie by labeling this post-war photo: "Guy Madison and his boy-friend during the war." If you look at fan magazines layouts from the 1930s, '40s and '50s, the actors are often put into poses that today some may presume to be suggestive or "gay." They weren't thinking about that back then; they were innocent poses for the camera—but try telling that to people who want to believe lies.

Which brings me to my bad rep. I have been called homophobic or a prude simply because I have crusaded these past 23 years against trash tomes. If so-and-so is gay, he must have had sex with . . . . Or, if so-and-so is straight, he must have had sex with... Then these "authors" make up a sex scene detailing what they *think* went on between these actors. I'm sorry, but I find this pointless and insulting to the reader. What happened to film scholarship? I am not against warts-and-all biographies, but I rebel against fantasy books disguised as serious non-fiction. Fortunately for truth seekers, these fake biographers often get their supporting facts wrong—sometimes ridiculously wrong. As long as I am here as book reviewer, I will tear these books apart.

I have written about actors I am pretty sure were gay but since I have no proof, I leave their orientation out of the story. I simply refuse to make up stories in order to assert an actor's orientation. I have been told that I have never mentioned in one of my profiles that an actor is gay, but that is false. I have done profiles on William Eythe and Thomas Beck, to name just two, because I had facts to back up my story.

I pay a price for being truthful. Around 2003, when I reviewed an awful Bogart book, I tried to spare my readers by not reprinting a bogus story. I said that the "author" put a "perverted spin" on an existing story. Of course, someone on a message board posted, "You have to go far these days to find somebody backward enough to refer to gay people as 'perverted,' but if that's your dish of tea, then Wagner's your gal." Actually, I was referring to a fake story about Ann Dvorak and Bogart. In this case, instead of merely dancing with Bogart (as she did with George Raft in the original story), Dvorak did a certain something to him as they moved around the dance floor.

First and foremost, I want facts—fully supported and not conjured up by someone trying to sell his books. Then there are the authors who just can't write, have bad attitudes, and simply don't know their movies. All too often they pad their books with laborious plot descriptions—something that should be outlawed.

Yet, despite all this, I am accused of being the only person to pan a certain book. I often hear the complaint, "But everyone else loved it!," which is then followed by accusations of me being jealous of the author, being mentally unstable(!) or of indulging in a personal attack. Funny thing about these so-called "personal attacks": They are always answered by personally attacking me!

I've actually had writers contact me, pestering me to review their books. Some of them bombard me with emails. One son of an actor desperately wanted me to review his book. When I finally did and it wasn't a particularly good writeup, he hit the roof: "Why did she review it?" Never mind that he had hounded me. This has happened quite a few times. Many authors feel that I should think only of them, not realizing or caring that I have other books to read. And other things to do and write myself.

Ah, but that's the thing: They truly don't want me to actually read their book. They think I should simply read the publicity and write from that. Some have wanted me to list upcoming books, as if my column was a "Coming Soon" they can use as a selling tool.

Permit me to describe an interaction with one particular writer. In his mind, it was taking too long for me to get to his book (600-plus pages of small print, a month's worth of reading). He wrote on Facebook, "When I read your reviews in *Classic Images*, usually very long evaluations of only one or two books, I wonder why you couldn't review several books with a single paragraph each and thus reduce your backlog." My taking the time to tell *CI* readers about the value (or anti-value) of a book is obviously something this guy doesn't care about. Lest you think he was truly concerned about my backlog; he was actually thinking only of his own book and his desire to unload his surplus copies. And it was apparent that he was taking it for granted that I was going to give it a good review. This bit of advice from him actually made me angry: "Read a few sample pages and base your evaluation on that." He, too, is a book reviewer and boasted that he must have reviewed 500 books or more: "I would read a couple of sample chapters because that was all that time allowed. I'm sure I was able to get a good handle on the author's research and ability from that."

How much value would there be in my reviews if I simply read a few pages? How helpful would that be to the readers of *Classic Images* if I did that?

Many writers don't want an honest assessment. They want someone to help them sell their book, whether it is good or not. Unfortunately, I know reviewers like this who think they're doing their fellow authors a favor. I will not be joining them. The way I write my column is the way I enjoy writing my column, and I'm not about to change my approach in order to fatten the wallets of others. I've done my column the way I want for years. I am not about to give in to those who think that my role on this Earth is to be their unpaid publicist.

So, here I am, trying to stand tall in a book industry that actually thrives on gossip and misinformation. I have made it my mission to attack the Darwin Porters and David Brets of the publishing world. I can only assure readers of *Classic Images* that I will always give my honest opinion as long as I am here.

Acknowledgments

I would like to thank the following individuals for their help, encouragement and friendship: Lisa Burks, Barbara Feldon, the late Sandra Grabman, Ray Hagen, the late Frances Ingram, Leonard Maltin, the late Doug McClelland, Ben Ohmart, James Robert Parish, Carol Peterson, the late Ruth Prigozy, Christina Rice, Janet Roitz, Robert Tevis, Barry Virshbo, Archie Waugh and Tom Weaver.

A screenwriter, producer, and novelist, Andrew J. Fenady (1928-2020) could do it all. He was a vivid writer, able to recount rousing battles and tender love scenes with equal ease. His was a special gift of storytelling and he completely enveloped the reader into his stories of the Old West. A.J. was a wonderful friend and I loved listening to his tales of working with Chuck Connors, Nick Adams, John Wayne and others. Gary Kent (1933-2023), actor and stuntman, was another great pal of mine and always encouraging. Not long before he died, he wrote me, "Laura, you have the patience of Job, and the cajones of Kid Rock...in fact, you rock!"

I love my remarkable nephews, Jake and Luke Vichnis, more than I can say, and I am very proud of their varied accomplishments. Thanks, too, to my awesome brother Tom, who I surely do not deserve. I am also blessed to have two sisters, Debbie and Patty, who make my life interesting. To say the least. Debbie's husband Larry deserves special mention; I am blessed to have him as another brother. I have cherished memories of my mother Fran Wagner and my Aunt Charlotte, and always will. Since I met Jackie Jones, my best friend and comrade in film, she has always encouraged me and been unfailing in her loyalty. And to the fabulous Eve Golden, who gave me such a wonderful foreword. To be mentioned in the same breath as Joan Crawford overwhelms me!

Sad to say, some of the writers whose work is covered in this book have passed away in recent years. Jeff Gordon (1954-2020) was an author extraordinaire, film historian and archivist. For his fabulous book *Foxy Lady: The Authorized Biography of Lynn Bari*, he interviewed Bari extensively. The volume was a labor of love and I am so glad he was able to see it published. Jeff was an enthusiastic movie buff and collector and he particularly loved 20th Century–Fox films. Thorough in his research and a conscientious writer, he left us with many wonderful articles in *Classic Images* and *Films of the Golden Age*.

Edwin M. Bradley (1958-2022) was McFarland's resident movie musical expert, authoring *The First Hollywood Musicals: A Critical Filmography of 171 Features, 1927-32* (1996), *The First Hollywood Sound Shorts, 1926-31* (2005), *Unsung Hollywood Musicals of the Golden Era: 50 Overlooked Films and Their Stars, 1929-39* (2016) and *Hollywood Musicals You Missed: 70 Noteworthy Films from the 1930s* (2020). In his last two books, he focused on actor-singers who never got their due—an approach I wholeheartedly approve of.

Published in 2014, *Peg Entwistle and the Hollywood Sign Suicide: A Biography* was James Zeruk Jr.'s (1961-2021) first—and last—book. He was an outstanding writer and researcher; his next project was to be a biography on Our Gang member Carl "Alfalfa" Switzer. How sad that the talent James showed in Peg Entwistle was stifled. I got the best response from any author from James. He wrote on social media:

> Author and film historian Laura Wagner of *Classic Images* is one of the most respected—and certainly feared—book

reviewers going. Her negative reviews are legend and hysterical. When my Peg Entwistle biography was released by McFarland & Co., back in 2014, I was nervous, for I knew she might one day review it. Well, that day has arrived in this July's issue of *Classic Images*!

Whew! I think she liked it!

I was trembling as I read it, waiting for the guillotine blade to drop. But I was spared and am deeply moved. As a gesture, I sneaked up to the Hollywood sign and read Ms. Wagner's review aloud as I stood near the H, where Peg entered the next world in 1932.

I hadn't been that close to it since 2014, when the book was released. But I've never read a review there before this, and I shall not do so again. Thank you, Laura Wagner, for your taking the time to not only read the book, but for having the insight into what I was trying to do and say for Peg. And THANKS OODLES for the wonderful review!

The dedicatees of this book, editor Bob King and my friend Peggy Biller, deserve more than a mere thank you. They made me the film historian I've always wanted to be.

The Reviews

Alan LeMay: A Biography of the Author of *The Searchers*
by Dan LeMay

Alan LeMay: A Biography of the Author of The Searchers by Dan LeMay (McFarland) is a volume that took me completely off guard. What a great read this turned out to be! I have to admit that I have never given much thought to Alan LeMay (1899-1964). He's just never been on my radar. I like *The Searchers*, of course, but never read the book. This, I realize now, was a mistake.

Author Dan LeMay, son of Alan, is a writer of skill, something he obviously inherited from his father. His background on his family, particularly of his grandmother's frontier life, is amazing, described with a pictorial vividness. (My mom would have loved this; she was always fascinated by life in the wilds. Her favorite book was *Betty Zane: Stories of the Ohio Frontier* [1903] by Zane Grey, based upon diaries kept by his ancestor. When I was growing up, she talked a great deal about this wonderful book.) Dan is his family's archivist, and he uses the wealth of material his family left him and his own memories of growing up to give us a terrific description not only of the grueling day-to-day existence, insecurities, and temptations of a pulp, magazine, and book writer, but also an insider's look at Hollywood in the 1940s and '50s.

Alan LeMay wrote long letters to his parents detailing his professional life, his fears, his struggles, and his work with publishers and Hollywood bigwigs.

In the latter category was Cecil B. DeMille, whom LeMay characterizes to his father as the "expert harasser of our time." Alan worked on the screenplays for *North West Mounted Police, Reap the Wild Wind, The Story of Dr. Wassell, The Adventures of Mark Twain, San Antonio, Cheyenne, Gunfighters, Tap Roots, The Walking Hills, The Sundowners, Rocky Mountain, High Lonesome* (which he also directed), *Quebec, I Dream of Jeanie, Blackbeard, the Pirate, Flight Nurse,* and *The Vanishing American.* (Unfortunately, the author dismisses the latter and tells us nothing. That is a movie I want to know more about. He, like his father, is status-conscious, so a little B movie isn't going to warrant much consideration.) There were also screenplays he did that went nowhere, notably *Calamity Jane,* which was intended for Ann Sheridan. He also wrote the source novels for the movies *Along Came Jones, The Searchers,* and *The Unforgiven.*

LeMay's letters are newsy and revealing of the inner workings of these movie projects. This is one of those books that does not require you to be familiar with the subject to enjoy it. All classic Hollywood fans will find something here. The troubles on the set of *High Lonesome* paint an especially revealing picture of what some filmmakers went through back then.

The author's comparisons of book vs. screenplay for both *The Searchers* and *The Unforgiven* are well done and interesting. He relates his father's thoughts, too, about the screen adaptations.

It's nice to see, in 2016, new information revealed about these classics. The photos are not numerous, but all are fabulous. Rare images like these totally make my day. This book is a treat. Give it a read. Not only will you learn more about the talented Alan LeMay, but you will gain new insight into some of your favorite movies. This is a great job all around.

Alan Sues: A Funny Man
by Michael Gregg Michaud

At first, I thought the title **Alan Sues: A Funny Man** by Michael Gregg Michaud (BearManor) was not only lame, but a bit pretentious. But, after reading this, I can't think of a better or more appropriate name.

Actor Alan Sues (1926-2011) was best known for his campy stint on TV's groundbreaking comedy series *Rowan & Martin's Laugh-In* (1968–73), particularly playing the character of Big Al the sportscaster. Of course, there was much more to Sues, but he was always the type of underappreciated performer who rarely got his due.

This is the first biography about him, and thankfully an excellent one, written by someone who was a close friend and interviewed him. In fact, this almost reads as an autobiography, so extensively does Michaud quote Sues. The author also interviewed other friends and colleagues, as well as providing his own insights into Sues' complicated psyche, to paint a balanced picture of the man. There is a rollercoaster of emotions going on in this bio.

While the author was friends with Sues, this is not a whitewash—quite the contrary. At times the narrative, while never mean, is brutal. Sues, like many comedians, had a lot of unhappiness in his life and suffered from addiction (alcohol, overeating). Much of this stemmed from his family and his sexuality. While he grew up in affluence, his parents alternated between being emotionally distant to overly critical. Somehow, Sues found humor and a will to survive.

Most of his life Sues wrestled with his homosexuality. For about five years in the '50s he was married and the author interviewed his wife (and stage partner) about their relationship. Sues' attitude loosened a bit when he met female impersonator Charles Pierce, who took him to gay bars. ("Charles led me astray," Alan said, "but he did it with style. And a sequined turban.") One of the saddest quotes from Sues: "You could PLAY gay if it was funny and NOT sexual, but you couldn't BE gay." This is a running theme.

During World War II, he served in the Army, and there is a hilarious story about how a mix-up sent him to the wrong unit—they thought he was African American!

Sues always had a wild sense of humor and that comes through loud and clear in this volume. I love that he wrote "Fuck you" on the bottom of his shoes to distract his tennis opponents.

The show business stories are pure gold. The orange hair dye story and his audition for the road company of *Mister Roberts* is classic. As is the one where he put raw egg whites on his face to look younger for an audition but ended up resembling a "six-foot tall Spanky McFarland" with extremely tight, unmovable facial skin.

His appearance on TV's *The Dating Game* resulted in a win for Sues, but when they went out to a restaurant on their date, he ended up loudly accusing her of peeing on his expensive shoes (she didn't, of course) and embarrassing the poor girl!

For fans of *Rowan & Martin's Laugh-In*, there's a lot of behind-the-scenes intrigue—some fun, some definitely not. The author interviewed cast members, including Ruth Buzzi and Jo Anne Worley. The latter made me laugh out loud with her statement that when Sues dressed in drag to imitate her, "he looked better than me." The following page has a priceless photo showing this moment and it's my favorite in the whole book.

Marvelous stories abound about the different actors and actresses he worked with on screen and in the theater. When he tried to upstage Miriam Hopkins during a play, she slapped him backstage. ("My teeth clattered. I didn't try it twice.") Former silent actress Enid Markey bit his hand so hard during a dance number, "it drew blood. And I thought, gee, this show business stuff is really rough." He had a supporting part in Broadway's *Tea and Sympathy* with Deborah Kerr-John Kerr and then Joan Fontaine-Anthony Perkins and there are some great tales from those productions. His recollection of an exchange backstage between Fontaine ("She was a genuine broad") and her sister Olivia de Havilland is superb.

He recalls that Mickey Rooney and Shelley Winters almost got into a fistfight—I would've paid to see that—while recording their voices for Rankin/Bass' Christmas special *Rudolph and Frosty's Christmas in July* (1979). Speaking of Rooney, my favorite story has to do with the outburst he directs toward Sues when they meet up years later.

Sues did a lot of theater, mostly stock, which surprised me a bit. Some venues weren't the best and his descriptions of these theaters are fun, especially the one with several mousetraps on stage. About his run in the musical play *Singin' in the Rain*: "This was a genuine road tour. I'm not sure I realized what I had gotten myself into. We traveled like a band of gypsies—without their flashy fashion sense."

You kinda feel bad laughing at his experience hosting the Macy's Thanksgiving Day Parade pre-parade show. The way he tells of the mishaps, it's uproarious, but it was ultimately very upsetting to him. Because of this, I won't look at Mason Reese the same way again. Horrifying and funny. Another side-splitting story about a child actor: He worked with Soleil Moon Frye on TV's *Punky Brewster* and she was so obnoxious, he wanted to "kick her like a football out the door."

Sues dishes about Deborah Kerr, Paul Lynde, Dom DeLuise, Vincent Price and his wife Coral Browne, James Coco, Janis Paige (wonderful), Leonard Nimoy, etc.

There are a few boo-boos here and there (*The Many **Lives** of Dobie Gillis* instead of *Loves*, for instance), but nothing to truly distract from the book's enjoyment.

His ex-wife pretty much sums Sues up: "I think being homosexual was ... a big problem for him. In a way, he was ashamed of himself, and he was also on the defensive at the same time. He was very conflicted. It's a shame because he was so talented. So creative and artistic. He was incredibly funny. That's what I fell for, his sense of humor. He was a fabulous story-teller, and could take over a room. And no matter how much people laughed, he never thought he was good enough."

Alan Sues: A Funny Man is more than good enough. It's well-written, very funny, poignant and insightful. Sues' voice is everywhere, commenting on all aspects of his life. Michaud is to be commended for writing this and helping us understand and appreciate Sues better. One of the most enjoyable, can't-put-it-down books I have read.

Ann Dvorak: Hollywood's Forgotten Rebel by Christina Rice/ The Inseparables: Images of Ann Dvorak & Leslie Fenton's 1932 Honeymoon from Their Personal Scrapbook by Christina Rice

In the 21st century, the pool of writers covering Classic Hollywood gets shallower by the year, so chances are that we occasionally swim in and out of each other's lanes. I don't usually review books by people I know, but when I do, I try to be as honest as possible. Being my friend does not guarantee a good review, however. On several occasions I have panned a pal's book. For many years I was friendly with actress Virginia Mayo. After I read her autobiography, I called her and told her that I didn't like it, and I felt uneasy about giving her a bad review. She was totally okay with it: "Do what you have to do. Be honest." She assured me she wouldn't be mad, and she wasn't. She even sent me an autographed copy. Another friend was less gracious, and he had no reason to be. I gave him a fantastic review, but I mentioned a few flaws, all minor. He never spoke to me again, telling a mutual friend that I had "lied" to him about loving his book. You cannot please some people.

So, full disclosure here: I am friends with Christina Rice, author of **Ann Dvorak: Hollywood's Forgotten Rebel** (University Press of Kentucky). We first became acquainted around 2003 when I was working on my Dvorak chapter in *Killer Tomatoes: Fifteen Tough Film Dames*. She had been researching Dvorak for a while and very kindly furnished me with information. As I researched

Ann, I found out what Christina knew all too well: This lady was an enigma, very little was written about her, and personal info was almost non-existent. Christina was continually frustrated by what wasn't available; there was no family to consult, no donated personal effects, and every time Christina tried to interview a surviving co-worker, she got the same response: Ann was professional and lovely. My chapter was meager, more of a tribute to a great actress, but I was so lucky Christina shared with me what she had at that time.

For the next few years, I was privy to Christina's efforts to gather more material on Dvorak for her book. It was discouraging, but she admirably forged ahead. A total of 15 years was spent bringing Ann's story to light.

To say I am proud of and astonished at the result is an understatement. Because of my own fruitless digging, I can really appreciate what it took to compile *Ann Dvorak: Hollywood's Forgotten Rebel*. Holes in her story I could never surmount were filled in by Christina. She was able to uncover some of Ann's letters and journals, which give us an idea of Ann's personality and the struggles she went through.

Dvorak has always been revered by those who appreciate her intense acting. She was absolutely amazing in the original *Scarface*, the pre-Code classic *Three on a Match*, and, my personal favorite, *The Strange Love of Molly Louvain*. In 1932, at the cusp of stardom, she decided to chuck it all and go on an eight-month honeymoon with husband Leslie Fenton. It destroyed her momentum and caused a lot of friction between her and Warner Brothers. She was never able to fully capitalize on her strong beginning and early promise. She was pretty much punished for her insubordination and assigned lesser parts by the studio, although she was always able to give something extra to the smallish and/or supporting roles she did play (for example, in *Heat Lightning*). Dvorak continued to turn in amazing vignettes in such later movies as *Our Very Own* and *A Life of Her Own*, not to mention the lead in *I Was an American Spy* and a riveting supporting job in *The Secret of Convict*

Lake. She's always been one of my top favorites. As a person, however, she was a mystery. Little was known about her except a few short chapters in film books, filled mostly with misinformation, and a couple of articles by other writers.

When researching Dvorak, I naïvely thought of Leslie Fenton as a villain. What little I knew of him suggested a controlling nature. And while this is partly true, Christina did not fall in the same trap as I did by portraying him as a one-dimensional figure; she was able to find something a little more poignant about their relationship and I began to actually like him and not see him solely as the one who ruined her budding career. A particularly interesting aspect that Christina explores is Ann's relationship with her mother, actress Anna Lehr. This, above all of Dvorak's associations, remained her most fractious and complex.

This is Christina's first book but the writing is better than that of most seasoned authors. Her sentences flow, her language is good, and she's straight to the point, never overdoing it. Her descriptions of Dvorak's films do not rely on plot summaries; instead, we get good background and pithy reviews of performances.

We have always been led to believe that Bette Davis and Olivia de Havilland were the first female stars to take on Warners, but before both of them, Dvorak rebelled and took the company to court. The back-and-forth between Ann and Warner Brothers makes for vivid, fascinating reading. There are two things going on, though: First, you simply can't understand why the studio is treating such a great actress so badly, but you can't help thinking that Dvorak was cutting her own throat—she should have waited to make her move. Davis' fights with the studio were calculated and ultimately successful, while Dvorak's were based purely on impulse and not well thought out. The realization that Ann threw her career away becomes painfully obvious in these pages.

Christina's voice throughout is realistic. She's not taking the approach of two Carole Landis books I've read that blame their subject's lack of fame on other people. Dvorak was the maker of her own career troubles; Christina knows this, and there's no excuses or pointing of fingers. I was very impressed by her ability to at once appreciate Dvorak but tell it like it was. Her approach should be a model for all writers out there.

One of the great mysteries of Dvorak's life was her time spent in London during World War II. This was probably my favorite part of the book, as I marveled at the author's uncovering of her movements at this time. Christina cuts through what was real and what was fan magazine-manufactured. This also applies to the later years of Dvorak's life in Hawaii in the 1970s. Until now, what little we thought we knew came from an exaggerated *National Enquirer* article. As sad as her life was, it's nice to finally know the truth. Christina was also able to shine a light on Ann's shadowy third husband Nick Wade, and it's not pretty. The author is the first to write about Ann's relationship with Wade. Material that Christina discovered at the proverbial 11th hour gave her a lot of valuable insights, and we are able to see Dvorak actually standing up for herself and finally being able to make a life for herself after years of being pretty much controlled by her mother and husbands.

This is simply a great book. No other author could have written this amazing story quite like Christina Rice. Thanks to her hard work and diligence, Dvorak has finally been given her due.

A gorgeous 88-page book, **The Inseparables: Images of Ann Dvorak & Leslie Fenton's 1932 Honeymoon from Their Personal Scrapbook** by Christina Rice (www.amazon.com), is a perfect companion to Rice's biography, *Ann Dvorak: Hollywood's Forgotten Rebel*. These rare, never-before-seen photos are accompanied by quotes by Dvorak from personal letters and interviews at the time. A treasure trove, to be sure, and an intimate glance back at an eight-month honeymoon trip Dvorak would recall as containing some of her happiest moments. She and her groom, actor Leslie Fenton, visited Paris, Berlin, Egypt, Rome, St. Moritz, and the Baltic Islands. Being a hardcore Dvorak fan, I absolutely adored this personal look into her private life.

Anne Bancroft: A Life
by Douglass K. Daniel

Douglass K. Daniel's biography, **Anne Bancroft: A Life** (University Press of Kentucky), is an intelligent, enlightening book about one of our most gifted actresses. Daniel doesn't merely give us a rundown of Bancroft's life and career or tell plots. He offers insights, allowing us a look behind her process as an actress, delving into how she transformed herself into her characters, how she studied for them, how she brought them to life. I never knew what a strain her acting put on her, emotionally and physically, and how this eventually led her to be very picky about what roles she would accept. (Her good judgment kept her out of *Myra Breckinridge*, *Mame* and *Mommie Dearest*.) The Actors Studio's Gene Frankel once warned his students that "talent is not enough—you must have courage, the courage to travel to those dimly lit places where the talent tells you to go." This quote would have surely fit Bancroft.

The period between her first stab at Hollywood in the 1950s, when she was not getting projects worthy of her, and her emergence as a serious theater actress with *Two for the Seesaw* (1958), is really well done. Not only does this contribute to our understanding of her as a performer, but as a person, as Daniel vividly gives us a peek into her temperament.

While the author was not able to interview Bancroft's widower Mel Brooks or their son, he makes up for that by talking with numerous friends and co-workers. This adds immeasurably to the story. It is especially valuable when it comes to her stage plays, which I believe are harder to research. Each is thoroughly discussed. The behind-the-scenes stories (and problems) relating to *Two for the Seesaw* and *The Miracle Worker* (play and movie) are marvelous. I will never look at *Seesaw* co-star Henry Fonda the same way again.

The movies, too, get great coverage. I really enjoyed reading about the making of *The Graduate* (1967) and *The Turning Point* (1977);

the latter has a story about how Bancroft and Shirley MacLaine's "fight" scene came about. It's content like this that really elevate biographies.

Bancroft's sense of humor really bursts through these pages. There's a story about how she had the opportunity to "flex her star muscle" during a stage rehearsal. There was no air conditioning and everyone was miserable; Bancroft told the producers to fix the situation and walked out until they supplied a cooler atmosphere. Workmen had labored all night to put in an air conditioning unit and they asked if "they could meet the star of *The Graduate.*" Actor Ray Stewart said to her afterwards, "Well, that's the least you could do." Bancroft responded, "Well, I could have fucked all of 'em."

There's a quote from Frank Langella about when they did *A Cry of Players* (1968). He protested when producers put his name first in the billing over hers; he didn't feel he deserved it, considering she was more accomplished. "That's the way it's gonna be, Frankie," she told him as she brushed her hair and put on her makeup. "You got the bigger hand last night. It's your show, and I'm gonna look like the gracious star giving it up to the new guy. Now get the fuck out of here and let me get dressed." Another anecdote from that show involves Ray Stewart, a stage mishap and Bancroft's priceless reaction.

Bancroft's no-nonsense approach is brought out most vividly during the making of the 1977 TV miniseries *Jesus of Nazareth* and how she handled Olivia Hussey's crazy breakdown on the set. Jeeze!

The author truly makes this a well-rounded picture of Bancroft and doesn't try to whitewash her, as friends talk about her temper and moodiness but also her many kindnesses. Still, it makes me like her even more, hearing both the good and the bad. This is a good woman—but don't mess with her! Sally Kellerman learned that lesson all too well on the set of an AFI project Bancroft was directing. Or the deli owner who told her she could use his establishment free for filming if she just autographed a photo so he could hang it up. "Why would I want to have a bloody picture on somebody else's wall that I don't even know?" she asked.

Bancroft's marriages to Marty May (1953-57) and Mel Brooks (1964 until her death in 2005) were like night and day. Her relationship with Brooks is poignantly described, especially during her last days. I actually teared up during this section, so well did the author go into her illness and death and Brooks' reaction to it. It packed an emotional wallop I did not expect.

This is a classy, first-rate biography. It really brings Anne Bancroft alive for readers and offers up more than most books of this type. Plus, the cover photo is simply gorgeous.

Australia's Sweetheart: The Amazing Story of Forgotten Hollywood Star Mary Maguire
by Michael Adams

I couldn't believe it when my friend Diane Byrnes told me there was a biography on Australian actress Mary Maguire (1919-74). U.S. movie buffs may know her for *That Man's Here Again, Alcatraz Island* (both 1937), *Sergeant Murphy* and *Mysterious Mr. Moto* (both 1938); she also made films in Australia and England. I can't imagine that she's on the radar of too many fans. I profiled her in *Films of the Golden Age* a few years ago so I knew of her; but as I read **Australia's Sweetheart: The Amazing Story of Forgotten Hollywood Star Mary Maguire** by Michael Adams (Hachette Australia), I became aware that I indeed knew very little. What a story!

One of five daughters, she was born Hélène Teresa Maguire in Melbourne, Australia, and nicknamed Peggy. Her father was a football player and welterweight boxer who later owned (with his wife) the Bull and Mouth Hotel in Melbourne and the Belle Vue Hotel in Brisbane. In 1933, the teenager film-debuted in a small, uncredited role in *Diggers in Blighty*. She got her big break the following year when she was brought to the attention of writer-director Charles Chauvel and cast in a major supporting part in his film *Heritage*. She was billed as Peggy Maguire, her performance was well-received, and she was touted as "Australia's Janet Gaynor." Director Miles Mander subsequently cast her as Charles Farrell's leading lady in *The Flying Doctor*, an Australian-British production. For this movie, she changed her name to Mary Maguire. She eventually made it to Hollywood and a Warner Bros. contract, but Maguire wasn't happy with the studio's B movie assignments.

At the beginning of 1938, she was released from her contract with the help of her new beau, Fox chairman Joseph M. Schenck, who was more than 40 years her senior. When she signed for a three-year stint at Fox, it was reported that she would be "given more important roles with the Fox organization than any she has yet had with a view to development to the ranks of the stars." Instead, she was cast as the ingénue lead in *Mysterious Mr. Moto* and then shipped to Fox's film unit in England to essay a supporting part in a Gracie Fields musical and a lead with George Sanders in *The Outsider*. Associated British Picture Corporation bought her contract and two leads came of this: *Black Eyes* and *An Englishman's Home*.

This is only part of the story. This biography had so many twists and turns. Maguire married Captain Robert Gordon-Canning, a controversial figure: A World War I vet, he was a member of the British Union of Fascists, the pro-German group The Link, and other such organizations, and became known for his anti-Semitic views. In July 1940, he was jailed as a Nazi sympathizer. She didn't agree with his politics but she found herself under scrutiny. The narrative is heavy on the events of World War II and often we go pages without mention of Maguire. But since it pertains to her husband, it eventually does involve her.

A pet peeve: In too many Hollywood books, we get writers heaping scorn on Michael Curtiz and/or B. Reeves Eason about the horses killed during the making of *The Charge of the Light Brigade* (1936). Adams writes that Eason "was most famous—infamous—

as the second unit director who had used forty-two cameras to capture the chariot race in 1925's *Ben-Hur: A Tale of the Christ*—and whose methods killed numerous horses to get it all on film. More recently he had used trip-wires on the 1936 epic *The Charge of the Light Brigade*, leading to the deaths of twenty-five horses and so much public outrage that the US Congress promised laws to prevent such cruelty in the future."

I emailed Alan K. Rode, author of *Michael Curtiz: A Life in Film* (University Press of Kentucky), to ask about this, and he answered: "I've been through the legal and production files at WB on how many horses died, what happened, depositions, court cases, etc. The Production Code was changed in 1940 outlawing the use of the Running W. Congress had nothing to do with it. The 'hundreds of horses' or 'twenty-five horses' stories from David Niven *et al.* have never cited any primary source documentation. My Curtiz book does. Until one of these accounts cites something other than a Charles Higham book, Errol Flynn's addled memoir or similar reference, I'll continue to discount it." Alan also sent me a blog post he wrote about *Charge*, "Separating Fact from Fiction": https://alankrode.com/the-true-story-of-the-charge-of-the-light-brigade. I bow to his knowledge of events, and I wish these facts were better known.

A big surprise to me was how sick Maguire was when she married. She had tuberculosis and she went through torturous treatments to get well. During all this, she had a son and almost died; ten months later, her son passed away. While Gordon-Canning was imprisoned, Maguire met Philip Legarra. After a scandalous divorce proceeding, she married him. They moved to the U.S., where she tried to revive her career with no success.

My research ended there. I had no idea what happened to Maguire after she lost a role in *Forever Amber*. I had hoped that her later life was a happy one. Unfortunately, *Australia's Sweetheart* tells us otherwise. Mary's later life was quite sad.

Running concurrently with Mary's story are the lives of her sisters Patricia, Joan, Carmel and Lupe: The author details their multiple marriages, affairs and drinking. It's dynamite reading.

Michael Adams is a superb writer and presents his multiple narratives well. He had help from the Maguire family and incorporated many other source materials. I was honestly shocked by everything Mary went through and on top of that—her sisters! There's also some wonderful info on their parents, Mick and Bina. They were quite a family. Who knew? I initially thought, "What could Adams possibly write about Mary Maguire to warrant 368 pages??" Well, it's a page-turner.

I wish there were more photos and not the few little ones scattered throughout. But that's a minor complaint. Even if you don't know Mary Maguire, I suggest you get this book and acquaint yourself with her and her family. There's a lot here of interest.

Barbara Payton - A Life in Pictures
by John O'Dowd

When most people think of Barbara Payton (1927-67), it is for her tumble from Hollywood starlet to prostitute, alcoholic and drug addict. They also recall how the Payton-Franchot Tone-Tom Neal love triangle led to a brawl that didn't do wonders for Neal's knuckles, Tone's face, Payton's reputation, or *any* of their careers. Most forget she was a human being whose personal demons destroyed a promising career as a more-than-competent actress in such films as *Trapped* (1949), *Kiss Tomorrow Goodbye* (1950) and *Only the Valiant* (1951). Author John O'Dowd has endeavored to bring a little dignity to her much-maligned life. He has already written an excellent biography, BearManor's *Kiss Tomorrow Goodbye: The Barbara Payton Story* (still available and highly recommended), which went a long way towards bringing her story to life with interviews with co-workers and relatives (including her son).

Now O'Dowd has given us a lavish large-format Valentine, **Barbara Payton - A Life in Pictures** (BearManor). This extraordinary tribute boasts more than 500 pages and tells Payton's life story with over a thousand images(!) on thick, glossy paper. It really is one of the best volumes of its kind, especially if you love to look at a beautiful lady such as Payton. I knew O'Dowd had great photos but this great? My God. There are so many amazing pictures, beautifully reproduced: publicity photos, portraits, candids, ads, etc., not only of Payton but other members of her family, one-time husband Tone and boyfriend Neal. Surrounding all this are quotes about Payton plus O'Dowd's sympathetic insights about her life and career.

I was simply bowled over by this gorgeous book and couldn't believe its giveaway price.

Barbarians on Bikes: Bikers and Motorcycle Gangs in Men's Pulp Adventure Magazines
edited by Robert Deis and Wyatt Doyle

New Texture strikes again with the fabulous **Barbarians on Bikes: Bikers and Motorcycle Gangs in Men's Pulp Adventure Magazines**, edited by Robert Deis and Wyatt Doyle with an afterword by Paul Bishop. This series celebrates men's adventure magazines of the 1960s and '70s and their "macho, over-the-top tales of alleged true-life adventures, flinty, opinionated takes on hot-button social issues, a spicy pin-up or two, and some of the most outrageous and arresting illustration art of the last century." For this volume, Misters Deis and Doyle point out that Hollywood biker movies of the late '60s were inspired by these lurid biker pulps.

Save for the intro and afterword, this is purely an art book—and what graphics! You get some vivid color and black-and-white images by masters Earl Norem, Bruce Minney, Al Rossi, Samson Pollen, Marti Ripoll, Gil Cohen, Charles Copeland, Mort Künstler, Norman Saunders, Norm Eastman, Ken Barr, Vicente Segrelles, Basil Gogos, Fernando Fernandez, Vic Prezio, Charles Fracé, Albert Pujolar and Victor Olson. A lot of covers but also many b&w interior art and splash pages of Nazi bikers, girls with machine guns riding on the backs of cycles, a lot of bondage (if you're into that), knife fights and, be aware, some nudity. The afterword by Bishop, a 35-year veteran of the Los Angeles Police Department turned novelist, tells of his real-life 1978 tense encounter with a biker.

Bebe Daniels: Hollywood's Good Little Bad Girl
by Charles L. Epting

Bebe Daniels: Hollywood's Good Little Bad Girl by Charles L. Epting, foreword by Annette D'Agostino Lloyd (McFarland), was a very uneven experience for me. Epting is a decent writer, if sometimes repetitious, and his research mostly cannot be faulted. There is a lot here that is worthwhile, not just for Bebe's fans, but film buffs in general. The early phase of her life has previously been bogged down by misinformation and just plain publicity lies. The author goes into detail and sets the record straight on many points. I was particularly impressed by his handling of Bebe's father's background while also disproving Bebe's own stories about him. I don't particularly like how Epting judges the father's character, without knowing him, but what the heck—it's his book. In the early going, all this fact-checking, although important, disrupts the flow of the narrative as he picks things apart. When he finally gets down to the business of telling *her* story, it moves faster.

Bebe Daniels (1900-71) started her career on stage as a child (a very well-researched portion of the book) and began in films in the silent era. She had a long collaboration with comedian Harold Lloyd, led a relatively scandal-free life, and married just once, to actor Ben Lyon, with whom she also acted. The Lyons went to England, where they became incredibly popular on radio, film and television, and Daniels worked tirelessly for the troops during World War II.

I found that while Epting offers some keen insights into Daniels, the person and the actress, he contradicts himself quite a bit. Foremost is his treatment of her stardom and her position as a top actress. Bebe was a star, that is true, but an icon? Maybe in England, where she and her husband spent many years. And how exactly does placing *sixth* on a 1930 popularity poll rival "her fame even at the height of the silent era"? In the mid-1930s, did Bebe and Ben Lyon rank as two of the most "beloved actors in the nation"? Again, they were beloved in England...but here?

This sort of exaggeration is something I was thankfully cured of by my friend Ray Hagen. When I just started writing, I was full of grand ideas of puffing up my subjects. Rightfully, Ray told me my "head was in the clouds" (his exact words) and I needed to look more clearly at the actors I loved. When I read some of my past articles, I cringe.

Epting has an inflated view of Daniels and I wish he would have toned it down just a bit. (A page after calling them beloved, the author quotes a review from the time that states, "Bebe Daniels and Ben Lyon may not be the biggest names in Hollywood...") According to Epting, during World War II, Bebe and Lyon "spoke with fellow Hollywood legend Clark Gable." Now they are legends?? When a reviewer praised Daniels for *Counsellor at Law* (1933), calling it "one of her best screen performances," Epting adds, "high praise for someone who had been making blockbuster films for over a decade." Really, "blockbusters"? And this from an author who complains of the quality of most of her films. He can't decide on the value of her Paramount films. Was she getting suitable material? I really can't say but he himself can't settle on an answer to that: She would be doing much better if she had better scripts; she was the studio's most popular actress; she complained about the quality of her stories; she was doing fabulous! Why does all this remind me of *Chinatown* (1974): "She's my daughter; she's my sister; she's my daughter; my sister, my daughter; she's my sister *and* my daughter."

In one of the many instances of backpedaling, Epting makes a very weird remark regarding Billie Dove, of all people. He groups her with Clara Bow, Louise Brooks and Greta Garbo as being "better remembered today than Bebe." Diehard film buffs might know Dove, but in general, especially because of *42nd Street*, Daniels has the edge. Heck, Almira Sessions has the edge over Dove.

Daniels' *Rio Rita* and Lyon's *Hell's Angels* were "renowned for their production values," yes, but that does not make the modest nature of their movie *Life with the Lyons* a "major risk." The author acts as if they never made a movie on a normal or even low budget before.

Referring to a 2008 article in *Style Weekly*, which quotes someone who knew Daniels as a child, Epting prefaces it with "While not an academic source, nevertheless it provides some interesting historical context." It's valuable, pure and simple. Who cares if it is academic?

"She did not sleep her way to the top of Hollywood, like Clara Bow." If Bow didn't have "It," she wouldn't have been a star—sleeping around or not. She had star quality and to imply otherwise is sour grapes.

The author says that *Hot News* (1928) was Bebe's first film with Neil Hamilton, but it was not. Their initial pairing was *The Splendid Crime* (1925), which Epting writes about. There's even a fabulous photo of the two from that movie. Similarly, I was confused about which film she made with Ben Lyon after their marriage— the author mentions the first as being *My Past* and then says it is *The Stolen Jools*. The author could have been clearer on this.

Referring to a 1930 movie premiere, he calls Claudette Colbert an "entertainment icon." The definition of "icon": "A person or thing regarded as a representative symbol of something." I don't see how this pertains to Colbert, especially in 1930, but…okay.

"Lloyd Bacon, who would later find success in musicals, directed." This is a narrow view of Bacon's multi-faceted career. I know the author is thinking specifically of *42nd Street* and *Footlight Parade*, but Bacon's musical output in his almost 100-film résumé was dwarfed by other genres.

About her failure as a producer for Hal Roach, which yielded only one film: "Whether or not this was due to Daniels' incompetence as a producer is difficult to ascertain, but it seems more likely that her failures were due to the fact that she was working at small, low-budget studios." Because we all know no one has ever succeeded as a low-budget producer.

Now we come to a running theme that slightly irritated me. Daniels was just a teenager when she hooked up with Harold Lloyd. They made 144 short films and by all accounts were romantically involved. Both Daniels and Lloyd were married to others for over 40 years—Bebe to Ben Lyon; Harold to Mildred Davis—but from time to time, Epting brings up Lloyd in the story, even though he had stopped working with Daniels in 1919. They remained friends, but didn't see each other *nearly* enough to warrant all this attention.

My major irritation comes after Epting cites Lloyd's death on March 8, 1971. Daniels had been sick for years when she passed away on March 16, 1971. "The news that broke on the morning of March 9 certainly did not help Bebe's frail condition. Harold Lloyd, who had been battling cancer for 18 months, died in Beverly Hills. Daniels' response to the news is unknown, although given the depth and longevity of their friendship it is a safe assumption that she was heartbroken. Although their love affair had ended more than 50 years earlier, their continued emotional attraction was undeniable. Bebe had found Ben and Harold had found Mildred—but the specter of lost love had never left either Daniels or Lloyd.

"Of course any impact of Lloyd's death on Daniels' condition remains only pure speculation, but the timing of the two events certainly seems more than coincidental. Did the shocking news of his passing take a toll on her physical health? Or did the sadness caused by his death cause Bebe to simply quit fighting, unable to live in a world without her first true love? The answer will obviously never be known."

But we can go on and on about it. Gag. And this from a guy who turns up his nose on writing that isn't "academic"!

If we go by this logic, can Epting answer this question: Did the death of Dennis Hopper (May 29, 2010) bring on the demise of Rue McClanahan (June 3, 2010)? Did anyone really expect Fredric March to soldier on for more than a few days after the world—and March—lost Marjorie Main? Surely no one thinks it's coincidence that anemia took the life of Dan Dailey just days before Smith & Wesson robbed us of Gig Young? Rondo Hatton shuffles off his mortal coil, and George Arliss follows suit … coincidence? Surely not. And as long as we're on this cause-and-effect kick, you know how Hollywood tongues wagged about the same-day death of Peter Lawford and Cheetah.

In all seriousness, I would also like to add this: Harold Lloyd was in his early twenties when he and a 14- or 15-year-old Daniels dated. Maybe I'm a prude, but I see something wrong with this. The author makes no mention of the age discrepancy, but chooses to take the view that Lloyd was the love of her life. Okay, fine, but he takes it to a whole new level of creepiness.

Epting could have supplied more of an assessment of Daniels' acting since it is apparent he has seen most if not all her existing movies. This would have helped the book considerably, instead of speculating on lost love or whether she was a huge star. If you are a fan of Daniels, I do urge that you get this, because there is some good information here. The author really goes out of his way to give Daniels her due—with mixed results, unfortunately.

On a side note, the 44 photos are excellent and well-reproduced. However, I found the cover photo atrocious. There are so many beautiful pictures of Daniels, and for the cover, they picked one where she looks as if she's wearing a rolled-up headband out of Olivia Newton-John's "Let's Get Physical" music video. A travesty!

The Boy with the Betty Grable Legs by Skip E. Lowe/ Hollywood Gomorrah: Sex Lives of the Hollywood Stars by Skip E. Lowe

I do not trust an author who writes two autobiographies with the second one adding a slew of scandalous stories. This smacks too much of wanting to sell books. This brings me to Skip E. Lowe (1929-2014), born Sammy Labella, an actor, comedian and, late in life, a public-access cable talk show host. He interviewed many celebrities and during his long career became acquainted with numerous personalities.

His first book was **The Boy with the Betty Grable Legs** (Belle Publishing). At times, the book is brutal, especially when he recounts a childhood rape by bullies, which he details graphically, and a horrible encounter with tennis star Bill Tilden in a public restroom. (Tilden was arrested at least twice in his life for contributing to the delinquency of a minor.) Lowe is not a good writer and his narrative is bursting with clichés, but early in the book, he does a fairly good job explaining his feelings about being different as a child and the efforts of his mother to get him into show business.

I *do* doubt his participation in movies of the 1940s—or at least his recollection of his extra work in them. His memory of *Song of the Open Road* (1944) is weirdly wrong, claiming that his character sang "till the 'massa' came home." That movie was about children working for the U.S. Crop Corps and not about slaves on a plantation. As for *Best Foot Forward* (1943), he says it was "one of [Lucille Ball's] first pictures." As far as I know, Lowe was never in an East Side Kids or Bowery Boys movie, but he writes, "Monogram Pictures kept me busy, playing wrong-side-of-the-tracks hoodlums in Maurice Duke's Dead End Kids' films. A tough Brooklyn accent, and I was all set." Duke never produced any "Dead End Kids" movies, he was the associate producer of The Teen-Agers series between 1946 and '48. IMDb only lists two 1940s credits for

Lowe, *Best Foot Forward* and *Song of the Open Road*, but I bet they are there because of this book. Or Lowe put them there himself.

The volume's timeline is screwy as he flits from one story to the next. You are really never sure what time period he is in; this is especially notable during the years he was "friends" with James Dean. Sorry, but everyone now who writes a book about their experiences in '50s Hollywood seemed to be friends with Dean (and Marilyn Monroe). Many of them, Lowe included, claim they had sex with him. In this case, however, Dean "forced himself" on Lowe. Yeah, right.

The section about entertaining in Vietnam is the best part of the book, as he details the struggles and feelings he went through during that difficult time. But I am leery of his character assassination of Bob Hope. Hope was far from perfect, but tearing down his service to his country via his entertainment shows is questionable. It sounds as if Lowe had some personal issues with Hope and this colored his storytelling.

He says one person was "blessed with a Bette Davis/Clifton Webb wit." Okay, but what does that mean?

He describes Nina Varela as an actress who "co-starred with Marlon Brando" in *Viva Zapata!* (1952). Varela was uncredited in that movie.

A few of the many misspellings: Roddy McDowell (should be McDowall); Hedy Lamar (Lamarr); James Farrentino (Farentino).

The Beatles' song "Hey Jude" could not be playing on a jukebox in 1966 since it wasn't recorded until 1968.

Aldo Ray did not rise "to fame in the 1940s," as his first film came in 1951. He also wasn't a "Latin hunk from San Francisco." He was born Aldo Da Re into an Italian family in Pen Argyl, Pennsylvania.

Lowe's whole chapter on Jean Wallace is filled with misinformation about her career (e.g., her heyday as a "star" was not the '40s) and exaggeration about the so-called love affair she and Lowe had in the 1970s or '80s—Lowe doesn't give us a clear indication when this "relationship" supposedly occurred. Cornel Wilde and

Wallace divorced in 1981 (although Skip doesn't tell us this), so I have to assume that's when all this took place. He also alleged to have been at Wilde's bedside when he died "at Christmastime." Cornel passed away on October 16, 1989, so it was more like Halloween time. Then, according to Skip, a heartbroken Wallace died six months later, although the date was February 14, 1990. Who was proofreading this book? *Was* there an editor? I recently asked a friend who knows both the Wilde and Wallace families about Lowe's claims of a sexual relationship with Jean and I was told, "She knew him when she was drinking heavily. I interviewed him, then ran everything past her brother Jack. All the Jean stuff is BS embellishment. She found him amusing and someone to drink with." As for Lowe holding Wilde's hand as he died, I was told, "Ha. Not. He did visit him in the hospital, though."

In this first book, published in 2001, Lowe claimed that he'd always been "sexually shy" and was content to "kick back and watch." Well, obviously such an attitude will not sell books. Come 2014 and Lowe changed his story completely: He is transformed into one of the most desirable men on the planet and many males, not just James Dean, force themselves on him. Most times, though, he does not need coaxing. Throughout his books, Skip disparages his own looks, calling himself overly effeminate and a hunchback—yet according to this second tome, he is absolutely irresistible to everyone. He prided himself on looking more like a woman than a man (yet, he doesn't), and gives this as the reason why David Carradine supposedly viciously raped him. I don't want to be judgmental about his looks but let me just say that Martin Short cited him as an inspiration for his Jiminy Glick character.

The title of his new book tells it all: **Hollywood Gomorrah: Sex Lives of the Hollywood Stars** (CreateSpace). Seriously? Yes, unfortunately. This book is basically *The Boy with the Betty Grable Legs,* but with much more smut added. All the good stuff in that earlier book is made null and void by a carload of vile and lewd additions. I am appalled that he claims to be close friends with the people in this book. Way to exploit your "friends," Skip!

Poor Barbara Hutton and Mary Rogers both are raked over the coals. Whether any of it is true, I have no idea, but it sure is not something a "friend" should be telling. One of the few people not shown in a bad light is Mamie Van Doren, and I am guessing it is because she's alive and he was worried about a lawsuit. (By this, I am not implying Mamie, a wonderful person, would have any dirt on her.) Christian Brando, another supposedly great friend, is also treated shabbily here.

In *Betty Grable Legs*, Lowe praised Lucille Ball for being so nice to him on the set of *Best Foot Forward*, going out of her way to make him feel comfortable. Here, he adds that she was drunk on the set and the director had to confiscate her flask. His James Dean section is given some gruesome details that were not in his first book—specifically a disgusting description of Dean's private area and body odor. This also plays a part in another loathsome story of the "sexually shy" Skip accepting a dare to do something underneath a table to a woman. Why he thought this stomach-churning account was appropriate is beyond me.

A story about him acting as a Good Samaritan, bringing a drunk Montgomery Clift home, now takes a creepy turn as Lowe alleges that Clift suddenly woke up from his stupor, grabbed him and tried to forcibly make him do a certain act. Troy Donahue, Cesar Romero, Aldo Ray and Christian Brando also all went after Lowe—as if I believe it for one second—and, of course, these are additions for this second book. Cesar supposedly said to him afterward, "Don't tell anybody. Promise me, Skip. It's nobody's business but ours." If this is true, how sad that Skip E. Lowe could not be trusted. As a passenger on a boat, irresistible Skip slips down to the engine room so he can carry on with all the sailors. Suuuuurre. His agenda is clear: "Straight guys are all pretenders."

Of course, we get the "shockers": He watched Marlon Brando being sodomized by a woman with a cucumber and George Raft having sex in a coffin. Even worse is the treatment of Martha Raye. Her great contribution to her country by entertaining soldiers has been reduced by Lowe to taking out her dentures and performing fellatio on a group of military men as they cheered her. Lowe even goes as far as claiming he and Raye had a contest to see how many Marines they could blow. Not only would this be illegal in any branch of the service, it is highly unlikely. Remember, too, that Lowe is supposedly "sexually shy." Seriously, who believes crap like this?

Misspellings include Peggy Cummings (should be Cummins); Katherine Hepburn (Katharine); "one of my *grate* traveling joys..."; and (multiple times) Joseph Cotton (Cotten).

Elizabeth Taylor and Eddie Fisher did not meet and fall in love during the filming of *BUtterfield 8* (1960); they met through Mike Todd, who was married to Liz from February 2, 1957, until his death on March 22, 1958. Fisher and Taylor wed on May 12, 1959; production on *BUtterfield 8* started in January 1960.

Tyrone Power and Cesar Romero were not contract players at MGM, but 20th Century-Fox.

Dan Dailey did not buy dresses, nylons and blouses at an Army Surplus store. I find it hard to believe that the notoriously private Dailey would enjoy parading around in front of Lowe in said apparel and a French maid's outfit.

When Lowe was interviewed for John O'Dowd's book *Kiss Tomorrow Goodbye: The Barbara Payton Story*, he gave the impression that he knew her only slightly, helped her out maybe once, but that's it. Now Lowe takes credit for bleaching her hair platinum and loaning her his apartment many times so she could have sexual trysts when she was working as a prostitute. Even weirder, he claims he joined in on the "fun." He also writes that Payton had dentures. Yes, she had some missing teeth after her sad decline, but she could never afford dentures. His account of her death is also erroneous. O'Dowd, an obsessive chronicler of Payton's life, makes absolutely no mention of these things in his biography and I have to lean in his direction when it comes to this.

As I read *The Boy with the Betty Grable Legs*, I found myself, at times, liking Skip E. Lowe. I felt sorry for his traumatic childhood and his stay in Chicago State Hospital for mental issues. I also wondered about how this affected him: "Still an infant, I stuck my curious nose into the tempting dark [of the cellar opening], and fell down 15 hard edged steps." But … any good or sympathetic feelings I had were destroyed by the despicable *Hollywood Gomorrah*. He comes across as an opportunistic back-stabber trying to profit from harming his friends. Whether anything is true or not seems irrelevant to him. My advice to all of you is to Skip this.

Bride of the Gorilla
by Tom Weaver

Tom Weaver has done a third volume in his *Scripts from the Crypt* series, this time a whole freakin' book on the 1951 grade Z thriller **Bride of the Gorilla** (BearManor) with a foreword by director John Landis. (While his foreword is entertaining, showing a love of gorilla movies, I don't think it truly fits here. A history of gorilla movies, yes; *Bride of the Gorilla*, no.)

Of course, this volume is more than just a script—although the script *is* interesting because of its variations from the finished product. As always, there's loads of good stuff for horror fans to savor. Weaver supplies the whole background and making of the film, "Fun Facts," a section on how the script and the completed movie differ, and the story of Realart Pictures and Jack Broder Productions. Dr. Robert J. Kiss, who I have come to appreciate through his contributions to Weaver's books, does a nice job chronicling *Bride*'s distribution history. David Schecter, an expert on movie music, comes through again with his astute discussion on the score—in a chapter amusingly called "Gorilla My Themes." Frank Dello Stritto writes a Lon Chaney Jr. tribute, while Scott MacQueen tackles writer-director Curt Siodmak, whom he had interviewed and befriended. To discuss the Barbara Payton-Tom Neal-Franchot Tone love debacle, Weaver brings in interviewees William Phipps, Tom Neal Jr. and Herman Cohen. There's much about the love triangle and the Tone-Neal brawl, which happened just before the release of *Bride of the Gorilla*. Phipps is always a welcome interview subject, fun and ready with great stories and perceptive comments. Most importantly, though, is the talk with Tom Neal Jr., the son of the B movie actor. Sadly, he died not long after this interview took place. He really delves deep into his troubled father and his insights help us understand the elder Neal better. Capping off this excellent volume is a life-and-career timeline of Lon Chaney by Greg Mank, with Tom on the assist.

As with all of Tom Weaver's books, this has a snarky, "punny" attitude. One thing that can be said for him: He makes film history lively and fun. His synopses are never dull and are chock-full of wry observations that (sometimes) leave you laughing.

"Apparently, it's not just rubber trees getting tapped on this plantation."

"It was love at first leer for Tone..."

"At PRC [Tom Neal] had his finest hour (and nine minutes) as the can't-catch-a-break chump in Edgar G. Ulmer's zero-budgeted noir *Detour* (1945)."

"The battle of the aesthete vs. the athlete began on the lawn with Neal hitting Tone hard. How hard? Hard enough that he flew through the air and landed on the front page of the next day's newspaper. EVERY newspaper."

What I didn't like about this book was Weaver's excessively bad treatment of star Barbara Payton. We all know about her downward spiral and the reasons behind it. Fun is fun until you start personally disparaging a person. Tom calls her a "mattress back," says that for her it was "always sex o'clock," and "Tone had lost the battle, but won the whore." Sorry, but no woman should ever be called a whore. There is a contempt for Payton that is disconcerting. "Do not judge, lest you be judged" is the appropriate phrase here. Life was not kind to Barbara, she had numerous problems and addictions that, unfortunately, she was only able to surmount near the end of her short life. I don't mean that he should have sugarcoated her life, but there are ways of giving the gritty details without nastiness. Do I think this shows that Tom hates women? No, I don't. I see this as an author, known for his sarcasm, seeing an ideal target and running with it. It will probably be funny to a lot of people—just not with me.

Still, *Bride of the Gorilla* makes for an intriguing addition to the series and no stone seems to have been left unturned. Everything you always wanted to know—or didn't know you wanted to know—is here. Highly recommended.

The Brute Man by Tom Weaver/**Rondo Hatton: Beauty Within the Brute** by Scott Gallinghouse

We are now on #10 of Tom Weaver's *Scripts from the Crypt* series (BearManor). While all the previous volumes have been outstanding, the best one yet is this newest one on **The Brute Man** (1946) and its star, Rondo Hatton. Which is ironic since *The Brute Man* is not the best of the films represented in the series. In fact, far from it. What makes this volume so great is the biography of Hatton written by Scott Gallinghouse.

Hatton tragically suffered from acromegaly, a disorder in the pituitary gland which results in an increase in size of the bones, including those in the hands, feet and face. This disease gave Hatton his distinctively "monstrous" look that was exploited by Universal when they cast him as "The Creeper" in *The Pearl of Death* (1944), *House of Horrors* (1946) and *The Brute Man*; the latter was made by Universal but sold to PRC who released it.

As I read Hatton's engrossing story, I realized how little I knew of him and how other authors have not only sensationalized him and his plight but just plain got it wrong.

Gallinghouse has already shown on other *Scripts from the Crypt* books how adroit he is at research—but he really comes into his own here. It's a long biography and so granular in its detail that it really takes you on a journey. Hatton starts off as a handsome young man and we experience the highs in his life at college, in athletics, and his newspaper exploits. The author clears up the reasons for Hatton's acromegaly and corrects past writers' assertions that it came from Hatton being gassed during the First World War.

Gallinghouse treats his subject with respect. I have often read and been annoyed at others who make fun of Hatton's looks. He had feelings, after all, and the author here is cognizant of that fact; the reader feels Gallinghouse's empathy and it adds much to the narrative. While Hatton suffered from his affliction, there is no "poor me" about his story—despite what others have written. He went on with his life as normally as possible and was not mentally deficient as reported elsewhere.

Tom Weaver follows the biography with the *Brute Man*'s production history and "Fun Facts." As always, Weaver does an excellent, thorough job and uncovers interesting tidbits and offers chin-scratching observations. For whatever reason, his humor hit the mark with me more than usual. I laughed numerous times. His pointing out of a typo regarding Rondo Hatton and Rhonda Fleming is a gem of absurdity. Some jokes (not many) fall flat, such as comparing photos of Hatton and FDR. Also, I didn't like some of the language used. It's one thing to *quote* someone cursing, but using these words in your own writing…well, I expect better from a film historian of Weaver's caliber.

Other features: Dr. Robert J. Kiss on *The Brute Man*'s release history; fascinating samples of Rondo Hatton's newspaper writing; David Colton telling the history of the Rondo Horror Awards; a few pages dealing with the Creeper's first appearance in *The Pearl of Death*; a reproduction of the *Brute Man* pressbook; George Chastain paying tribute to other "Brute Men" of the movies; Andrew J. Fenady remembering producer Ben Pivar in a very lively, entertaining piece; Gary Rhodes (dryly) talking about postwar horror films; and an unused story idea by Dwight V. Babcock meant for Hatton. There is also a reprint of an article published after Hatton's death in *Pageant* magazine: "Hollywood's Strangest Love Story." It's an error-filled article and very dramatic but it gives one a sense of how Hatton was treated back then (and up until this present book).

It should be pointed out that the *Brute Man* script is not included, but the continuity script. Kerry Gammill outdid himself with the stunningly lifelike Rondo Hatton illustration on the cover.

There is a second version of this book: Weaver and his colleagues wanted Hatton to have a biography of his own, the way all the other classic horror stars do, and they weren't happy that it ended up as just part of a book on the actor's worst movie, *The Brute Man*. So, a few weeks after the publication of the *Brute Man* book, a "sister version" was designed: the *Brute Man* continuity, production history and pressbook were deleted, a new cover and back cover designed, so that Rondo now had the spotlight on him from cover to cover. **Rondo Hatton: Beauty Within the Brute** is shorter (200 pages rather than 300) without the *Brute Man* emphasis, and therefore cheaper, and its cover is a knockout original painting by pop culture artist Drew Friedman, another Rondo Hatton fan from way back.

Charlton Heston: Hollywood's Last Icon
by Marc Eliot

I have reviewed Marc Eliot's previous books on Cary Grant, Ronald Reagan and James Stewart. All received good reviews elsewhere, and have all been "bestsellers" (it says here), but I found them lacking and filled with errors. His newest, **Charlton Heston: Hollywood's Last Icon** (Dey Street Books/HarperCollins), is no different: It has been described by others as a definitive biography and it will undoubtedly match the $uccess of his earlier books. But, yet again, I found it sloppy and inadequate. However, *Hollywood's Last Icon* is a slight cut above his norm, simply because he had access to Heston's personal papers and diaries and was able to interview his children.

In past books, Eliot has taken a bit of delight tearing down his subjects. Not here. Heston is treated reverently—whether it's because of the family's involvement, I cannot say. I *have* read some not-so-nice comments about Heston from others, but here we get truly only one negative remark from Richard Harris. Eliot seems to place the blame on Harris for their bad relationship, even though it seems obvious (to me, anyway) that Heston was being a jerk to him.

Heston's marriage to Lydia Clarke is painted in a weird light. At times their union was strained, but Eliot implies that it's basically one-sided; her chronic migraines and dissatisfaction had little to do with Heston (and his womanizing) and he simply endured it as best he could. Hmmmm.

While there are some interesting backstories, mostly for the bigger films in Heston's canon, Eliot tends to overwrite—a lot— but at the same time leaving out fascinating tidbits. I compared the sections of the Heston-Cecil B. DeMille movies to Robert S. Birchard's *Cecil B. DeMille's Hollywood* (University Press of Kentucky) and found Birchard (a higher grade of historian than Eliot) more readable and interesting.

Tangents are Eliot's specialty, and the book groans under the weight of them. The page count is close to 500 (not counting bibliography, filmography and source notes), but this volume would have been *much* better half that size. Was there even an editor on this? It didn't feel like it. I know for certain there was no fact-checker.

The writing is generally competent, although unexciting. However, Eliot has an inclination toward run-on and non-sentences. He isn't too inventive with how he starts a quote from someone, overusing the phrase "So-and-so had this to say" followed by a colon.

> [Charlton's father] Russell, who had learned construction
> from his father, John Carter, a poor Yorkshire County
> coal mine pit boy in the United Kingdom who came to

America in search of freedom and fortune, and landed
a job as a lumberjack with the Stevens Logging company of Roscommon, Michigan, a town named after the
county in Ireland.

Notice that that wasn't even a sentence; it never gets back to
Russell after going off on the tangent about his father.

"She came from a very interesting family," according to Holly
Heston Rochell, Charlton Heston's daughter.

It was run by a strict, Victorian-style matriarch, my
grandmother, Lilla's mother—'Ladybird,' as she was
sometimes called by other kids in the neighborhood, or
'Josie,' or 'Uncle Joe,' which referred to Joseph Stalin, that
ought to give you an idea of the kind of person she was.

Well, this is the interviewee's run-on sentence. Eliot could have
fixed it but...

Again, not a sentence:

Bars and grills all over the city one night a week when
hot dogs boiled in huge vats were given away with drinks,
while piano players pounded out show tunes and singers
sang and dancers danced, with each other or alone, the
bar floor their stage.

My head hurts:

[Nicholas] Ray was a product of the Group Theater of
the '30s, where he had met and worked with Elia Kazan,
after Kazan hired Ray to be an assistant on his 1945 film
debut, *A Tree Grows in Brooklyn*, he quickly climbed the
Hollywood ladder, along the way working with some of
film's [*sic*] biggest stars, including Humphrey Bogart in
Knock on Any Door (1949) and *In a Lonely Place* (1950).

Methinks Eliot's record of attendance in fourth-grade sentence
construction class may not have been perfect.

So dramatic: "The fall cross-faded into winter and the city turned
biting cold, the streets filled with relentless snow, the days dark by

late afternoon." Now he's got me wondering how to tell if the snow on the ground in my town is "relentless" or better-behaved.

The "Professor Irwin Corey Double-Talk Award" for this one: "When [Lydia], which was increasingly the case, stayed behind and managed the affairs of the house." Now I'm starting to suspect that Eliot's editor missed a similar number of fourth-grade classes.

"Lydia's doctors decided to have another thyroid operation she had been putting off for awhile." Her *doctors* had the operation when their patient wouldn't? That doesn't sound very helpful.

"As midnight approached, [Heston] went outside, stood by the pool, and stared up at the sky, lost in his own thoughts as he listened to the sound of reindeer." How does Eliot know he did this? Were Heston's children spying on him that night and then told Eliot?

Eliot's "clever" description of television: "It was something like radio, only better, or worse. It had live pictures, sort of, that appeared on ten-inch black-and-white screens that jerked around as if suffering from some sort of nervous condition, with weird horizontal lines that sometimes turned into disturbing zzzzs, tinny sound, and a lot of cornball content." Time to get a new TV set, Marc.

The success of the film *The Caine Mutiny* (1954) did not inspire Herman Wouk to adapt his novel into the Broadway play *The Caine Mutiny Court-Martial*: The latter premiered on Broadway in January 1954; the movie opened in June '54. Twice Eliot calls Captain Queeg's ball bearings "pinballs."

Hal Wallis did not resign a day after the March 2, 1944, Academy Award ceremony. Wallis actually left Warners on April 1, 1944.

Wallis did not produce *The Killers* (1946); Mark Hellinger did. *The Strange Love of Martha Ivers* (1946) was released by Paramount, not Universal. Also, that latter film did not make Kirk Douglas (in his film debut) a star; *Champion* (1949) lays claim to that.

Eliot refers to Martin & Lewis films as "light comedies." And here I was thinking that *I* was the only one who felt they exhibited that ethereal Lubitsch Touch.

More Wallis nonsense: According to Eliot, the producer made the Martin & Lewis "light comedies" and Elvis musicals and then "returned to more serious filmmaking" with *Becket* (1964) and *True Grit* (1969). Eliot obviously has never heard of *Come Back, Little Sheba* (1952), *About Mrs. Leslie* (1954), *The Rose Tattoo* (1955), *The Rainmaker* (1956), *Gunfight at the O.K. Corral* (1957), *Summer and Smoke* (1961), etc.

It is misleading to say Judy Garland being "unstable" was the reason she was replaced on *Annie Get Your Gun* (1950). Judy had personal problems (exhaustion, the break-up of her marriage, addictions), but she had just as many, if not more, issues with director Busby Berkeley.

Lucille Ball, not Paulette Goddard, was the first choice for the role of Angel the elephant girl in *The Greatest Show on Earth* (1952); she turned it down because she was pregnant. Regardless of what Eliot writes, Goddard wanted the part but DeMille rejected her—not the other way around.

"The big coup was getting Jimmy Stewart to play 'Buttons,' the fugitive disguised as a clown, for the bargain rate of $50,000. Stewart's career had not as yet fully recovered the Oscar-worthy momentum [*sic*] it had gained prior to his wartime service, and it would take a series of increasingly brutal westerns by Anthony Mann and three suspense pictures by Hitchcock to put him on top. He was grateful for the work..." Oh, yes, Stewart was so desperate when he made *The Greatest Show on Earth*. After the war, he did *Call Northside 777* (1947), *Rope* (1948), *The Stratton Story* (1949), *Winchester '73*, *Broken Arrow* and *Harvey* (all 1950), to name a few. He was perhaps the first Hollywood star to become a profit participant in one of his movies (*Winchester '73*) and was on 1950's Top Ten Money Making Stars Poll. Meanwhile, Eliot makes Stewart, one of the movies' hottest stars, sound like an unemployable naif standing out by a pool at midnight listening to reindeer.

"Despite lukewarm reviews, *Ruby Gentry* was a major hit at the box office; from a $535,000 budget it earned $1.75 million in its initial domestic run, making it the highest-grossing Hollywood movie of the preceding twenty years." *Ruby Gentry* wasn't even the highest-grossing Hollywood movie of its *own* year, much less "the preceding twenty years." According to *Variety's* January 1954 list of 1953's top grossers, the #1 moneymaker ($20 to $30 million) was *The Robe*; take *that, Ruby Gentry's* $1.75 million! Other movies that ran laps around *Ruby* in 1953: George Montgomery's 3-D Western *Fort Ti* ($2.6 million), *Ma and Pa Kettle on Vacation* ($2.2 million), *Abbott and Costello Meet Captain Kidd* ($2 million), *Francis Covers the Big Town* ($1.8) and ... let me see ... 2, 4, 6, 8, 10, 12 ... bear with me ... 26, 28, 30, 32 ... talk amongst yourselves ... 50, 52, 54 ... getting there! ... *Ruby Gentry* was outgrossed by about 65 other 1953 movies. Has Eliot even heard of *Gone with the Wind* (1939)? Highest-grossing movie of the preceding twenty years, my foot! You have to be wary of Eliot's box office totals. He says *The Ten Commandments* (1956) made more money overall (including reissues) than any film released in the first seven years of the 1950s. Actually, Disney's *Peter Pan* (1950) and *Lady and the Tramp* (1955) both made more. Methinks Eliot played hooky during math classes, too.

Also, *Ruby Gentry* is not a knock-off of *A Place in the Sun* (1951), although Eliot snarks that Jennifer Jones and Heston were no Elizabeth Taylor and Montgomery Clift—like anyone here cares.

Just because *The Greatest Show on Earth* won the Best Picture Academy Award, does that mean we need a total rundown of the whole Oscar telecast, what was said, how they said it, etc.? About Gloria Grahame, who won for *The Bad and the Beautiful*, he absurdly writes, "[She] had a habit of stuffing cotton along her gum line to straighten out and thicken her upper lip, had not removed it and came across sounding as if she had had one too many." Absolutely not! If you watch a clip of her speech (did Eliot??), a surprised and breathless Grahame simply says, "Thank you very much." (At this point, I'd like everyone who's wondering why a Heston biography includes a false and demeaning description of Gloria Grahame on Oscar night for *The Bad and the Beautiful* to join me in singing "Ah! Sweet Mystery of Life.") At least Eliot didn't repeat the obnoxious urban legend that Grahame tripped on the way up the podium and exclaimed, "Oh, shit!"

Bad for Each Other (1953) was not an "updated remake" of *The Citadel* (1938). Although the stories are superficially similar, *Bad for Each Other* was based on the novel *Scalpel* by Horace McCoy.

Eliot gets confused as to what Heston movie inspired Indiana Jones' look (brown leather jacket, fedora, tan pants) in *Raiders of the Lost Ark* (1981). He says it was *The Greatest Show on Earth*. While Heston's garb in that has some similarities, the movie in question is *Secret of the Incas* (1954). Alan Ladd (1943's *China*) and Ronald Reagan (1952's *Hong Kong*) had earlier worn the leather jacket-fedora combo, but in an interview, *Raiders* costume designer Deborah Nadoolman acknowledged her debt to *Incas*. The plot has familiar elements, too: Heston's adventurer looks for a lost artifact and there is a tomb scene with a shaft of light similar to *Raiders'* map room scene. (The aforementioned *Hong Kong* is also cited as an inspiration and its plot has similarities to *Indiana Jones and the Temple of Doom*.)

"In the late '40s to mid-50s, [comedy] parts usually went to [Cary] Grant, if he wanted them, or Gregory Peck or William Holden, while Heston remained, to the studios, best suited for westerns, historical films, or action-adventure flicks." Yes, Peck and Holden got all the comedy parts.

William Boyd was up for the lead in *The Ten Commandments* (1956), but Eliot goes on for an uncomfortably long time telling us why he was not ultimately chosen. *This* is why this book is so freakin' long. Editor!

According to Eliot, Gertrude Lawrence introduced Cecil B. DeMille to Yul Brynner backstage after a performance of *The King and I* in February 1953. If she did ... then who's that buried out at Greenlawn Cemetery? Lawrence died in September 1952.

Jack Palance was considered for the part of Dathan in *The Ten Commandments*. Writing about the actor's prior work, all Eliot singles out is that Palance was Brando's understudy in *A Streetcar Named Desire* on Broadway. No mention is made of his important roles in the movies *Panic in the Streets* (1950), *Sudden Fear* (1952), and *Shane* (1953), among others. He was nominated for Best Supporting Actor Oscars for the last two. Palance turned DeMille down (and was replaced by Edward G. Robinson) and then "inexplicably," writes Eliot, Palance signed to do *Sign of the Pagan* (1954). Maybe *Pagan* was not an epic on par with *The Ten Commandments*, but it gave Palance a helluva great role as Attila the Hun.

Eliot calls Debra Paget a "pretty starlet who had been knocking around Hollywood in minor roles for nearly a decade." I would not call her parts in *Broken Arrow* (1950), *Bird of Paradise* (1951), *Belles on Their Toes*, *Les Misérables*, *Stars and Stripes Forever* (all 1952), *Princess of the Nile* (1954), etc., minor. He should say what he means: He thinks the films themselves were minor. Maybe they were, compared to a DeMille epic, but let's not forget that Paget was a star.

It's made to seem that Heston gave "TV actor" Dennis Weaver his "big break" in *Touch of Evil* (1958). It was his 21st film, and he'd had bigger roles in his previous features.

It really isn't fair to blame Rudolph Maté for Heston's (supposed) lackluster showing in *Three Violent People* (1956). "Without DeMille's craftsmanship that had now twice custom-fitted Heston like a polished gear into a high-powered machine, lesser directors like Maté had trouble illuminating the characters he played off the gleam of his real-life persona." Later, the author blames Anthony Quinn's direction for Heston's performance in *The Buccaneer* (1958). This happens often here. It's never Heston's fault, always the writer or mainly the director. Barbara Stanwyck, for one, had her share of lousy or mediocre directors, but she rose above her material; a true professional always does. Just sayin'.

I do not see how *The Big Country* (1958) is "essentially the same tale" as *Shane* (1953). *Shane* comes up later when he unfairly compares it to *Will Penny* (1967). The only similarities are that Will is a loner and there is a child actor involved with the plot. *Planet of the Apes* (1968) is likewise compared to *2001: A Space Odyssey* (1968).

Was it Rock Hudson's "pretty face and muscular build" that got him an Oscar nomination for *Giant* (1956)? Perhaps Eliot does not feel it was his acting ability.

I am not understanding the comment that Heston's wife Lydia "suffered a hysterectomy and couldn't have any more children..." She might have *suffered* a miscarriage but you *undergo* a hysterectomy. Did she have something wrong with her that she had to have a hysterectomy? The way the author writes this, it sounds as if Lydia was forced to have the surgery against her will. Anyway, it's an odd way to put it. Also, why didn't her doctors undergo her hysterectomy for her, the way they did her thyroid operation? This is not addressed.

Another puzzler: "As I was maturing, and getting to know Chuck better, I felt he always appreciated so much from everybody." I have no idea what this quote, from Stephen Macht, even means.

How was Jack Lemmon's Oscar nomination for *Some Like It Hot* (1959) affected by the movie not being nominated for Best Picture?

Eliot also had this to say: "If Americans thought about Muslims at all, it was mostly from the way Hollywood portrayed them in films like *Road to Morocco* (1942), a Crosby-Hope comedy in which all Muslims are insane and all women look like Dorothy Lamour running around in negligees, or *Casablanca* (also 1942), where everyone is either a Nazi, a European freedom fighter, or an American, the only visible natives selling trinkets in the street or making corrupt side street deals."

James Dean did not make his feature film debut in *Rebel Without a Cause* (1955); he had small, uncredited movie roles starting with 1951's *Fixed Bayonets!* and continuing with *Sailor Beware* and *Has Anybody Seen My Gal* (both 1952). If Eliot means his debut as a starring actor, he's *still* wrong: *East of Eden* (1955) was filmed from May 27 to early August 1954; *Rebel* was in production March 28 to May 26, 1955.

I am *so* glad Eliot cleared up for me that although Sid Grauman owned Grauman's Chinese Theatre, he was *not* Chinese. Whew.

It's also good to know that Eliot thinks that Best Art Direction-Set Direction, Best Original Song and Best Score of a Dramatic or Comedy Picture are all "minor" Academy Awards. Miklós Rózsa, in particular, would be pissed.

Writing about *55 Days at Peking* (1963), Eliot refers to an "aging" Ava Gardner. Heston was just months younger; why isn't he also described as "aging"?

Nicholas Ray "never directed another foot of film the rest of his life" after *55 Days at Peking*, claims Eliot. Maybe he means a commercial film. Ray directed *We Can't Go Home Again* (1973), the segment "The Janitor" in *Wet Dreams* (1974), the short *Marco* (1978), and *Lightning Over Water* (1980).

"The that'll-be-the-day sentiment, which permeated the Hollywood film industry from its inception and continued into the '60s, was that a black man could be elected president easier than he could star in a major Hollywood film." Seriously, this is what Eliot writes. The reverse was certainly true. Obviously, he forgets Harry Belafonte and Sidney Poitier, both of whom starred in Hollywood films.

The Arrangement (1969) did not put an end to Elia Kazan's directorial career; he did *The Visitors* (1972) and *The Last Tycoon* (1976) after that.

In his *Planet of the Ape* section, Eliot wrote, "Ape movies were nothing new," citing as examples *Blonde Venus, Tarzan the Ape Man, King Kong, Mighty Joe Young, Bedtime for Bonzo, Bringing Up Baby, Monkey Business* and *2001: A Space Odyssey*. I kid you not. Eliot had nothing to say regarding the question of why *Bringing Up Baby* is on his ape movie list.

Skyjacked (1972) would "do for disaster films what *Planet of the Apes* did for science fiction movies, giving Heston the opportunity to kick-start another dormant genre. The last tragedy-in-the-sky disaster film that hit big had been William Wellman's *The High and the Mighty* eighteen years earlier…" Wrong and wrong! It was never a dormant genre. What about *Zero Hour!* (1957), *Jet Over the Atlantic* (1959), *The Crowded Sky* (1960), *The Doomsday Flight* (1966), the mega-hit and Best Picture-nominee *Airport* (1970), etc.? If any film "kick-started" the disaster film craze of the '70s, it was *Airport*, not *Skyjacked*, which, by the way, is a much better film than Eliot leads us to believe. Another Heston "disaster" film, *Two-Minute Warning* (1976), is passed over rather quickly (and snidely), although elsewhere I have read interesting stories about its production. Eliot generally spends the most time on Heston's "biggies" and as the actor gets older and movies get "lesser," Eliot is not interested enough to cover them. I would rather hear about *Two-Minute Warning* and *Secret of the Incas* then endure another tangent totally unrelated to Heston. I wish authors like Eliot used their page count more wisely.

Instead of relating the plot of *Diamond Head* (1962) himself, Eliot lazily quotes an extensive summary from TCM's website. Obviously, the movie, like many the author deemed minor in Heston's filmography, did not interest him and he hastily dismisses it. Some minor plot points of other films are off, such as the ones for *The Wreck of the Mary Deare* (1959) and *Soylent Green* (1973).

As with all of Eliot's writings, politics are a large part of the book. This would be fine if he stuck to his subject, but he rarely does. Mentioning Paul Robeson leads to a prolonged bracketed comment explaining who he was and his political leanings. Same with Burt Lancaster and his almost-involvement with *The Greatest Show on Earth*. After quoting DeMille about Burt's politics, Eliot notes, "Not that it really mattered," before telling us the "real reason" Burt couldn't do the picture. If it really didn't matter, why mention it? Especially in a book about Charlton Heston? There is so much unnecessary background about Ronald Reagan. We do not need Reagan's life story—we have Eliot's (horrible) separate biography on him. There's also too much on Lyndon B. Johnson. Way too much.

Do I believe that the always-busy Ed Asner was blacklisted because of comments he made about Heston? I do not.

The Blacklist is repeatedly referenced in this and other Eliot books. You can bet if someone had a problem with HUAC (even a passing difficulty), it's discussed here.

In a book about Heston, no one gives a flying damn about why John Wayne turned down *High Noon*. We also get histories of the USO, the American Film Institute, Lincoln Center, the National Rifle Association and the conflict in Vietnam. Why do we have to hear about Richard Lester's career and his association with the Beatles, just because he directed a Heston picture? Why go to the trouble to explain what the TV series *Sea Hunt* is about just because it is a fleeting reference in a quote? The same occurs when he tells us who Catherine the Great was!

Eliot overwrites to the point of overkill. Tightening would have helped make this an easier read. Talking about Tom Gries, he allows a quote to go unedited and then adds a note correcting it. I mean, why quote it in the first place if it's wrong?

If you are a Heston fan, be prepared for a hard slog. There are some good things; Heston's children supply insights into his character and Heston's diary excerpts are interesting. The reviewers telling you this book is terrific, without mistakes, and definitive, are full of baloney. They have no grasp of film history and probably didn't bother to read the whole book. Well, like Lydia's doctors, I've read it *for* them.

Consider Your Ass Kissed!
by Ruta Lee

Ruta Lee is best known for her roles in *Seven Brides for Seven Brothers* (1954) and *Witness for the Prosecution* (1957), has worked extensively in film and television and has been a major force in the charitable organization The Thalians (thalians.org/) since the mid–1950s. Her autobiography, **Consider Your Ass Kissed!**, is even sloppier grammatically than actress Tisha Sterling's book *and* more expensive. Is it really that difficult to find someone to proofread your book? Don't you think your readers—or skimmers—will notice? Isn't it worth it to have your story told properly?

The floating apostrophe reared "it's" ugly head throughout, along with misplaced commas and quote marks and capitalized Words that Shouldn't be. Added to that, the often-wonky sentence structure and a back-and-forth timeline made this a mess. Italics and quotes are used for TV shows and films and it just looks unprofessional.

I am sure Miss Lee is a very nice person. I mean, seriously, the book brims with gushy references to her "dear friends" who are like sisters or family to her. She continually harps on it; I understand Debbie Reynolds was like a sister to her but does she have to mention it EVERY TIME SHE BRINGS UP HER NAME? Are all these tons of people truly her dear friends and family? And, if so, why do we care? Could the book's title be connected to the constant name-dropping? I bought this book to hear about her experiences in Hollywood. We do get that and there are some interesting stories about Frank Sinatra and others, but you have to get through a lot of trivial things she thinks are important; you know, like her dogs, houses, friends, and how wonderful she is at this or that.

There's some good stuff here and there so it's not a total waste of time. I think Ruta Lee has accomplished many good things in her life. As Don Rickles would say, "Ask her. She'll tell you."

By the way, the binding on the copy I bought was not very well made and fell apart. Serves it right.

Crane: Sex, Celebrity, and My Father's Unsolved Murder
by Robert Crane and Christopher Fryer

Crane: Sex, Celebrity, and My Father's Unsolved Murder, written by Robert Crane (son of *Hogan's Heroes* star Bob Crane) and Christopher Fryer (University Press of Kentucky), has a sensational but ultimately deceiving title. Like a lot of potential readers, I was initially interested in this because of Bob Crane (1928-78), his career, and murder.

First, let me say that this is a well-written and (at times) engrossing read. I was particularly interested in the opening passages, as the authors interwove the murder of Bob Crane and the investigation of the homicide with the years leading up to it. Some have stated that this approach was confusing, but I thought it easy to follow and it added dramatic tension to the account. Unfortunately, this narrative device was abruptly abandoned after several chapters.

There's a lot to learn about the "real" Bob Crane. We really get a sense of who he was and how he ended up leading such a sordid life after living in Connecticut and New York and moving to Hollywood. His son was a witness to much of this and in this book, he offers up some enlightening material and observations about his father, mother and stepmother. Some of it is distasteful and I have admiration for how the authors handled this touchy subject. Writing about your father, his sexual addictions, and murder, cannot be easy.

And yet…

Let's compare this with Peter Ford's biography of his father, Glenn Ford (2006's *Glenn Ford: A Life,* University of Wisconsin Press). While Glenn was not into the crazy stuff that hooked Crane, he had multiple affairs with co-stars and some difficult patches in his personal life. Peter covered it all with objectivity. But he also knew that his father's fans expected him to write about Glenn Ford and his work.

Crane and Fryer could have taken a lesson in this respect. Less than half of the book is devoted to Bob Crane, who is the book's major selling point—perhaps the book's *only* selling point. Bob's life just kinda flies by and instead we find ourselves getting into his son's life, loves, and work in minute detail. Sorry, but I did not read this to learn about the son, his interviewing for *Playboy,* and his personal and professional relationship with John Candy. Look, I like Candy—he was talented and he struck me as a genuinely caring man. (There's a great story on the set of *Only the Lonely:* Candy, learning that co-star Maureen O'Hara had a tiny dressing room, gave up his own to her and moved into hers—that is, until the producers got him another.) However, there's more on Candy here than on Bob Crane, which cheats the reader. The authors try to compare Bob Crane with Candy a few times, but this just rings hollow and seems like a strained attempt to tie these two unrelated men together somehow.

The authors have a sort of stuffy attitude when it comes to Hollywood. During 1964-65, Bob Crane was lucky enough to get a recurring role on TV's *Donna Reed Show*, which Crane-Fryer dismiss as "sweet but corny, and certainly not at all hip." Donna Reed, not hip? Imagine that. The Reed show is even compared to a totally different series, *The Dick Van Dyke Show*. Here and there, the "old establishment" in Hollywood is disparaged, and I found this annoying and unnecessary. Once again, we see the old problem of authors not understanding their target market. When you are writing a book about a sitcom star, you should have the sense to not offend people who are interested in sitcom stars.

Near the end, interest picks up with Robert Crane's dealings with his stepmother and half-brother, Scotty. In the book, it is alleged that Crane's second family tried to capitalize on his murder by selling (online) the videotapes he made of his sexual encounters. This was a very distressing section of the book. There is an undercurrent of bitterness throughout the book and while that is understandable, it is unpleasant. A lot of vindictiveness is reserved for the stepmother and half-brother. Implying that Scotty might not be his father's biological son is a little strange; just looking at photos of Scotty is enough to see a strong resemblance to Bob. There's also insight into (and enmity toward) the main suspect in the murder, Bob's friend John Carpenter (not the director, of course). Again, this is entirely understandable.

There's also some intriguing stuff about Paul Schrader's *Auto Focus* (2002), a thoroughly disturbing movie starring (a perfect) Greg Kinnear. Robert Crane had some input in the screenplay and added touches to the production, and even had a small part as an interviewer.

Although I really enjoyed most of *Crane: Sex, Celebrity, and My Father's Unsolved Murder*, I wished the authors would have concentrated exclusively on Bob Crane. They write poignantly on the illness and death of son Robert's first wife, but when a book is sold to you on the celebrity of Bob Crane, the story of Bob Crane's daughter-in-law, touching as it is, just seems to be a digression.

If you are interested in Bob Crane, you will find some new material here, but you must be prepared to read a lot about his son. While Robert led an interesting life, his story should be presented in a whole other package.

The Creature Chronicles – Exploring the *Black Lagoon* Trilogy
by Tom Weaver, with David Schecter and Steve Kronenberg

Don't let the price tag discourage you: **The Creature Chronicles – Exploring the Black Lagoon Trilogy** by Tom Weaver, with David Schecter and Steve Kronenberg, with an introduction by *Creature from the Black Lagoon* star Julie Adams, is well worth it. The McFarland hardcover is devoted to *Creature from the Black Lagoon* (1954), *Revenge of the Creature* (1955) and *The Creature Walks Among Us* (1956). I am always suspicious (and always let down) when such volumes make the usual "Everything you ever wanted to know" boast—but, in this case, this is totally right-on.

According to McFarland's blurb, the Gill Man "was the final addition to Universal's 'royal family' of movie monsters... With his scaly armor, razor claws and a face only a mother octopus could love, this Amazon denizen was perhaps the most fearsome beast in the history of Hollywood's Studio of Horrors. But he also possessed a sympathetic, poignant quality which elevated him fathoms above the many aquatic monsters who swam in his wake." At 400-plus pages, this is the definitive history of the trio of Gill Man movies, a day-by-day, detailed report of what went on during filming. There are notes about the designing and construction of the Creature suits, the weather and how it affected the shooting schedule, camera breakdowns, mishaps, preview reactions, behind-the-scenes intrigue, etc. To this is added cast biographies, story analyses, a comparison of different script drafts and how they stack up against what ended up on-screen, interviews with filmmakers, in-depth discussions of the films' music, etc. All this is complemented by 295 photos, many of which may never have been previously seen.

Tom Weaver is an inspired and astute tour guide on this Amazon expedition. His wordplay is especially noteworthy, and keeps the narrative fresh and lively—particularly when relating the films' plots. A few of his turns-of-phrase are clever and I got a kick out of most of them. (His photo captions are always extra special in his books and are never throwaways; be sure to read them for added information and, of course, for choice puns.) Some highlights— for me, at least:

His reaction to John Agar's umpteenth drunk-driving arrest is "D-U-I-yi-yi!"

A shot of underwater swimmer Ginger Stanley at the bottom of a spring, cooking dinner on a stove: Wet-ty Crocker. (Groan!)

About cantankerous, credit-grabbing makeup department head Bud Westmore: "Even when it appeared as though all the bugs had been ironed out of the plan, things were still not All Quiet on the Westmore Front."

A photo of Julie Adams on the *Black Lagoon* grotto set, being attended to by a nurse after hitting her head on a plaster "cave wall," is labeled "Lady sings the bruise." (I believe I've used that phrase in my writing, too.)

An unconscious Creature being brought to Ocean Harbor by hunters hired to "Bring him back alive": "Fishin' Accomplished!"

The Creature goes for a "breath of fresh water."

During a fight in the original *Creature*, they go "mano a claw-o."

My favorite: The scientists setting out for the Black Lagoon, to look for limestone fragments on the lagoon bottom, are "gonna take a sedimental journey."

There's a lot of fun stuff here. I am still laughing at one of Universal's marketing ideas for *Black Lagoon*: "[A] roundup on monsters highlighted by our Gill Man from this picture, and including King Kong, the WereWolf of London, Frankenstein, Buddy Hackett, etc." After Hackett's name, Tom writes "[sic!]."

Ginger Stanley—the underwater swimming double for Julie Adams and Lori Nelson—tells some great stories. I love the one about Esther Williams having to wear a fake ear in *Jupiter's Darling* (1955). Dancer Larri Thomas, ex-wife of John Bromfield, is another good interviewee; one of her best anecdotes is about her and Beverly Garland on the set of *Curucu, Beast of the Amazon* (1956) wading through mud. It just goes to show that the best tales from the sets don't always come from the "big" stars.

The cast bios (Richard Carlson, Julie Adams, Richard Denning, Antonio Moreno, John Agar, Lori Nelson, John Bromfield, Nestor Paiva, Flippy the Educated Porpoise[!], Jeff Morrow, Rex Reason, Leigh Snowden, Gregg Palmer and, of course, Gill Men Ricou Browning, Ben Chapman, Tom Hennesy and Don Megowan) are very lively. Perhaps too lively in the case of Agar and all his problems with alcohol and the law. His relationship with one-time wife Shirley Temple goes on for a little too long, but there's no denying that it's good stuff. While I don't think the author is very sympathetic to Agar or even Richard Carlson, at least he does not resort to just spewing facts. I've read too many books with short, very dry, impersonal actor biographies—a lot of times just consisting of a list of movies culled from IMDb.

I was surprised by Tom's handling of Creature actor Ben Chapman's story. As some of you might know, after Chapman's death, it was revealed that he had apparently lied in many interviews about his Korean War exploits. I was sure Tom would make some snarky remarks but, no, he handled that section with respect and a balanced view which showed both sides of the story. Tom Weaver is never dull, always gets to the heart of the matter, and the personal information he gleans from interviewees and other sources are always interesting, enlightening and engaging. The writeup on

Don Megowan (the Land Gill Man in *The Creature Walks Among Us*) is significant as there has previously been nothing chronicling his life story; Tom is helped in this respect by his interview with Megowan's daughter, who paints a sweet portrait of her father.

Tom's own portrait of director Jack Arnold is not-so-sweet, but he backs up his claims with many disturbing eyewitness accounts. He also challenges Arnold's assertions that he was a one-man band on his movies, the sole reason they were successful. Writer Harry Essex is another target; Tom makes mention of him trying to take credit for *It Came from Outer Space* (1953) and *Creature of the Black Lagoon*, "accumulating thousands of frequent liar miles talking to interviewers about his input." Yet Tom is fair, and helps others, notably designer Milicent Patrick, get the credit long denied them.

Tom's attention to details—okay, minutiae—is fabulous. He has so many great tidbits, including relating the "screwball" plot given *Revenge of the Creature* on the back cover of a 1993 VHS release. One slight jarring note comes in the section about *Creature* rip-off *Octaman*. Tom's explanation about star Pier Angeli's death is off. (For more information about the mysterious nature of her passing, consult McFarland's topnotch *Pier Angeli: A Fragile Life* by Jane Allen.)

We get some great stuff about the *Creature* rip-offs *Curucu, Beast of the Amazon, The Monster of Piedras Blancas* (1959) and *Octaman* (1971). There's background about a Gill Man parody made in 8mm by Florida residents during the making of *Revenge of the Creature* called *The Return of the Creature*, including an interview with its star-director-writer, Mike Gannon. I've seen this short film and it is indeed hilarious; it's nice to be able to learn how they made it on such a shoestring budget.

David Schecter's and Steve Kronenberg's contributions are excellent, too; Schecter writes expertly about the music in the films, while Kronenberg analyzes the content of the trilogy. I particularly enjoyed David J. Schow's recounting of the history of *The Black Lagoon Bugle* (his fanzine about the Gill Man movies) and

Dr. Robert J. Kiss' wonderfully researched bits about the films' playdates.

McFarland really went all-out with the book design. Bigger than the usual (8.5 x 11) McF volumes, this has glossy pages and an attractive color scheme using a lot of reds and greens. But what really counts, after all, is the content and it just can't be beat; it's an exhaustive, lively and essential work of scholarship. You often hear film fans say of a 60-year-old movie, "What more can be said after all this time that hasn't been said?" Well, throw that notion out the window; Messrs. Weaver, Schecter and Kronenberg have plenty to say, and most of it is completely new. A must read and the best book of its kind, bar none.

Daddy Cool: Finding My Father, The Singer Who Swapped Hollywood Fame for Home in Australia
by Darleen Bungey

A singer not well known, especially in this country, is Robert Cutter aka Lawrie Brooks. It was by accident that I found the book **Daddy Cool: Finding My Father, the Singer Who Swapped Hollywood Fame for Home in Australia** by Darleen Bungey (Allen & Unwin). One day, I was searching for information on singer Lawrence Books (1912-94), the star of Broadway's *Song of Norway* (1944), and *Daddy Cool* came up. At first, I thought it was "my" Brooks and was disappointed when it was not. Then, I was intrigued.

"He was a glamorous heart-throb, a famous American singer performing in front of Betty Davis, Katherine Hepburn, Clarke Cable and other stars." I was impressed that all three stars' names were misspelled ... but not in a good way.

"In the 1930s, his recording of 'Hawaiian Paradise' outsold those of Bing Crosby and Guy Lombardo." If this is true, could it be that the main reason was because of Andy Iona and His Islanders? After all, Cutter would have only done the brief vocal refrain.

"So how did he become an Australian infantryman, fighting alongside and performing for his fellow Diggers in Palestine, Beirut, Egypt and New Guinea? Why did he leave Hollywood and the ritziest hotels in America for a modest Californian bungalow in suburban Sydney? And what caused him to cease his endless drifting from one woman to another, one marriage to another, and settle with the love of his life?"

I had to read this book. I knew Cutter-Brooks vaguely, having heard only a few of his songs. But I am always interested in learning about "new" singer-actors. I am glad I did.

Cutter-Brooks' daughter Darleen Bungey tells her father's story in an engrossing way, and captures the 1930s and '40s in an engaging style. Her frankness was refreshing; she wasn't afraid to say some unflattering things about him. The picture that emerges of Cutter-Brooks is a fascinating one, and he truly came alive on the page for me. Nothing against Bob Dylan, but I laughed out loud at Cutter-Brooks' opinion of him: "[He sounds like a] constipated manic howling over the asylum wall."

While I agree with Bungey's assertion that Cutter-Brooks was popular in Australia, I think his accomplishments here in the U.S. are wildly exaggerated. Be that as it may, he was a good singer and worthy of this excellent biography. His daughter did a fine job investigating his life and discovering what made him tick.

Doris Day: Reluctant Star
by David Bret

"Meticulous research…Bret cleverly conjures an overview of this intriguing story."—*Sunday Express*

"Excellent. After reading this revealing book, you see how she grew to prefer puppies to people."—*Daily Express*

Those who believe that reviewing books is easy are out of their cotton-pickin' minds. It never ceases to amaze me how many so-called biographies out there seem to be written by people who can barely make a credible statement and whose main emphasis is on scandal. Fortunately, there are authors who care about getting it right—Tom Weaver, Scott O'Brien, and Eve Golden to name just a few. Too often I have to endure some truly awful writing. Or worse. In that last category is the David Bret book before me now. I keep wishing someone would wave a magic wand over him and his next book would be judiciously written, believable and reliable. I live in the real world, however, and I was sure his **Doris Day: Reluctant Star** was going to be bad—and, oh, is it bad! Of course, if you read other, more prestigious reviewers, this is a tell-it-like-it-is book—a revealing, and wonderfully written biography. The word "excellent" has been used to describe it, which is why, although the book is a few years old, I decided to see for myself.

Like other volumes of its ilk, this one has an agenda: to tear down its subject, strip her of all dignity, and make wild accusations about her and others in her life. Well, I am sick of it.

I know actors are not perfect—nobody is!—and I wouldn't care to read a sugarcoated version of anyone's life. This, however, is a very bitter portrait of Doris Day, and it is not based in reality. This is not balanced reporting, but an attempt to knock a much-loved person down several pegs through innuendo and outrageous claims. There is no denying that Doris led a tough life, endured quite a few hardships, and married the wrong men. She talked about her trials and tribulations in *Doris Day: Her Own Story*, written with A.E. Hotchner back in the 1970s. Bret claims that "in trying not to offend her readers and risk many of them losing respect for her that had built up over the years, and on account of her strong, if not frequently misguided religious principles, she was not always entirely honest about herself and those around her." So, now we are to believe the author is here to save the day? *He* is going to reveal the truth about Doris, telling us what "really happened"? Hogwash.

His bibliography is comprised of the usual suspects: *Hollywood Babylon* and *Hollywood Babylon 2, The Illustrated Who's Who of the Cinema, The Gay Book of Days, The Celluloid Closet* and three of Bret's own books. *Doris Day: Her Own Story* was his major source here, but I have the feeling Bret used Doris' volume as a mere container to fill with garbage. He apparently wouldn't have known much about her troubles if she hadn't written her book first. About the only "new information" in Bret's book is nasty, unsourced gossip. Since Bret does not give us endnotes, we have no idea where he got any of his sensational assertions.

There is no source for a quote from Doris' mother (who died in 1976) wherein she claims her brother would have "gladly killed [Doris' first husband] Al Jorden on the spot if need be."

Bret obsesses about the wrong things. Who cares if Doris' mother never found another man after she divorced? This happens later when Doris herself, burned after four marriages, decided to remain single. Is it really necessary for a woman to be married at all times? He makes a comment about her dying an old maid because her standards were too high. Ugh. In Doris' case, it is entirely understandable that she wanted no more drama in her life. Bret even questions her devotion to animals and goes on far too long criticizing her belief in Christian Science. What Doris did or didn't do and what religion she chose to practice is her own business; she doesn't have to answer to David Bret.

I was not happy with the treatment given singer Frances Langford. Bret gives two versions as to why Langford left Bob Hope's radio show. First, that when Les Brown was hired, Hope wanted to keep Langford and did not want Doris with the band, but Brown insisted, "No Doris, no Les," so Langford was canned. Langford's purported reaction was to raise a fuss and call Doris "that Cincinnati bitch." Then he alleges that, in fact, the show's producer was happy to get rid of the popular and established Langford because of her "escalating personal problems." These so-called problems involved, claims Bret, "having sex with a fighter pilot while at the controls of his plane." He then turns around and says that this incident led to her firing and the hiring of Doris—forgetting about his earlier remark about Les' ultimatum.

First of all, Langford was not fired. In 1946, Hope's show was going in another direction, to that of situation comedy. Frances had been making sporadic appearances on his show and was a regular on 1945's *The Chase and Sanborn Program*. She always found time to work with Hope, though, but ultimately left to star in her own airwave series with Don Ameche, *The Drene Show*, where they played The Bickersons. In regards to Langford, Bret knows so little about her that he says she "starred" in *Broadway Melody of 1936* and had "just completed" *Yankee Doodle Dandy* (1942)! The truth is that Doris guested on Hope's show in '46, but did not become a regular until 1948. Bret has screwed up the entire timeline.

Bret writes that, at Columbia, Doris had her say on who she sang duets with—Dinah Shore, Frank Sinatra, Johnnie Ray, Guy Mitchell, Frankie Laine, and Donald O'Connor. He even makes the absurd statement that the singers "had to be Jewish also like herself, descendants of immigrants." Doris was (a) not Jewish, and (b) not able to dictate to Columbia execs. (He later contradicts himself—again—and mentions that Columbia organized the duets.)

Then we get to Bret's main interest: "And was it merely by chance that some of these men happened to be gay at a time when Doris was starting to develop such a following and when, like Elizabeth Taylor and Judy Garland, she possessed a sixth sense for detecting a man's sexuality?" Seriously? What is going on here?

Next, it's poor Buddy Clark's turn in the barrel. "Doris found Buddy attractive, and was not put off by him being gay, though needless to say they never had an affair." There is no source for Buddy being gay. He was married twice and had children, and at the time of his recordings with Doris he did have a wife. I know these facts don't necessarily mean he was straight, but what is the source of Buddy being gay? It gets worse: According to the author, Buddy's "last hit recording in his lifetime—dedicated to an unnamed male lover—had been 'I Love You So Much It Hurts.'"

Funny, I didn't hear that dedication, even whispered, on his record. Also, Buddy did not make his debut with Benny Goodman in 1934; it came in 1932 with Gus Arnheim.

More drivel: Doris would "never forgive" Buddy for recording a duet with her rival Dinah Shore. "To exact her revenge," remarks Bret, she "persuaded Shore to duet with her on the deprecating, appropriately titled 'You Can Have Him.'" So, we are supposed to believe that Doris orchestrated this to get back at both Buddy and Dinah? What book publisher-editor would allow this kind of absurdity to get by?

Now we get to director Michael Curtiz, a handy target in other Bret books. Most of what Bret writes about Curtiz is crude and totally off-base. He says that the director called George O'Brien a "prickless faggot" on the set of *Noah's Ark* (1928), which prompted O'Brien to "burst into tears"; he repeats an incident on the *Captain Blood* set about Ross Alexander and his "exuberant armpits" and Errol Flynn threatening Curtiz with a razor; and writes out a lot of profanities Curtiz allegedly said to and about Doris during her screen test and on the set of *Romance on the High Seas* (1948); Doris allegedly responded with more cursing. (Practically everyone in Bret's book has a potty mouth.) According to Bret, a comment made to Doris by Curtiz, in which he used the expression "do not disturb," was later borrowed by Doris for her movie *Do Not Disturb* (1965). Yes, Doris really told the producers and songwriters, "Hey, Curtiz said something to me in 1948 that would make a great title and name of a song." No, I think not.

To get the true story about Michael Curtiz, I went to the best source, Alan K. Rode, who has a Curtiz book coming out from the University Press of Kentucky (see review below). I know Alan's a stickler for facts and he takes his research seriously. When I made him aware of Bret's claims, he emailed back that this was utter nonsense. When prodded further, Alan wrote, "[George] O'Brien admired Curtiz's obsession with realism that turned other people off. He let Curtiz have an actual hot iron held near his face during a blinding scene and was also literally impaled with a collapsible spear that didn't collapse. There is a lot of folklore about *Noah's Ark*. No one really knows if people actually were killed as has been written about ad nauseam. As for the Day episode, it is contrary to everything she has said or written about her initial audition and subsequent screen test with Curtiz that earned her the role in *Romance on the High Seas*. She had the highest respect for 'Mr. Curtiz.' This book sounds like more made-up junk by a successor to Charles Higham." Amen, Alan.

To set the record straight:

Doris Kenyon was not Rudolph Valentino's leading lady in *Monsieur Beaucaire* (1924), Bebe Daniels was.

The song "The Bird on Nellie's Hat" was written by Arthur J. Lamb and Alfred Solman, not singer May Ward. I think Bret's a bit confused here. He says that Maidie Scott popularized the song and while she did have success with it, Ward had the hit first.

Doris could not have sung "That Old Black Magic" in 1939 since it was not written until 1942.

In her autobiography, Doris detailed her life as an abused wife. First husband Al Jorden was undoubtedly troubled. Bret goes a step further and says that Doris enjoyed this treatment and wore her "bruises with pride." He also diagnoses Jorden as a closeted homosexual simply because of the way he treated Doris! I have no idea where that "logic" comes from, nor do I want to know. Doris' second hubby is also pegged as bisexual. The "author" blames Doris' "bad table manners" for Jorden's mood swings and abuse. He also says that Doris was a nymphomaniac—a rather extreme claim.

Would Doris name her son Terry after "her favorite book from her childhood," *Terry and the Pirates*? Or, could it be, that she named him after the comic strip of that name created by Milton Caniff?

Calling the Williams Brothers "the original boy band" is laughable. That quartet (Bob, Don, Dick and Andy) sang on radio and did backup on recordings and in movies. Wikipedia's definition of a boy band is "a vocal group consisting of young male singers, usually in their teenage years or in their twenties at the time of

formation, singing love songs marketed towards young females."
This kind of popularity the group did not enjoy and they were
mostly anonymous during this time—until Andy broke away to
start his own career.

"Gargantuan wisecracker" Jack Carson was typecast as the "inar-
ticulate guy-next-door with the heart of gold who invariably lost
the girl at the end of the picture," Bret says, showing that he knows
little about the actor.

Bret makes much throughout about how Doris and Frank Sinatra hated each other's guts and they "loathed" sharing the recording booth together. Of what I read, from far more reliable sources,
the opposite was the case. Also, I have heard outtakes of their
recording and they seem to be having fun with each other when
Frank ad-libs.

Another thing: Why in the world would Warner Brothers "hit
on the idea" of publicizing *My Dream Is Yours* (1949) by pairing
her with Frank Sinatra on a Columbia recording of a song not in
the movie, "Let's Take an Old Fashioned Walk"? The answer is
they didn't. Warners didn't run Columbia Records. Also, WB had
no interest in Sinatra at the time and didn't care one way or the
other if he had a hit song. "It would take another six years—and
the success of *From Here to Eternity*—for Sinatra to get back on
his feet." The time between *My Dream is Yours* (1949) and *From
Here to Eternity* (1953) is four years, not six.

Lee Bowman was hated by everyone and considered a "nasty
piece of work"? By whom? Bret also says that Lee was "popular
with audiences." I wish that were so.

David Butler directed *It's a Great Feeling* (1949), but he was not
in charge of hiring the songwriters. Bret refers to Doris' "so-so
cover of Marlene Dietrich's 'You Go to My Head.'" While Dietrich recorded it, it was hardly "her song" and she was not the first
to sing it. Likewise with Kate Smith and the song "Imagination."

Jazz cornetist Bix Beiderbecke died of lobar pneumonia and
alcoholism, and to insinuate murder or suicide is ridiculous. The
m.o. here is to suggest scandal where there is none.

Lynn Root and Harry Clork's play *The Milky Way* was filmed first under that title in 1936 with Harold Lloyd in the lead; Danny Kaye's *The Kid from Brooklyn* (1946) was the second filmed version.

I cannot believe Bret left out some dirt, especially when it's true. Talking about Steve Cochran, Bret says he was regarded as one of the "gentlest" men in Hollywood. Numerous arrests during Cochran's lifetime say otherwise; he was accused of beating and tying up women. Mamie Van Doren, in her autobiography, mentions that he got violent and she had to end their relationship because of it. Of course, many thought he was a wonderful, funny guy, but the fact remains that he had anger issues.

Bret does not miss out on the chance to mention Cochran's "legendary appendage." That Doris had an affair with Cochran has never been proven, but that doesn't stop the "author" from going on about it.

On Moonlight Bay (1951) was not based on Booth Tarkington's novel *Alice Adams*. The screenplay was culled from the Tarkington novels *Penrod* and *Penrod and Sam*. His info on the album of songs Doris did from *On Moonlight Bay* on Columbia is wrong; Jack Smith did not sub for Gordon MacRae (who was under contract to Capitol) on the songs done in the movie; Jack sang two of the songs he did in the film, "I'm Forever Blowing Bubbles" and "Love Ya." James Emmons was the singer who took MacRae's place on the records, dueting with Doris on "Till We Meet Again" and "Cuddle Up a Little Closer."

Did Johnnie Ray really ejaculate during a live singing appearance? I hope not. Bret's dirty writing gets into high gear when he claims that the song "Candy Lips" was really an "ode to oral sex," but its meaning went "over the heads of the general public." But not Bret, by golly; with a subterranean mind in which he takes great pride, he's as sharp as a tack when it comes to stuff like this! Along the same lines, *On Moonlight Bay* had strong lesbian overtones with an "actual" character whom Bret claims was supposed to be gay. The same goes for *Calamity Jane* (1953): three of the songs have "homosexual overtones" and Doris' Calamity has an attraction to the character played by Allyn Ann McLerie. The Oscar-winning song "Secret Love" is about lesbianism, natch. Rock Hudson and Tony Randall's relationship in *Send Me No Flowers* (1964) also has a gay subtext. *Please Don't Eat the Daisies*, *Midnight Lace* (both 1960), *Come September* (1961, not with Doris), and *That Touch of Mink* (1962) all have a wealth of gay in-jokes. Or could it be that Bret finds double-entendres and gay vibes everywhere he wants to find them?

The 1984 television movie *Calamity Jane* was not a remake of Doris' film. While he disparages this later movie, it actually won some awards and lead Jane Alexander was Emmy-nominated. In discussing the real-life Calamity Jane, he attacks her for what he says are falsehoods, the result of an "overactive imagination." Is the pot calling the kettle black here? More hypocrisy: Talking about Rock Hudson's last days with AIDS, Bret actually writes, "Over the next few days the public were fed the most lurid resume of his personal life—very dubious 'exclusives' acquired from suspicious sources: insiders, talent scouts, so-called close friends and prominent doctors, who were of course unnamed and in almost every instance pure editorial fiction; the oldest trick in the book." Apropos of nothing, did you know that there's an ego defense mechanism called "projection" that compels people to accuse others of doing the shameful things that they themselves do?

It says here that Al Jolson's version of "I'm Just Wild About Harry" was done "as an appreciation of his lover, American-Hungarian dancer Harry Pilcer." Wow, okay, no. By the way, Pilcer was born in New York City.

Calling the Lane Sisters "a popular musical comedy act of the day" is really misleading. They made movies together, but to call them a musical comedy act is incorrect.

He says Gordon Douglas, compared to Curtiz, was an amateur when he was assigned to direct *Young at Heart* (1954). Douglas' career went back to the early 1930s and he was a more-than-competent craftsman.

Ava Gardner did not regularly visit the *Young at Heart* set, as she and Sinatra had broken up. Also, Ava was not dubbed by Gogi Grant in *Show Boat*; Annette Warren was her voice double. Bret is thinking of Grant's singing for Ann Blyth in *The Helen Morgan Story*.

Regarding a bad review Pauline Kael gave Doris for *Love Me or Leave Me* (1955), Bret states that Doris' response was "said to have been unprintable."

The film version of *The Women* was released in 1939, not 1936.

"Diminutive" is the sole word used to describe Alan Ladd. The man was 5'6"—he was not a midget! Stop slamming Ladd about his height. Cagney was almost two inches shorter, who cares? Reta Shaw has the adjective "roly poly" attached to her name. Ethel Merman gets the delightful "motormouth chanteuse."

During the making of *Julie* (1956), Bret still has Louis B. Mayer head of MGM but on the "verge of retirement." In fact, Mayer resigned in 1951.

The Pajama Game (1957) was not Bob Fosse's film debut. *The Affairs of Dobie Gillis* (1953) was his first as an actor; as a choreographer it was *Kiss Me Kate* (1953).

The song is called "I'm Not At All in Love," not "I'm Not An All In Love." The accompanying musical scene for this is compared to something out of the Australian soap opera *Prisoner* (aka *Prisoner: Cell Block H*), which was about women behind bars. I kid you not.

The old story about Clark Gable having bad breath is brought up yet again, because Doris couldn't have possibly swooned when he kissed her in *Teacher's Pet* (1958).

During *Storm Warning* (1951), Ronald Reagan was not newly divorced from Jane Wyman; they untied the knot in 1948.

It's *The Caine Mutiny Court-Martial*, not *The Caine Mutiny Court Marshall*.

It's Helen Forrest not Helen Forest. Tim Conway not Tom Conway.

Rod Taylor did not make a "series of science fiction films" before co-starring with Doris; prior to their teaming his only sci-fi films were *World Without End* (1956, a supporting part) and *The Time Machine* (1960).

Clint Eastwood did not replace Eric Fleming on TV's *Rawhide*, the two had co-starred on the series together from the beginning and then Clint went on alone after Fleming left.

Stephen Boyd is said to be gay and he would rush "home to his boyfriend" after leaving the girls he escorted around town. Source?

On a Doris Day TV special, she jokes around with Rock Hudson and introduces him as Tab Hunter. Bret interprets this as a "real surprise" slipped into the script to slyly reference Rock's homosexuality, because "Tab never made any secret of his homosexuality while Rock always fought to conceal his." I seriously doubt Doris would have allowed this to happen.

To back up his statement about Doris not doing more for Hudson when he was dying of AIDS, Bret quotes Marlene Dietrich, condemning Doris for putting her animals first. This is unreasonable.

He repeats an "ungallant report" by someone saying Doris went out in public in her later years looking like a bag lady. His repeating it is just as bad, especially since he seems to agree with it.

Bret's remarks about the TV series *Dynasty* are more than a little strange. I watched that show and the idea that the characters played by Rock Hudson and Michael Nader were "fuck buddies" is just too weird for words.

Nick Adams was not a household name because of the short-lived TV series *Saints and Sinners* (1962), but for *The Rebel* (1959-61), where he played Johnny Yuma. Clark Gable, on the set of *Teacher's Pet*, was worried that Adams knew all about his "secret gay past"—baloney. Supposedly, Adams also supplied James Dean lookalikes to big name male stars to have sex with. Uh, yeah, sure.

Loretta Young did not star in *It Happened One Night*, it was, of course, Claudette Colbert in her famous Oscar-winning role.

Bret, to strengthen his snide assertion that Cary Grant was gay and there was "something wrong with him," makes a boo-boo by saying that none of his "four marriages" bore any children. In reality, he was married five times and Dyan Cannon gave birth to his daughter Jennifer.

Brian Wilson was not involved professionally with Charles Manson, it was his brother, Dennis Wilson.

Much space is devoted to laboriously recounting in tedious detail the plots of Doris' films. It's endless and if you brave this creepy book, you will find this filler a complete waste of time. Also, although Bret really admires her singing, most of her movies are panned. He says her performance in her debut, *Romance on the High Seas,* was awful and that "she is not allowed enough time to deliver each line, resulting in her speech being gabbled and frequently incomprehensible." Something tells me Bret has been watching poorly duped copies of her movies. Can anyone be so ignorant that they do not know that major Hollywood studio films of that day were made with an extremely high level of technical skill?

None of her co-stars seem to be good enough for Doris, and he particularly dislikes Rod Taylor, Frank Sinatra, and James Garner. More seriously, every movie's storyline reflects in some way her personal life, a sadistic ploy by husband Marty Melcher to drive her to mental ruin; much is made of her Method acting, and Marty's glee in watching her suffer. I don't think Marty was a nice man and he undoubtedly was not good to Doris, but he's made over-the-top evil here.

In Bret's atrocious Clark Gable book, he fawned over Doris. In this book, Bret's attitude toward her is completely reversed. What accounts for this extreme change in treatment? The only explanation I can imagine is that the author thinks that the best way to sell a book is to fling mud at the subject.

Dorothy Lee: The Life and Films of the Wheeler

and Woolsey Girl
by Jamie Brotherton and Ted Okuda

I just love knowing that we live in a world where we can read a book like **Dorothy Lee: The Life and Films of the Wheeler and Woolsey Girl** by Jamie Brotherton and Ted Okuda (McFarland). That this book is also a fascinating and breezy read is absolutely awesome.

Dorothy Lee (1911–99) was a singer-actress of the early sound era best known for her films with the comedy team of Wheeler and Woolsey. She was a talented little performer, appearing in vaudeville, singing with Fred Waring and His Pennsylvanians, acting on stage, and seen in the movies *Take Me Home* (1928), *Syncopation, Rio Rita* (both 1929), *The Cuckoos, Dixiana, Half Shot at Sunrise, Hook Line and Sinker* (all 1930), *Laugh and Get Rich, The Stolen Jools* (short), *Cracked Nuts, Too Many Cooks, Caught Plastered, Local Boy Makes Good, Peach-O-Reno* (all 1931), *Girl Crazy* (1932), *Mazie, A Preferred List* (short), *Take a Chance, Plane Crazy* (short), *Signing 'Em Up* (short, all 1933), *Hips, Hips, Hooray!, School for Girls, Cockeyed Cavaliers, If This Isn't Love* (short), *The Curtain Falls* (all 1934), *In the Spotlight* (short), *Without Children, The Old Homestead, The Rainmakers* (all 1935), *Silly Billies* (1936), *Twelve Crowded Hours, S.O.S. Tidal Wave* (both 1939), *Laddie* (1940), *Repent at Leisure, Roar of the Press*, and *Too Many Blondes* (all 1941). Two of my favorite songs by Lee were duets with Bert Wheeler: "From Niagara Falls to Reno" from *Peach-O-Reno* and *Hips, Hips, Hooray!'s* "Keep on Doing What You're Doing."

The quality of the writing is superb; the pages rustle by at a fast clip and it's never boring. This is helped immeasurably by input from Lee herself. The authors interviewed her—and what they got were wonderful reminiscences about her movies, her co-workers, her aborted love affair with Fred Waring, and the relationships with her six husbands, which including columnist Jimmie Fidler.

There are choice quotes throughout, and a warmth, which gives this biography a glow. This extends to the terrific foreword by Nick

Santa Maria, who also knew Lee. The authors add some great details about all the movies, and do not rely solely on plot summaries.

The book, while rightly complimentary about Lee and her films, never overstates her stardom. If they don't like a movie, the authors say so. Lee's own modest assessment of her (vast) talent is fun to read: "When I watch myself—oh, brother! I have no idea how I lasted as long as I did. I guess I got by on whatever charm I might have had. And the movies were pretty bad too. A couple of the Wheeler and Woolsey pictures are cute, but most of them just aren't very good, and it makes me wonder why these films were so popular..."

Charm is what Lee and this book have in spades. There are some first-hand stories about such stars as Buster Keaton, Marion Davies, Al Jolson, Harold Lloyd, and Ginger Rogers— and, of course, Wheeler and Woolsey who are, in my opinion, one of the most underappreciated comedy teams ever. (A nice companion volume to this book is McFarland's *Wheeler & Woolsey: The Vaudeville Comic Duo and Their Films, 1929–1937* by Edward Watz, forewords by Tom Dillon and Dorothy Lee.)

The saucy cover shot perfectly conveys the fun that Lee exuded on screen. I totally loved this book, and you will, too. Full filmography and marvelous photos complete the package. A must-have!

Ed Wood and the Lost Lugosi Screenplays
by Gary D. Rhodes

The BearManor *Scripts from the Crypt* series sails into new territory, UN-made scripts, in its fifth entry, **Ed Wood and the Lost Lugosi Screenplays** by Gary D. Rhodes.

For decades, fans of the Worst Director of All Time (Wood) have been reading in books and magazines, and hearing in documentaries, about his plans to make two more Bela Lugosi vehicles,

The Ghoul Goes West and *The Vampire's Tomb.* The movies never got made but the scripts did get written, and now diehard Wood fans can read them. As pointed out in this book, as you read them, you'll see Lugosi in your mind's eye playing the parts and hear him in your mind's ear reciting the dialogue, accent and all.

First is *The Ghoul Goes West*, which might have paired Bela with Gene Autry if it had ever come to pass. The storyline is "*Bride of the Monster* [another Wood-Lugosi film] in cowboy hat and Western chaps," according to Tom Weaver, another contributor to the book. He makes this comparison: "In *Bride of the Monster*, Lugosi is a foreigner-scientist, banished from his homeland, who has set up shop in a desolate American locale and has henchman Tor Johnson kidnapping locals for his experimental use (he intends to create a race of supermen). In *The Ghoul Goes West*, the Lugosi-like main character is a foreigner-scientist, banished from his homeland, who has set up shop in a desolate American locale and has his *two* Tor Johnson–like henchmen stealing corpses for his experimental use (he intends to create a race of supermen)."

The second script, *The Vampire's Tomb*, is a cross between *And Then There Were None* and *Mark of the Vampire*, with murder most foul taking place in an old dark house where a sinister bunch plots a rub-out—but then they start getting knocked off themselves. The Lugosi character this time is a mysterious stranger who is either a Prof. Van Helsing–like vampire hunter ... or a vampire. If you remember *Mark of the Vampire*, I bet you could guess right now who Lugosi really is, even though you've never seen the movie through no fault of your own because it was never made. (Leave it to Ed Wood to make a movie so predictable that you can guess the ending without him even making it.) Meanwhile, there is a Girl Vampire "in the long flowing robes of the dead" that's obviously a rip-off of *Mark of the Vampire's* Luna (Carroll Borland). *The Vampire's Tomb* is especially fun reading because Wood knew who he wanted to cast in all the co-starring and supporting parts, and now we the readers know, so while reading the script you can picture these actors throughout: Lyle Talbot, Loretta King, Dolores Fuller, Duke Moore, Bobby Jordan(!) and more.

This book is much more than the two scripts. After an intro by a guy who knew Ed Wood when both worked in the "adult book" biz, Gary Rhodes is first up at bat (pun) with "Unfinished Symphonies: A Non-Production Background," over 30 pages of everything that's known about Wood's plans for these two pictures. A good bit of it is derived from items printed in *The Hollywood Reporter, Variety*, etc., but there are also comments from interviewees (including Alex Gordon), quotes from personal correspondence and more.

Tom Weaver is aboard with "Annotated Synopses" of the two movies. His synopses would be useless to anyone who intends to read the scripts, but the saving grace is that throughout his two lengthy recaps, he points out bloopers, makes various observations and, most interestingly, points out the *other* Lugosi movies (beyond *Bride of the Monster* and *Mark of the Vampire*) from which Wood stole bits and pieces of plot, even lines of dialogue. The list includes *Dracula, Murders in the Rue Morgue, The Raven, The Wolf Man*, even *Abbott and Costello Meet Frankenstein*. In Weaver's description of a *Ghoul Goes West* scene in which a beating victim is left lying in a doorway, then revives and staggers to the sheriff's office and collapses in the doorway, he adds parenthetically, "This guy must just *like* to lie in doorways."

The lineup of extras continues with Lee R. Harris' everything-you-always-wanted-to-know essay on the making of Wood's TV pilot *Final Curtain* (a treatment for that film is included too).

Sorry, Rhodes, Weaver and Harris, but the best contribution (saved for last) is by Robert Cremer. Cremer wrote the first Lugosi bio, *The Man Behind the Cape* (1976), and here he materializes out of the past with the essay "A Tale o' the Cock: My Weekend with Ed Wood," in which he describes the experience of hanging with the snockered Wood and picking his brain for *Man Behind the Cape*—with Wood bitterly complaining that a Lugosi bio is a book that he, Wood, not Cremer, should be writing. The far-out "Weekend at Brewskie's" saga culminates in a …

No, I'm not going to tell you, you have to read it yourself. A member of the Classic Horror Film Board described this Cremer chapter in a way I couldn't hope to match, so I'll just quote him: "Cremer's account of an evening with Ed Wood and friends is … incredible. The story simultaneously makes me wish I'd been there and also feel so very very grateful that I wasn't."

The icing on the cake: the brilliant *Ghoul Goes West* and *Vampire's Tomb* posters that artist George Chastain created for this book. Now, in addition to scripts and production histories, even posters exist for these non-existent movies. Ad lines for *Ghoul Goes West* include "More THRILLS than SHANE & HIGH NOON" and "More CHILLS than DRACULA & FRANKENSTEIN."

Like parts of other Rhodes (and Weaver) books, *Ed Wood and the Lost Lugosi Screenplays* isn't for the casual schlock movie fan but for the advanced student: The authors assume that you know all the basics about these people (Wood, Lugosi, more) and their movies and then they lead you down many very obscure and arcane paths to further knowledge. Do fans need to know all these things? Do fans need to know *any* of these things? Perhaps not. But as Criswell says in Wood's *Orgy of the Dead* (1966), "It pleasures me" to know them. So maybe it'll pleasure you too.

Ed Wood's *Bride of the Monster*
by Tom Weaver

Tom Weaver's *Scripts from the Crypt* series rolls on with #4, **Ed Wood's Bride of the Monster** (BearManor), the 1955 sci-fi/horror starring Bela Lugosi. This volume is filled to the brim with goodies: foreword by Sam Sherman; "'He Tampered in God's Domain': The Horrible History of *Bride of the Monster*" by Gary D. Rhodes; "Fun Facts" by Weaver; an examination of *Bride's* music by Michael Lee; *Bride's* release history plus a bio of character actor Ben Frommer by Dr. Robert J. Kiss; the pressbook; Buddy Barnett's *Cult Movies* interview with co-star Loretta King; Alex Gordon's "My Favorite Vampire" (an article that originally appeared in a 1963 issue of *Fantastic Monsters of the Films*); a 1978 Ed Wood interview conducted by filmmaker Fred Olen Ray; the divorce papers of Bela and his fourth wife Lillian(!); a 1986 interview with Richard Sheffield by Gary D. Rhodes; reproduction of the playbill for Bela's *Arsenic and Old Lace* (1954); press clippings and script for 1954's *The Bela Lugosi Revue*; the full transcript of his 1955 Senate testimony on his drug addiction; Bela's foreword to Ed Wood's book *Your Career in Hollywood*; a personal, typewritten recollection of Bela by his fifth wife Hope; and Bela's death certificate, mortuary charges and last will.

The centerpiece, of course, is the *Bride of the Monster* screenplay. I know, you are probably thinking, "It had a script??" Yes, it did, and over the years there's been much haggling about who actually wrote it. Gary D. Rhodes, the leading Lugosi expert, takes all this conflicting information and does a terrific job of sifting through it. There was also a lot of drama going on in Lugosi's life during this time. It's sad, to be sure, but Rhodes treats Bela with the respect he deserves. I have read little of Rhodes' work, but he is a fantastic writer. Years ago, I reviewed his scholarly *White Zombie: Anatomy of a Horror Film* (McFarland).

Tom Weaver makes his typically wry observations in his "Fun Facts" section. He uncovers some real finds such as Conrad Nagel's nephew Don being part of the cast and he quotes from a *Scary Monsters* interview with Don. I am always amazed by the obscure stuff he unearths and brings together. His informal tone puts the fun in the facts. Weaver's "Fun Facts" concentrate mostly but not exclusively on the movie; he begins with the story of the partnership of Ed Wood and *Bride* co-writer Alex Gordon and then picks apart *Bride*, pointing out bloopers, interesting trivia (including a cast member's visibly missing finger) and questioning some of the things that happen in the movie. My favorite: In the finale, the almost skeletal Lugosi character is transformed into a rampaging man-beast *much* larger than Tor Johnson, and yet little Lugosi's clothes still fit him. Because so much of Tim Burton's *Ed Wood* (1994) is devoted to the making of *Bride of the Monster*, Weaver spills lots of ink on that movie also, up to and including star Johnny Depp's arrest for trashing a NYC hotel room around the time of *Ed Wood*'s release, outrageous behavior that some speculated was purposeful (to increase interest in the actor and his newest movie). Weaver also points out that Martin Landau, accepting his Best Supporting Actor Oscar for playing Lugosi in *Ed Wood*, was building in his acceptance speech to a salute to Bela Lugosi—but the Oscar gods must have thought he was taking too much time and struck up the band, drowning him out just as he was about to sing Bela's praises from the Shrine Auditorium stage to a worldwide audience of a billion people. As Boris Karloff always liked to say, "Poor Bela!"

One of my favorite parts of the book is Dr. Robert J. Kiss' write-up about Ben Frommer (1913-92). I love forgotten players, those actors not typically written about, and Dr. Kiss brings Frommer to life in his astute piece. He also had access to his personal scrapbook!

Bride of the Monster was the only Ed Wood movie to feature an original score. Michael Lee does a bang-up job of analyzing it and furnishing some info on composer Frank L Worth (1903-90), heretofore unheralded.

The Rhodes chapter is the main course, tracking the confusing history of the making of the movie, which was begun in one year and, after a long hiatus, finished in the next. A large number of news blurbs from *Variety* and *The Hollywood Reporter* help him create a plausible-sounding timeline and to speculate on What Was Shot When. Along the way, there's lots of interesting tidbits, including the fact that actress Helen Gilbert (who counted among her many husbands gangster Johnny Stompanato) was in the running for the picture's lead. Rhodes, like Weaver, is a film historian who wants to get it right and not rely on the mounds of misinformation out there. They go the extra mile. It's amazing to me that here it is 2017 and these two are supplying fresh information and insights about a more than 60-year-old movie.

The photos are exceptional and reproduced very well: scene stills and candids, clippings, ads, many rarities never seen before.

Hard-core Lugosi and Ed Wood fans will eat this up but, truly, any movie fan will find something here to pique their interest.

Errol Flynn: Gentleman Hellraiser
by David Bret

"Author" David Bret has reached a new low with his "biography" **Errol Flynn: Gentleman Hellraiser,** a revision of his earlier *Errol Flynn: Satan's Angel.* You really can't blame Bret, though. In my opinion, he's giving his readers exactly what they want—trash and fantasies disguised as biography and fact. Sadly, reviewers also are guilty of eagerly lapping up this slop. "With the same gusto and verve of his subject, Bret plows through Flynn's escapades and accomplishments," wrote Publishers Weekly. "A generally unprejudiced look at a man who left a lasting mark on the cinema and many in it." No wonder the gullible innocents fall prey to such writing when even Publishers Weekly seems to believe what Bret is writing. Or do they? Does anyone? Is the acceptance of such books merely a knowing surrender to fantasy?

Admittedly, Flynn is a perfect target for celebrity fantasy books. We all know the Flynn legend, of his adventures, drinking and womanizing. He's so outrageous that it's very easy for writers to add to that legend. After all, it sounds like something Flynn would do, right? So, it must be true. Some authors approach Tallulah Bankhead the same way, attributing to her every raunchy quote they can find or fabricate. How do we know if even half the stuff printed about her is even remotely true? At this late date, it is hard to tell.

Not surprisingly, David Bret projects these fantasies without substantiating them with endnotes, or lists of credible sources. He typically claims that a "friend"—in this case the long-dead Marlene Dietrich—told him of the sordid goings on in Flynn's life.

Let's first take a look at this book's bibliography, which Bret calls "Primary & Secondary Sources." Twenty-three are listed, but too many of them are either very questionable overall, or of little use in substantiating a bio of Flynn. His list includes: *Hollywood Babylon* (volumes one and two) by Kenneth Anger; *The MGM Story* by John Douglas Eames; *The Secret Life of Tyrone Power* by Hector Arce; *The Gay Book of Days* by Martin Greif (whose subtitle should give you an idea of the rubbish it is: An Evocatively Illustrated Who's Who of Who Is, Was, May Have Been, Probably Was, and Almost Certainly Seems to Have Been Gay During the Past 5000 Years); *Errol Flynn, The Untold Story* by Charles Higham; *Hollywood & the Great Fan Magazines* by Martin Levin; *The Sewing Circle* by Axel Madsen; *Quinlan's Film Stars* by David Quinlan; *High Camp, A Gay Guide to Camp & Cult Film, Vol. 1* by Paul Roen; and *The Secret Sex Lives of Famous People* by Amy and Irving Wallace (which is actually the wrong title—it is *The Intimate Sex Lives of Famous People*).

Even though Bret mentions Flynn's friend Buster Wiles in some stories in the book, never once does he appear to have consulted the invaluable *My Days with Errol Flynn: The Autobiography of Stuntman Buster Wiles*. We have no idea where Bret gets the notion that Wiles served as Flynn's pimp, obtaining both young girls and boys for him. Bret also ignores three other credible books: Flynn's second wife Nora Eddington's *Errol and Me*, *The Young Errol: Flynn Before Hollywood* by John Hammond Moore, and *The Baron of Mulholland: A Daughter Remembers Errol Flynn* by Rory Flynn. It also seems he never bothered to check any of the files or production reports for Flynn's movies, but he seems to "know" stories from the locations, accounts that are always dirty and sound highly suspicious. Nor are any autobiographies of Flynn colleagues referred to. Instead, we get unsubstantiated quotes from Flynn and others detailing all kinds of crazy things.

Weirdly, the book promises "extraordinary revelations" in this "compelling and affectionate portrait." Affectionate? Is it rational to claim that an affectionate look at Flynn includes painting him as a crude, dishonest, selfish pedophile who is into pornographic films featuring bestiality? Is this the "unprejudiced look" Publishers Weekly was thinking of? No, don't be misled: if David Bret has a definite agenda here, I would opine that it is to top every other Flynn biography for outrageous, salacious accusations. "Bret explores the star's love of underage girls, young men, binge drinking and drug experimentation," the back cover crows.

I simply don't understand what passes for "humor" in this book and I seriously doubt that Errol would have done any of the "funny" things Bret claims: farting in front of director Michael Curtiz, masturbating in omelets to serve to unsuspecting friends, using mortuary instruments for cutlery, etc.

In truth, the main focus of this book is sex—lots of sex. If you are to believe this book, Flynn had sex with virtually every single person he ever bumped into, male and female alike. Of course, many of these liaisons make their debuts here in this book ... no other source I know of has yet latched on to them. (That, I assume, will come later, if the course of celebrity fiction runs true to form as the false statements of one book carry over into a slew of new ones.)

Bret seems to have a fascination with the tragic Ross Alexander. It's never been proven that Ross was gay; these rumors started with a 1989 book on Bette Davis that had some really hilarious, absurd stories about Ross, including the topper in which he has sex with a hobo. Since then, Ross has been the go-to guy to have sex with alllll of Hollywood's male stars. Bret, in his "biography" of Clark Gable, claimed Franchot Tone and Ross had an "intense" relationship. Here, we are served more of the same. There's just something so special about that Alexander boy! Who could possibly resist those sad, tormented eyes, that physique! Not Errol, that's for sure. "Tall, dashing, extremely handsome and muscular,

Alexander had made a name for himself on Broadway in the now appropriately titled *Let Us Be Gay*, during the run of which he had had an affair with the leading man, Rod La Roque." (It's actually spelled La Rocque, by the way.) In fact, Alexander was in the 1929 Broadway play, while La Rocque was in a 1930 movie version, and they never appeared in the property together. Remember, in a book like this, you can't let facts get in the way of a racy story.

Supposedly, Errol and Ross "camped it up" on the *Captain Blood* set, making no secret of the love they shared. Bret, true to form, sees sex everywhere, including a scene in the movie where Dr. Blood (Flynn) tends Jeremy's (Alexander) injured knee, "massaging the shapely limb perhaps a little TOO sensually." Bret also says that Flynn stepped "out of character" to call the "homophobic" and "outraged" Lionel Atwill "my dear" and "darling." There was also a "problem" on the set when the "homophobic" Michael Curtiz and Flynn got into a row over Alexander's "somewhat exuberant armpits which, Errol declared, 'turned him on like hot twin fannies.'" It gets worse. When Curtiz decided that Alexander's hairy underarms in the whipping scene would get them in trouble with the Hays Office, he came to the set with a razor, ready to shave Alexander's armpits himself. The smitten Flynn objected, took the blade and threatened to cut Curtiz's throat if he "removed so much as one hair from Alexander's 'magnificent oxters,' so the scene was left uncut, and received few complaints."

Bret's claims about Ross Alexander are all false, saying that he killed himself in January 1937 because he was in debt and his career was "on the skids." More absurdity comes with the comment that Alexander believed that Ronald Reagan was signed to the studio to replace him and this sent him over the edge. Flynn would always "detest" Reagan and "hold him personally responsible for his lover's death." In fact, Reagan wasn't signed to Warner Bros. until April 1937, four months *after* Alexander's suicide.

Many years later, when Flynn became involved with Beverly Aadland, it was "probably the most tender, sincere relationship Errol had experienced since the one with Ross Alexander, twenty years before." This made me wonder, was it Beverly's "exuberant armpits" that won him?

I found this passage especially telling, in regard to Errol's early years in New Guinea: "All we have to rely on is Errol's account of his adventures, and the somewhat dubious reminiscences of several American and Australian soldiers who served on the island during World War II, a decade after he had left (by this time, of course, his actor's status added considerably more interest to the subject). It would appear more sensible to dismiss most of these handed-down 'tales' and rely upon Flynn himself, whose honesty through-out his autobiography—written towards the end of his life when he no longer cared what others might have thought of him—has never been doubted by his critics, friends and colleagues." How is it sensible to dismiss eyewitness accounts ... unless, of course, they conflict with your agenda. In fact, Flynn's autobiography has had its share of detractors who believe he exaggerated or simply left out things. And if his memoirs are so reliable and trustworthy, how come Flynn never once mentioned any of the alleged sexual relations he had with men, especially Ross Alexander?

He attributes quotes to Errol without telling us where he got them. Would Flynn really tell an unidentified reporter in the 1950s, "Whilst I was in New Guinea, I allowed my cock to rule my head. And, just as you sometimes end up with a sore head through thinking too much, so I ended up with a sore dick on account of my other pursuits."

Somehow Bret was privy to director Robert Florey telling Flynn that his "greatest regret" was never directing Rudolph Valentino, with whom he "had a passionate affair." What follows is a highly questionable exchange between Florey and Flynn that is unprint-able here. In my opinion, if anyone still thinks this book has any credibility, they should read this passage—a choice gob of trash if ever there was one.

Marlene Dietrich is given the dubious distinction of being Bret's scapegoat. It was supposedly she who told the "author" about the Flynn–David Niven and Randolph Scott-Cary Grant relationships. Of the latter twosome, she says they were lovers "for donkey's years."

The "tall, extremely handsome but somewhat naïve" Patric Knowles "fell under Errol's spell at once" and joined his same-sex parties. They never had an affair, says Bret, because although Knowles "wanted to," he was afraid of a scandal that might "force" him to give up his career. Hmmm ... but the alleged same-sex parties were okay. I wonder who Knowles told about his crush on Flynn? Bret, of course, neglects that crucial point.

William Lundigan is described as a "blonde, ethereal-looking former radio announcer," so, of course, he must be gay and he must have an affair with Errol. Even though Lundigan was under contract to Warners in the late 1930s, Flynn was the one assigning him parts, according to Bret. Oh, sure. Also, did you know that Carole Lombard introduced them? Carole hosted fabulous gay parties and was the "undisputed doyenne of Hollywood's so-called lavender set." This is so very interesting, it's a shame that Bret did not include this in his Clark Gable book. Bret somehow is in on a conversation between Flynn and Lombard about how good the sex with Lundigan was. Also, he was the proverbial fly on the wall to hear Errol make a crude sexual remark to Basil Rathbone during a sword fight—because, of course, Basil was always after young boys.

Errol tried to "make" Robert Taylor, but was unsuccessful, causing intense hatred on Flynn's part. How Bret would know of the dialogue shared by the two when Taylor supposedly turned him down is a real mystery.

Lupe Velez, it says here, devastated John Gilbert so much with her "sexual appetite" that he "ended up a shivering wreck whose only solace had come with the bottle." Lupe also ruined the lives of Lawrence Tibbett and Gary Cooper, according to Bret.

The weirdest mistake comes from listing some of the guys who joined Errol in drinking and carousing. Bret lists John Decker, Alan Hale and Alan Mowbray(!), and then ... drum roll ... Grant Mitchell. I am guessing that Bret actually meant to write Grant Withers, who was notorious for his drunken escapades, and not the bespectacled character actor Grant Mitchell, who was born in 1874. Mitchell's inclusion is perfect in a way since it adds to the overall absurdity of the book.

Errol's voice, Bret says, was "certainly not as grating as Cary Grant's."

Tallulah Bankhead had the Scarlett O'Hara part but was dropped when "in a drunken outburst she had threatened to spill the beans about the director George Cukor's earlier relationship with Clark Gable."

Errol had an affair with director Edmund Goulding during the filming of *The Dawn Patrol*. Goulding, who "never made a secret of his homosexuality," also had relationships with Robert Taylor, Edward Everett Horton and Tyrone Power. You heard it here first. Flynn also had an affair with Power. A few other biographies have stated this—such "reliable" sources as Charles Higham and Hector Arce—but each time the details change. In this biography, Ty is hopelessly in love with the self-involved Flynn, but in other books, it's the other way around. Later, Bret himself says that during *The Sun Also Rises* (1957), Flynn was "still carrying a torch" for Power, but that Tyrone was "no longer amorously interested in him." He claims Annabella started the rumor (stated here as fact) that Power was a coprophiliac (look it up, I ain't explaining it here); however, this was in an early edition of *Hollywood Babylon* and was taken out of later printings.

I am not sure Bret has actually seen *Dodge City*, although, like many of the movies in the book, he goes into its plot (mostly wrong). He certainly is not fair to co-star Ann Sheridan, who plays a saloon singer, comparing her unfavorably to Dietrich. Sheridan, he says, "does not merit second female lead," an opinion with which she herself would have agreed. Her billing was for publicity purposes, inspired by her new Oomph Girl status. To say that she sings her songs "indifferently" ... them are fighting words, mister! Strangely enough, no mention is made of Sheridan's long-term relationship with Flynn; nor does Bret bother to quote from Ray

Hagen's excellent interview with Ann (reprinted in the book *Killer Tomatoes: Fifteen Tough Film Dames*).

Instead of giving intelligent overviews of the movies *The Sisters* and *The Private Lives of Elizabeth and Essex*, Bret quotes from the book *High Camp, A Gay Guide to Camp & Cult Film, Vol. 1* ... which tells us zilch.

Virginia City (1940) has "stunning" photography, "albeit in black and white." Yes, it's too bad they made b&w films back then. Ruins them for me, too.

Bret cannot understand why Bruce Cabot, a Flynn friend-lover and fellow carouser (supposedly of both sexes), was not cast in another Warner Bros. film after *Dodge City*. He was: *Wild Bill Hickok Rides* (1942) and *The Desert Song* (1943). But, more importantly, Mr. Bret, he was under contract elsewhere. You wouldn't know that by this book, though: Cabot was always at Warners hanging out with Flynn on his sets, he had no movie work of his own to do. Let's not even get into the character assassination of Cabot. He, too, has had a bad rep elsewhere, but these new biographers are adding more to his indiscretions.

The personal life of FBI head J. Edgar Hoover was not common knowledge back in the 1930s and '40s. There is no way that Errol knew every detail of Hoover's secret life, the bizarre explanation given here for him not being arrested for having sex with minors.

We are supposed to believe that the death of Jack Budlong during the filming of a scene (erroneously described as the Little Big Horn one) in *They Died with Their Boots On* was one that Flynn never got over.

The "dashing" Helmut Dantine became the object of Flynn's lust while making *Edge of Darkness*, but the Austrian actor was "saving himself" for Tyrone Power who was away at war. This, according to Tallulah Bankhead ... where she said this, I have no clue.

Thank Your Lucky Stars had "no running storyline." Of course, it does; it is not as Bret claimed "just one mostly forgettable song and dance routine after another."

Here, Flynn "detested" Dick Haymes because he was married to Nora Eddington after Flynn. Actually, reliable sources say Flynn and Haymes were pals.

The whole business about Rory Calhoun and *Confidential* magazine is wrong. He was not outed for his supposed homosexuality, but a story was leaked about Rock Hudson's friend (not lover) George Nader. Calhoun had a criminal past which had nothing to do with Hudson. I also seriously doubt that Flynn had an "occasional" one-night stand with Rory. Who else has heard the story that Lana Turner hired a hit man to kill *Confidential* publisher Robert Harrison?

Bret sees homosexuality in the plot of the war movie *Objective, Burma!* (1945). No, I am not kidding.

A lot of space is reserved for Errol's mother and his hatred of her. Bret says that her birth name was Lily Marelle Young, but it was in fact Lily Mary Young. She later dropped Lily and changed Mary to Marelle because she thought it sounded more exotic. He says that Flynn's mother "doled out" beatings with "almost sardonic relish." How he came to that conclusion, is beyond me.

It's *The Garden of Allah*, not *The Garden of Alla*—a mistake that happens multiple times, as does calling Jerry Giesler "Geisler." Flynn's friend Hermann Erben is referred to as "Herman" three times.

At the time of *The Roots of Heaven*, Bret says that Orson Welles was a "huge box-office draw." If that were true—which it is not—Welles would not have had a chronic problem raising money for his film productions.

Earl Conrad, Flynn's ghostwriter and biographer, concludes Bret, was "obsessed with Errol's penis, a subject which would take up FOUR pages in *Errol Flynn: A Memoir*." That's nothing. Bret spends about 200 pages in this book obsessing over Flynn's organ.

Dennis Morgan did not sing "Home Is the Sailor" at Errol's funeral. According to many sources, including Morgan's wife (who was there), he sang Robert Louis Stevenson's poem "Requiem."

Warren William was a "former silent star"? Actually, he had leads in two silents in the early '20s but was not a film star until after the silent era ended.

Max Steiner "moved to Hollywood, where an early success had been his score for *King Kong*—the first of his twenty-six Oscar nominations." Steiner was not nominated for *King Kong*. In all, he was nominated 24 times, and won three times.

In *The Prince and the Pauper*, the twins do not change clothes as a prank; they are playing a game.

Busby Berkeley, not Berkely. Bret also gets the details about Busby's manslaughter charge wrong; he did not knock down and kill three pedestrians. Three people were killed when Busby's vehicle hit head-on a car and sideswiped another.

Where did Bret get the quote from Errol about Gérard Philipe? It's not something Flynn would be telling any reporter in the early 1950s.

Patrice Wymore was a dancer-actress, not a singer-actress; she always utilized a voice double on screen. Alexis Smith also had a voice double for her singing, but Bret credits her with songs in *San Antonio* (1945) and *Montana* (1950). Regarding Wymore, Bret says that when Flynn first saw her, he supposedly told someone that he fell for her "hook, line and scrotum."

Flynn did not choose actress Micheline Presle for the movie *Adventures of Captain Fabian* (1951). Actually, even though it is not mentioned in this book, Presle was married to the film's director, William Marshall, from 1949 to '55, and that was the reason she was in the movie.

Bret claims that Flynn did the very dangerous leap down the stairs in *Adventures of Don Juan*. Director Vincent Sherman's autobiography (another source not consulted) related who did execute the stunt, Jock Mahoney. Jock, in interviews, verified this; because the jump was so dangerous, he insisted on being paid extra for it. Bret also says that Flynn did a dangerous stunt in *Against All Flags*. Again, no.

According to Bret, Flynn and screenwriter George Oppen-
heimer had sex with the entire male fencing academy featured
in *Adventures of Don Juan*. And in some mystical interview not
sourced, Robert Douglas talks about his "relationship" with Flynn.

The story about the last time Olivia de Havilland saw Errol happened two years before Bret claims it did.

I've saved the best mistake for last. Bret messes up royally when
he has Diana Barrymore dead of a suicide in 1957 and has Flynn
"unable to stop himself" from commenting crudely on her death.
In the real world, Flynn never commented on Diana's death
because she died in 1960, outliving Flynn by a few months.

Vile.

Oh, there's so much more. You should be glad I read this, so you
don't have to. This whole book is just one sickening story and stupid
phony quote after another. I felt like taking a shower after reading
this book. We learn nothing about Errol Flynn, man or actor. He
was a complicated man, to be sure, but the "author" utterly fails to
delve into Flynn's psyche. Selling books seems to be the purpose
here, not adding to our knowledge of Flynn. Your best bet would
be to get McFarland's *Errol Flynn: The Life and Career* by Thomas
McNulty, now in softcover.

Bret says that *Confidential*'s Robert Harrison never bothered
checking the authenticity of his stories before printing them. How
could someone write such a line without questioning himself and
his own writing? (More projection!) When I first started reading
film bios years ago, I never imagined I would read a book this
bad; one chapter is even called, "If It Moved, Flynn Fucked It!"
Pathetic. Truly pathetic.

✳

Eva: Men's Adventure Supermodel
by Eva Lynd and edited by Robert Deis and Wyatt Doyle

New Texture has truly outdone themselves with their new book. Classic movie and TV fans know Swedish-born Eva Lynd for her guest spots on TV's *The Thin Man, Peter Gunn, The Texan* and *Hogan's Heroes*, and the movie *That Lady from Peking* (1975); sometimes she was billed as Eva von Fielitz (her real name). She was also seen as the "girl in the tube" in Brylcreem TV commercials. Mostly, she was an extremely popular model for artists and photographers and her image appeared on countless book, magazine and pulp covers, ads, catalogues and album covers. No wonder, since she was, and is, a gorgeous lady.

Eva: Men's Adventure Supermodel (New Texture) by Eva Lynd and edited by Robert Deis and Wyatt Doyle is a remarkable volume brimming with rare illustrations of covers, ads, LPs, original art, etc. There are a lot of doozies here of Miss Lynd being held captive, posing half-clothed, holding guns, and just standing there looking beautiful. It is astounding, the amount of work she did as a model.

But this isn't merely a book of pulp art. This is also the autobiography of Miss Lynd as she tells her life story and what it was like working with photographers, artists and actors. She has a nice story about Henry Fonda when she did a bit in the film *Stage Struck* (1958)—with a photo of them to go along with it.

Like all of New Texture's books, this one is magnificently produced in color and black and white. The design work is inventive and eye-catching. Even if you aren't into pulp, there are many other treasures here to pique your interest. And the words of Miss Lynd, a very likable person, are fascinating. It was wonderful to learn more about someone I only knew by name and face. I commend Deis and Doyle for taking the time to tell her story and honor her with this lovely tribute.

Evelyn Dove: Britain's Black Cabaret Queen
by Stephen Bourne

I admire the work British historian Stephen Bourne does on his books about African-American performers: Ethel Waters, Butterfly McQueen, Elisabeth Welch, Adelaide Hall and Nina Mae McKinney. If *Classic Images* readers will recall, I had issues with the latter mostly because of editing and the meagerness of the research. But I can sympathize with him on the last point: Researching black entertainers is not an easy task. The mainstream press rarely published articles about African Americans and sometimes it is difficult to locate black newspapers of the day.

Bourne has no such problems with his newest book, **Evelyn Dove: Britain's Black Cabaret Queen** (Jacaranda). It clocks in at just 160 pages but there's a lot here, mostly incorporated from Dove's own personal scrapbook.

Jacaranda, a new-ish London-based publisher, has created a compact, nice-looking book with glossy pages. The layout is quite attractive and the many unpublished, rare photos make this even better.

I read an online review in which Dove is called a "forgotten singer" and that Bourne "provides scant evidence that she should be as famous as the author seems to think." The review goes on to say that she never was famous to begin with. What a jaded, foolish idea. Yes, Dove (1902-87) is forgotten now, but starting in the 1920s and stretching into the 1960s, she was well known internationally on the stage, in movies, on radio, recordings and television. She was a name in her time but like most performers, she faded into obscurity. I commend any author who makes the immense effort to rescue these lost performers. It's more difficult to do than, say, Marilyn Monroe, and much more rewarding. There are a lot of details here about Dove's personal and professional life, and that of her family, that you will not read anywhere else.

That said, the text still needed tightening, and there is some repetition. It's not overly distracting, though. While Bourne goes on a bit more than I'd like about Josephine Baker and Ethel Waters, he does so to explain what Dove had to go through during her career due to racism. The excessive Eartha Kitt material, however, could have been seriously trimmed—it was very self-indulgent on the author's part as he met Kitt and felt the need to explain this laboriously. (Dove played Kitt's mother on television in *Mrs. Patterson*.)

Chances are you have never heard of Evelyn Dove, but if you are interested in show business, she is someone you should be acquainted with. There are so many singers like her who have long been relegated to the shadows. Thanks to Stephen Bourne, we now have her story.

※

Fall Girl: My Life as a Western Stunt Double
by Martha Crawford Cantarini and Chrystopher J. Spicer

By the time I finished reading the glowing **Fall Girl: My Life as a Western Stunt Double** by Martha Crawford Cantarini and Chrystopher J. Spicer (McFarland), I had grown to admire Martha, her general outlook, and the way she put her beloved horses, particularly Frosty, first in her life.

Martha practically grew up on a horse, learning to ride from her stepfather Carl Crawford, who rode and raised polo ponies when that sport was the Hollywood "in" thing. While still a teenager, she won trophies for her horse-riding abilities. Going to Hollywood, she was a stunt double (and sometimes just a regular stand-in) for numerous actresses: Anne Baxter (*Yellow Sky*), Carroll Baker and Jean Simmons (*The Big Country*), Debra Paget (*Love Me Tender*), Eleanor Parker (*Interrupted Melody*, *The Man with the Golden Arm*, *The King and Four Queens*, *The Seventh Sin*), Claudette Colbert (*Texas Lady*), Martha Hyer (*Kiss of Fire*), Dana Wynter (*The View from Pompey's Head*), Anita Louise (TV's *My Friend Flicka*), Linda Darnell (*Dakota Incident*), Rhonda Fleming (*The Killer Is Loose*, *Gun Glory*), Janice Rule (*Gun for a Coward*), Betsy Palmer (*The Tin Star*), Shirley Jones (*April Love*), Shirley MacLaine (*The Sheep-*

man), Patricia Owens (*The Law and Jake Wade*), etc. In *The Killer Is Loose* (1956) she also played (uncredited) the gunned-down wife of Wendell Corey, although you never see her face. Among the treasure trove of candid photos is a dandy of Martha sitting with Corey on the set.

Martha was known for her expert fast mounts and jumping abilities and was in demand for movies, commercials and TV series such as *December Bride, Cheyenne* and *Have Gun – Will Travel*. She also had glamorous good looks which made her ideal as a double for actresses. "I must have looked such an oddity amongst [the other stunt women]…I never quite fitted the mold of a stereotypical stunt girl…"

Some stunts didn't make the final cut, most memorably her ride full-gallop into the flames in *Interrupted Melody*. She also relates her harrowing experiences as an extra in the earthquake sequence in *The Rains of Ranchipur* (1955): "Every day it felt like you took your life in your hands just to walk out there. There was no doubling on this job, just utility stunts, and sometimes the real stunt was just to finish the day's work in one piece."

Martha's stories are honest, lively, chatty. She devotes whole chapters to certain productions; it's nice to read an autobiography by someone who was a keen observer. Her experiences with Clark Gable and Eleanor Parker are especially insightful and give us a better understanding of them. I laughed at her recollection of Guinn "Big Boy" Williams bulldogging a polo pony. While Martha liked many of the actors she worked with, she does let us know when they were less than nice and calls out a few of 'em for having egos and putting on airs. In the case of Anne Baxter, she just avoided Martha during the *Yellow Sky* shoot; Gregory Peck, Jock Mahoney and Richard Widmark, however, all get nice mentions.

Her co-author Chrystopher J. Spicer is one of the better writers out there; his *Clark Gable: Biography, Filmography, Bibliography* (also from McFarland), which I reviewed in 2002, is a marvelous book which I highly recommend.

The tone of *Fall Girl* is a pleasant one and there is never a dull moment in this insider's look at '50s Hollywood. The very first chapter, about a stunt gone wrong, is amazing and vividly told. Interwoven with her moviemaking tales are her efforts to raise and train the horse Frosty, who later had his own local TV program. The way Martha writes about and describes Frosty, all horses in fact, is sweet and very heartfelt and gives this book a lot of heart. Martha has guts and proved it throughout her life. This book is a pretty terrific, fun read and I strongly urge you to get this one.

Feuding Fan Dancers: Faith Bacon, Sally Rand and the Golden Age of the Showgirl
by Leslie Zemeckis

Stripper Faith Bacon has long fascinated me. Years ago, I did some research and was disappointed at how little I could find. She was the originator of the fan dance, but her thunder was stolen by another burlesque dancer, Sally Rand, who also claimed to be the first to use a fan in her act. Rand had better luck than Faith, as Bacon's fame faded with the years and she is unfortunately not remembered for her trailblazing.

Faith's suicide was especially sad to me: She threw herself out of a Chicago hotel window. Newspapers described her sole personal belongings as "Miscellaneous clothing, one white metal ring, a train ticket to Erie, Pa., and 85 cents." In 2011, my friend Barry Virshbo and I went looking for the hotel where she killed herself, but it was no longer there.

So, as you can see, I was hyped to read **Feuding Fan Dancers: Faith Bacon, Sally Rand and the Golden Age of the Showgirl** by Leslie Zemeckis (Counterpoint Press). Bacon's and Rand's personal and professional histories are concurrently told in this dual biography. Both ladies had to be strong to deal with the struggles to survive in a grueling business. Anyone who thinks being a stripper is all fun and games is totally wrong. Burlesque was not an easy life, and the author is at her best capturing this.

There are many similarities to their stories, but their differences are striking. Bacon's fate was sealed by her mother, who was not the best influence, shall we say. Rand was able to cope better in her personal life, despite a few wrong men, and stuck it out with style, something Bacon was not equipped to do. "The press would chronicle Faith's hard times, but not Sally's," Zemeckis writes. "Sally hid it better, behind dimples and confidence."

The problem I have with this book is one I have with many volumes these days: the lack of fact-checking and editing. I have no idea why publishers cannot employ someone who knows about entertainment history. While Zemeckis has done good research and knows her burlesque, she is weak in other areas.

Spelling mistakes: Ronald Coleman (Colman), Coconut Grove (Cocoanut), Bill "Bo Jangles" Robinson (Bojangles), etc. She calls Helen Hayes a Ziegfeld Girl and Texas Guinan a "society hostess." I believe Zemeckis is getting showgirl Helen Brown mixed up with Hayes. (Hayes' real name is Brown, you see.) As Eve Golden remarked to me, "It is to laugh."

The author claims that Harry Richman got Joan Crawford her big break by introducing her to Joseph Schenck, but Richman actually contacted producer Harry Rapf.

Rand didn't attend the wedding of Eddie Fisher and Debbie Reynolds in the 1960s at the Tropicana. The wedding she went to was Fisher's to Connie Stevens. (Fisher and Reynolds were married from 1955 to '59.)

"In a year that saw *Gone with the Wind* and *The Wizard of Oz*, her film was a trifling," Zemeckis writes about Rand's *The Sunset Murder Case*. There is a better backstory to the film than the author tells us. First, it was supposed to be released in 1938 but wasn't. (There was, however, a preview in '38.) A lawsuit delayed its release and then the following year Grand National canceled distribution on the picture. It was finally shown theatrically in 1941 with some sources claiming that Rand's dance was omitted. I also do not understand the *GWTW* and *Oz* reference; comparing a small indie with two major studio releases is ridiculous. In addition, *The Sunset Murder Case* wasn't even shown at the same time as those two biggies.

At one point, talking about a publicity stunt with a fawn, Zemeckis writes that the animal was "bleeding slightly." I hope to God the author meant "bleating," because the image the other conjures up is not good.

The worst error (for me, anyway) was mistaking Eleanor Powell and "*Sound of Music* actress" Eleanor Parker. The author meant Powell, by the way; and I don't think I like Parker, a three-time Oscar nominee, being labeled as the "*Sound of Music* actress." Just saying.

Sloppy editing and fact-checking aside, I did enjoy the book. It was continually interesting and offers fascinating portraits of these two women. The author had the help of Rand's son and Bacon's cousin, which is a bonus. I do wish there were more photos. And, for some reason, there is no index!

Some fun stuff here and great quotes from the women, particularly Rand, who knew how to work the publicity. I have a newfound respect for both of them, especially after reading the gruesome stories of accidentally cutting and impaling themselves on stage but still going on with their acts. You get a real sense of how they did what they did, what made them do it, and how they survived. Bacon continues to be a heartbreaking show business figure to me and I am glad that Zemeckis was able to fill in the blanks of her story.

Counterpoint Press is a new publisher to me. I like that they took a chance on two arcane performers.

Film Noir FAQ: All That's Left to Know About Hollywood's Golden Age of Dames, Detectives, and Danger
by David J. Hogan

I always look forward to a new book on film noir. Unfortunately, this year, I have been disappointed with the pickings. Finally, however, I have a volume that I thoroughly enjoyed, written by someone with a strong sense of what makes *noir* tick and a writing style that is fluid, interesting, and a pleasure to read. **Film Noir FAQ: All That's Left to Know About Hollywood's Golden Age of Dames, Detectives, and Danger** by David J. Hogan (Applause) is, in my humble opinion, one of the best on the subject.

The chapters are broken up into sections, grouping films that share the same themes, etc. Interspersed within are "case files," little, pithy write-ups that nicely sum up the careers and styles of key *noir* figures. Others have tried to explain the mysteries of *noir*, but Hogan comes closest to describing it as concisely and vividly as possible:

> You do not control the circumstances of your life. Choices you agonize over are likely to be bad ones. Choices you make without thinking are likely to be worse. Whatever you love and value can be taken from you at any moment. Forces greater than you, and greater even than your leaders, can conspire to destroy you. Those forces are no smarter than you, but they have the power and you don't. You are not a true participant in events, only an observer. If you are particularly foolish, or just unlucky, you will be a victim.

Hogan writes that film noir "forced us to acknowledge that the presumably solid foundation upon which we base our assumptions and our very lives is temporal and dangerously unstable. It's likely to not merely shift beneath our feet, but give way completely, turning the routine of our lives upside-down and annihilating our expectations. We're plunged into a disorienting place where everything we thought we knew is wrong." I really enjoy the way Hogan turns a phrase. In addition to his meaty, well-thought-out critical analyses, there are some juicy tidbits here and there that really stand out:

"Sexy with her baby face, pillowy lips, and taut little figure, Veda is a gaily decorated box of poisonous candy."

"And yet, despite its smooth glow, *Mildred Pierce* has an almost unbearable edge of ragged emotion."

"Vaguely comical at first (she pointlessly brushes her lusterless hair after Roberts gives her the lift), Vera quickly becomes fate's own blunt instrument, a perfect bully who wears Roberts out with unending carping and bossiness. She's unsympathetic but pathetic, as well, and it's sad that she's already been ground down by life."

"Key sequences ... are gorgeous with menace."

"... Legenza is stitched by police machine gun fire and falls alive onto the tracks, where's he's squashed by a speeding train."

"Brown's brutal fistfight with a mobster in a tiny sleeper-compartment bathroom must surely have inspired the similar dustup in *From Russia with Love*."

"Finally, a gold star to hairdresser Kay Shea, who gave Robert Wagner a towering pompadour with the curvature and stiff swirls of a conch shell. *A Kiss Before Dying* is glam-noir."

"The sequence unreels—bam bam bam—and hits us right in the gut."

"Resplendent in color so luscious you want to bite it..."

While Hogan knows his *noir*, there are some blips along the road:

Talking about *The Strange Love of Martha Ivers* (1946), Hogan claims that, on the set, "Stanwyck was helpful to [Kirk] Douglas." In his autobiography, *The Ragman's Son*, however, Douglas alleged that during shooting she was "indifferent" to him.

"*Decoy* was produced by Jack Bernhard and Bernard Brandt, and directed by Bernhard, for the most prosperous of Hollywood Poverty Row outfits, Monogram." The most "prosperous" (even Hogan says it is a relative word) of the low-budget companies was Republic.

Richard Basehart was not signed by MGM after *He Walked by Night* (1948); he left Eagle-Lion to become a 20th Century-Fox contract player. He was loaned to Metro for *Tension* (1949).

In the case file about John Payne, the author says that "before the 1940s were out" he had "opportunities to experiment with heavier character characterizations, notably in *To the Shores of Tripoli* and *The Razor's Edge*." The latter fits into this category, but the 1942 wartime romance *To the Shores of Tripoli*?

"Glenn Langan, taking a bit part far removed from his leading roles at Fox barely ten years later." As much as I love Langan, Fox never gave him a lead, unless you count his role in 1946's *Margie*. I get what Hogan is saying here, though.

Gaby André was in *Highway 301* (1950), not Gaby Rodgers. The latter was in *Kiss Me Deadly* (1955).

The Doris Day recording is "'S Wonderful" not "'S Marvelous."

William Lundigan, says the author, "seldom enjoyed leading roles."

He writes that Mascot's main claim to fame was Rin Tin Tin movies, but actually it was their serial output.

About Elisha Cook Jr.'s famous, kinetic drum solo in *Phantom Lady* (1944), it has been "variously credited to Buddy Rich and Gene Krupa." In actuality, drummer Dave Coleman assisted Cook.

He says that *Beware, My Lovely* (1952) was adapted by Mel Dinelli from his play *The Man* (1950). That is true, but the story started life as a *Suspense* radio show by Dinelli from 1945: "To Find Help," starring Frank Sinatra and Agnes Moorehead. It was redone on *Suspense* in '49 with Gene Kelly and Ethel Barrymore.

The Killers (1964) "gave Ronald Reagan ... a startling opportunity to shoot Angie Dickinson." I believe he means slap, not shoot, as Lee Marvin does the shooting honors.

These minor problems should in no way deter you from the many wonders of this book. There is so much to enjoy and learn. It's very hard, at this late date, to find a book which offers a fresh perspective, especially about some movies that have been written about to death (e.g., *The Maltese Falcon*, *This Gun for Hire*, *Phantom Lady*, *Mildred Pierce*, *Detour*), but the author manages it.

How nice, in his discussion of *The Big Combo* (1955), that he didn't resort to mentioning the much-talked-about "love" scene between Richard Conte and Jean Wallace. Sometimes, it becomes annoying when writers (and fans) repeat the same things over and over. (Don't get me started on "That's *Hedley!*" the exclamation every nitwit uses when they see an image of Hedy Lamarr. This has become my biggest pet peeve, ever. Thanks, Mel.)

Even with opinions that I do not entirely agree with, the keenly insightful Hogan explains himself so well that his argument seems totally plausible. I especially enjoyed the write-ups on the usually maligned *Pickup* (1951), *Niagara* (1953), and his particularly incisive commentary on another film often given a bum rap, *Party Girl* (1958). The book vs. film analysis of *Nightmare Alley* (1947) was also well done. At the conclusion of the book, there is a brisk afterword devoted to neo-noir, where I was pleased to see references to *P.J.* (1968) and *Poodle Springs* (1998). The photos throughout are excellent, especially the shadowy, menacing shot of the awesome Lawrence Tierney from *The Devil Thumbs a Ride* (1947). The cover photo, a moodily lit portrait of Glenn Ford from *Gilda* (1946), is just perfect. The title of the book is misleading, though, as it is not the typical FAQ (an abbreviation of "frequently asked questions") published by Applause. I hope this does not fool readers into thinking this is a superficial question-and-answer volume—it is a substantial, thoughtful discussion.

Hogan's economical writing is a marvel; he effortlessly explains so much in a short amount of space, and he really gets to the heart of what is and isn't *noir*. The book is a must-have for all noir enthusiasts.

Foxy Lady: The Authorized Biography of Lynn Bari
by Jeff Gordon

Foxy Lady: The Authorized Biography of Lynn Bari by Jeff Gordon (BearManor) is one of the very best movie biographies in an extremely crowded field. Lynn Bari never became a major A-list star (and never pretended otherwise) but she's always had a solid fanbase. As a long-time admirer of Bari's work, I was hoping for the best but expecting the worst from this book. Thankfully, I got the best.

Bari was in contact with author Gordon beginning in early 1989, when he started conducting a long series of phone interviews with her. She was brutally honest about every aspect of her long life and career. Her memory was razor-sharp and, often, self-mocking and blazingly funny. Sad to say, Lynn died near the end of that year just as they'd planned on their first in-person meeting.

Lynn's extensive, clear-eyed quotes from those conversations appear throughout the book, in bold print, discussing her troubled relationship with her alcoholic mother, her three disastrous marriages, her 12 years as a mostly frustrated contract player at 20th Century-Fox, her relationships with Darryl Zanuck and fellow actors and directors, her later years in television and on the stage (which became her favorite performing venue) and her own later-life problems with alcohol. Gordon chose to repeatedly interrupt his well-researched narrative to let Lynn have her say, and this (along with interviews with many of her friends, family and co-workers) is what makes the book shine. Lynn seems to have remembered every detail of every movie she ever made, and reading these commentaries is a joy. You don't have to be a fellow Lynn Bari worshipper to enjoy this illuminating look behind Hollywood's closed doors.

Favorite passages include Lynn's reminisces of two projects that had problems during production. She started work on *Charlie Chan at Ringside*, but Warner Oland's personal troubles shut the movie down and the film was refashioned as *Mr. Moto's Gamble*.

Lynn's observations about Oland and Peter Lorre are eye-openers. Another film, *Bon Voyage!*, with Lynn and Jeanne Crain, started but was canceled altogether. I laugh every time I recall Lynn's comments about Crain's bizarre behavior on the set. Side-splitting stuff. Lynn's wry sense of humor is fully captured by Gordon within the book. Another brilliant section: Lynn's tale that opens the volume. Her train ride with her mother and Ronald Colman perfectly sets the tone of what is to come.

The book includes hundreds of well-reproduced photos, a detailed filmography of her 140-plus movies, and a listing of all her TV appearances.

Full Service: My Adventures in Hollywood and the Secret Sex Lives of the Stars
by Scotty Bowers with Lionel Friedberg

When **Full Service: My Adventures in Hollywood and the Secret Sex Lives of the Stars** by Scotty Bowers (with Lionel Friedberg) was first published by Grove Press, I could not get a review copy. Finally, after hearing from a few film fans who mistook the book for gospel truth, I decided I needed to act, so I splurged and bought the book on Amazon. Luckily, I was able to get a copy for one cent, but even at that price, I overpaid.

"This manuscript is based on my memory and, to the very best of my ability, reflects actual incidents and personalities as I recall them," writes Bowers. His co-author Friedberg adds, "This manuscript is based on roughly 150 hours of recorded interviews with Scotty Bowers. I have added only factual details regarding studios, productions and various film shoots to augment Scotty's recollections, specifically where he could not remember exact details himself." Notice how the two of them are protecting themselves: These memories are, to the best of an 80-something Bowers' ability, as he recalls them, and when needed Friedberg fills in the blanks. Believe me, this happens a lot, and many times Friedberg also seems to have no idea, so we get, "I don't remember what happened next," etc. Yes, very reassuring.

Here's a little passage I found interesting. Ex-Marine Bowers was working at a gas station when two service buddies pulled up to get gas: "I asked them how they had found me. I hadn't given my work address to anyone. 'C'mon, Scotty.' 'Course you did.' 'Where? When?' I asked. And then they reminded me about the ex-servicemen's contact office down at the Crossroads of the World in Hollywood. 'You filled out a card, dumb head,' they chided. Of course! It had been a couple of weeks since I filled out the card." So, 67 years ago he couldn't remember what happened two weeks earlier. Now, he is recounting a series of rather bizarre 67-year-old memories, and we're supposed to believe what he says?

First things first. Bowers' childhood is particularly disturbing. While living on a farm, he claims to have regularly watched animals having sex. He also peeked in his parents' bedroom: "And why not?" he reasons, "As far as I was concerned, they were only doing what nature intended them to do. But for some reason society seemed to follow more antiquated values." This is the theme of the book—everyone is doing what comes naturally, and who is Bowers to judge them?

Okay, but Bowers also applies this attitude to the sexual abuse he endured at the hands of older men—when he was eight years old. Bowers gives me the impression that he sees nothing wrong with pedophilia. When he was nine, he had to leave the farm, and his secret molester:

> On his way out that evening he gave me a look that I will never forget. It was one of genuine love, of pity, of remorse, of affection for me. But he couldn't say anything and neither could I. Deep down I knew I was going to miss him. He was a warm, tender man, and in a special way I knew that he cared for me.

Also, Bowers claims that he "satisfied" numerous priests as a pre-teen: "I felt no shame, no guilt, no remorse for what I had done. In fact, I derived an undeniable sense of satisfaction knowing that I had brought a little joy into someone's life." *Seriously?* I found this sickening and it is hard to understand how anyone could see nothing wrong with men taking advantage of a little boy. This passage also gave me a strange feeling that there was something missing from the story here—that something was being hidden from the reader. So, right off the bat I began to seriously doubt the credibility of the book.

Also bothersome: I read elsewhere about someone doing some checking on Bowers on Ancestry.com found that he was not living where he claimed when he was eight years old; not on a farm in LaSalle Co., Illinois, but in Wills Co., where his father was a prison guard, not a farmer. So, what should we believe about his sex-filled farm days??

When he moves to Hollywood after World War II, he claims to be the go-to guy for "arranging tricks," his base of operation being a gas station. "If you ever ask a middle-aged queen to keep a secret, you can be absolutely sure that it will spread like wildfire," he says. Strangely, however, the owner of the gas station never knew what was going on under his nose.

Bowers insists over and over he was never a pimp, yet he says he set up everyone in town. He also supposedly never got paid, even though he struggled to make a living. How noble! Yes, he just was a good-hearted person who wanted to make our troubled world a happier place. Gee, that's *so* nice!

As for his live-in girlfriend (at the time) and their daughter, they often did not see him for days as he spent his time having sex with several partners a day. "I would be out all night sleeping in a different bed, then go home, do my laundry, change my clothes, make sure my two girls had everything they needed, throw a sandwich together, and then head back to the gas station for my evening shift." Bowers expects us to believe this? It sounds weird and phony, as if he is depicting himself as some sort of selfless sexual missionary. We're supposed to like him for being so generous with his private parts? Once again, we see another strange disconnect in the writing because, in fact, Bowers comes across here as immoral, empty and shallow. In real life, he could be a generous man, but in that case, I would say his writing ability is so poor that he is unable to express his own true character in print.

Bowers was the "very best of friends" with Katharine Hepburn even though he does not know how to spell her name. He also was the "very best of friends" with Marion Davies, George Cukor, Tennessee Williams, Cole Porter and others. How strange that there seems to be no photos of Bowers with any of these celebrities. One "friend," writer W. Somerset Maugham, couldn't have been too close: The file photo Bowers uses in the book is not Maugham, but writer David Goodis. Whoops! So not only does he not know how to spell the names of some of his friends, he does not even know what they look like!

About Porter he writes, "Over the years I fixed him up with many tricks and he valued my friendship. In some odd sort of a way he eventually looked upon me as a sort of confidant ... Cole shared a lot of his innermost dreams, desires, and fears with me." Of course, Bowers doesn't care to go into this "innermost" stuff because, hey, why waste time on that when we have so much sex to talk about instead? There's really no deep thinking here; just a series of sex acts described graphically with some immature comments from Bowers ("Do you get what I mean?" he writes several times). No offense to Mr. Bowers, but, basically, *if* what he is saying is true, wasn't he actually more of a servant than a friend?

Sex. It's everywhere in the book and if we are to believe him, Bowers had sex with almost everyone in Hollywood, or at least helped them get sex. Seriously, do you think Errol Flynn, Tyrone Power and Desi Arnaz needed help finding partners? I think not. Bowers claims to have had a threesome with Cary Grant and Randolph Scott at their beach house. Boring. Actually, by the time Bowers showed up after the war, the two former housemates no longer had their 1930s beach house. Duh.

What I find strange about these gay fantasy books is the false social atmosphere they present. We all know the attitudes gay people endured during the 1940s and '50s when the events in this book supposedly took place. One could not be open with their orientation and could not openly indulge in it. Yet, in these books, prominent people whose careers could be destroyed by exposure flaunt their lifestyles without a trace of fear. Even more unrealistic is that in these books it seems as if *every single person* was gay or bisexual. Unable to connect the dots in his narrative, Bowers says that in the Marines there was a hostility toward homosexuality, yet when he works at the gas station his Marine buddies "jump" at the chance to make extra money having sex with men.

I am reminded of a recent Facebook discussion about Patsy Kelly. It is the standard belief that Kelly was a lesbian. Whether she was or not is not the issue here, and I don't care one way or the other. But as these stories snowball, people increasingly embrace speculation as "fact," with many going so far as to say that Patsy was "very open" with her lesbianism in the 1930s onward, and didn't care who knew about it. How do they know this? Were there interviews with her telling us this? In fact, the Hollywood studios and columnists back then never would have allowed her to talk openly about it. So … where do these "facts" about Kelly come from? Bowers and others of his ilk are attempting to rewrite history to be what they think it should be. Yes, actors should have been able to be open about their sexual orientation, but the sad truth is that they could not.

That said, some of the more high-profile (but closeted) actors back then who were gay aren't even in this book (e.g., Van Johnson, Cesar Romero, Tab Hunter). Instead, we get the "shockers"—Walter Pidgeon most prominent among them. The desire to shock seems to be the main motivation behind this misinformation, and I'm guessing that is why stories about real gays are overlooked.

I don't get this new breed of "biographers" who create new stories for each new book. Bowers also adds to stories started in *Hollywood Babylon* about Tyrone Power and Charles Laughton doing various things with, um, waste. He says that he talked a Power "biographer" out of including information about Ty's supposed scatological interest. He's so proud of himself for protecting Power's memory, but what does he do? You guessed it—he tells all. How is all this enlightening? The stories, too, about Hepburn, Spencer Tracy, and the Duke and Duchess of Windsor in particular sound very suspect. ("Call me Edward," the Duke absurdly tells him—even though his pals called him David. That's as stupid as claiming to be a friend of Barbara Stanwyck and her saying, "Call me Babs.") More questionables: Edith Piaf "loved the time" she spent with him, Vivien Leigh begged him to stay with her, and "What a Man" Bowers helped Dr. Kinsey immeasurably on his sex "research."

"She strutted around, cocksure; she was clearly cognizant of the fact that she was a rapidly rising superstar," he writes about Katharine Hepburn. This is supposed to be the early '50s. That's right, in this book Hepburn still was just a starlet after World War II!

Were Tracy and Hepburn really chased by paparazzi when they were making their movies together? Their romance was only written about later, not at the time as he claims.

The story keeps changing about why Gable did not want George Cukor to direct him in *Gone with the Wind*. Bowers says that the story of Gable not wanting a gay man to direct him was planted in "the gossip columns of the Hollywood trade papers simply to undermine George's reputation." What trade papers would print something like that back then?

Let's say for a moment I believe everything in this book. Can I ask what purpose it truly serves except dragging people through the mud, betraying their confidence, and hurting their families and fans? Why do some film fans want to read this garbage? I am all for a well-rounded biography on an actor describing their true characters, but a lot of stuff in this book is just degrading and sickening. Believe me, you do not want to read about Charles Laughton and William Holden. File all this under "too much information" we do not need to know. Bowers wants us to believe he's a happy-go-lucky guy who is proud of his sexual prowess and "crotch bulge," likes girls more than the thousands of guys he's had sex with, likes homely girls, and as a "trick" arranger, gas jockey, waiter, handyman and bartender, etc., was close buddies with every important person in Hollywood.

The Bowers I became acquainted with in these pages is unlikable. The pages simply reek with ego. The movie *My Fair Lady* would never have been made without Bowers and he tried to warn Ross Hunter about remaking *Lost Horizon*, but the producer would not listen, dammit. I laughed out loud when, according to the modest Bowers, he, a lowly shoeshine boy, entered a bar, and big, burly, married male patrons got misty-eyed when they saw him. He says he didn't care whether someone was gay or straight or what problems they had, but such a pronouncement is always a precursor to several pages explaining all about those gay people and their hygiene or proclivities involving poop. Of course, he cares; he knows what sells.

His "friend," Tennessee Williams, allegedly, "began writing his own account of my life but before it saw the light of day, I told him to destroy it." Oh, so that's why Williams never published a story about Bowers. You know, if Williams' manuscript was even half as tedious as this book, I wouldn't blame him for destroying it!

Bowers and Lionel Friedberg's *Full Service* is poorly written, filled with clichés, many of them straight from the pages of the worst romantic fiction, and a lot of disgusting, uninteresting stories. There's no depth. The co-author's idea of adding "factual details regarding studios, productions, and various film shoots to augment Scotty's recollections" is to merely list the names of movies.

We should all make an effort not to support such trash, but I fear this trend to shock schlock, faux-tell-alls is here to stay. "For whatever reason," Bowers remarks, "people have always found me easy to trust." That's probably the saddest comment in the whole book.

※

Getting Smarter: A Memoir
by Barbara Feldon

On TV's *Get Smart* (1965-70), Emmy-nominated Barbara Feldon, as Agent 99, was the intelligent, beautiful, engaging cohort and romantic foil to Maxwell Smart (Don Adams). As a kid I looked up to her as a strong role model, as I'm sure many young girls did. She was also someone I looked forward to seeing in other TV series and movies. I never knew anything about her personal life, so when *Classic Images* columnist Robert Tevis told me she had written her autobiography, **Getting Smarter: A Memoir**, I was eager to read it.

In my 20-plus years as a reviewer, I have read many an actor's autobiography; some were good, some were just plain awful. In all honesty, *Getting Smarter* is the—and I mean *the*—best written. Miss Feldon is not only a very capable actress but she is an excellent and persuasive author. It's not easy to transmit your personality onto paper, to lay out the details of your life in a manner that is absorbing. To capture that and keep the reader interested is a gift.

Her voice is a distinct one and you cannot help but to empathize and identify with her vulnerability, from her childhood days, to the moment she leaves home to live on her own in New York City, to meeting and falling in love with a charming Frenchman with too many secrets. The main body of the book deals with this relationship, and I will not give it away as I want the outcome to surprise you as it did me. I found myself quickly turning the pages, engrossed in the crazy merry-go-round he put her through. Each revelation was a head-shakingly sharp detour into something else. And Miss Feldon writes it in such a way that you don't mind that much of her acting work is not mentioned. There's a charming separate chapter about *Get Smart*, of course, and she also talks about winning the grand prize on *The $64,000 Question* (her category: William Shakespeare), modeling, doing TV commercials, appearing on *East Side/West Side* with George C. Scott, etc. The bulk of the book, as mentioned above, covers her marriage and the process she went through in therapy. In all, her unflagging humor, which is never bitter, comes through.

The photos, 60 of them, are chic and gorgeous, some of them taken when she was a model. The layout is extremely nice; this is a high-quality volume. This honest memoir, filled with assorted unexpected and dramatic twists and turns, is a real winner.

⁘

The Girl Who Fell Down: A Biography of Joan McCracken
by Lisa Jo Sagolla

I have been watching FX Network's miniseries *Fosse/Verdon* (2019) starring Sam Rockwell as director-choreographer Bob Fosse and Michelle Williams as actress-dancer Gwen Verdon. I am generally enjoying it, although there have been some expected liberties taken.

What got me was a recent episode that featured Fosse's second wife, actress-dancer Joan McCracken (played by Susan Misner). Many casual viewers are probably not aware of McCracken. Broadway fans know her for *Oklahoma!* (1943), *Bloomer Girl* (1944), *Billion Dollar Baby* (1945), etc. Movie buffs would remember her as the best thing in MGM's version of *Good News* (1947), where she socked over "Pass That Peace Pipe." She was a comedy-dance innovator and was influential in helping Fosse and also Shirley MacLaine. For years, McCracken suffered from diabetes and it was this and heart disease that ultimately killed her at age 43.

Fosse/Verdon pretty much relegates McCracken to the sickly, bedridden wife Fosse leaves for Verdon. We never really get the idea of her true importance; she was not a mere footnote in Broadway history, but an important performer. I get that the miniseries is centered on Fosse and Verdon, but McCracken's character should have been better written and defined.

To get the whole story, I strongly urge you to get Lisa Jo Sagolla's **The Girl Who Fell Down: A Biography of Joan McCracken**

(Northeastern University Press). McCracken's tragic story is worth reading about. Alas, it was McCracken's role in shaping Fosse's career that she is now known for. She was the one who influenced and pushed him to move his talents away from dancer and more toward choreographer. I applaud Sagolla for taking the time to chronicle her life, career and achievements and not just paint McCracken as merely a Fosse girl.

Sagolla is a dance critic, so she knows her stuff, but her writing is accessible to those with less knowledge of dance. I am glad this is out there to spotlight the considerable talents of the wonderful Joan McCracken.

Go Slow: The Life of Julie London
by Michael Owen

Since I started reviewing for *Classic Images*, I have read every book in its entirety—except two (so far). **Go Slow: The Life of Julie London** by Michael Owen (Chicago Review Press) is now the third. I tried, I really did, but to paraphrase the title, it went very, very slowly. I made a good effort, got past the 100-page mark, but it became senseless to continue and I got fed up with Julie and the author.

Owen, a popular music historian with some impressive credentials, is a fairly good writer and he interviewed the right people (e.g., family, friends, co-workers). But, after a while, he resorted to listing all the musicians performing with London on stage and in the studio. We go from recording session to recording session while he analyzes her songs and how they did on the charts (not very well, for the most part). It becomes less a biography than a notebook about London's music. This would be fine, if you are prepared for that and you are into that.

Personal stuff is thrown in, of course. But as I read about her continual drinking to get through days and her performances, I kept thinking, "When is the author going to address that Julie is possibly an alcoholic?" He never does and, for some reason, it really bothered me. I found myself not liking Julie as a person. To me, she was too self-absorbed and her interactions with others, such as her children and husbands (Jack Webb and Bobby Troup), were odd. There was an undercurrent here that simply turned me off to whatever charm she supposedly holds.

I also felt that she didn't come across as a particularly successful singer or actress (save for a few things). This was probably because of how Owen interpreted every project. He alternated between trashing a movie because of its B status or overdoing his praise for her in an A movie (1956's *The Great Man*). According to the author, the reason some of her performances were not successful was not because she was subpar but because of something else. Owen didn't really want to admit that London was merely okay in most of her movies. *Man of the West* (1958) with Gary Cooper and London gets an excellent write-up, but that was a major movie. The author is not a fan of the Bs and when talking about London's movie career—what you B is what you get. No, instead, we hear how short Gordon MacRae was in *Return of the Frontiersman* (1950). Why? I have no idea except maybe Owen wanted to deflect blame.

Many of London's albums didn't do well and there seemed to be a lot of negative feelings throughout about the course of her music career. Owen loves her singing and even claims that London's version of "The Man That Got Away" was better than Judy Garland's. (Yes, you read that correctly.) At one point he compares London's voice to a passage from *The Great Gatsby*, of all things.

He also critiques the covers of her albums, always a major selling point of her LPs (which should tell you something). A lot of her appeal came from her looks. She was gorgeous and, naturally, the book's colorful, luminous cover shot is a dandy.

Go Slow was just not my cup of tea. The personal angle was handled competently (except for the drinking) but be aware of what this book focuses on. You might like *Go Slow*, but I grew tired very quickly of the book's aimlessness and Julie London's (and the author's) attitude.

Grant Williams
by Giancarlo Stampalia

Grant Williams (1913-85) is best known today as the star of the sci-fi classic *The Incredible Shrinking Man* (1957) and, to a lesser extent, the same year's *The Monolith Monsters*. He was a serious-minded actor who studied with Lee Strasberg and did stage work, so it was a letdown for him personally to be "reduced" to B movies and then TV (guesting and a recurring role on *Hawaiian Eye*).

There has been very little written on Williams and what is out there is untrustworthy. Much of this is due to Williams himself, who led reporters astray with fake "memories." Also, his private life has been open to conjecture, especially his sexuality. Since the blond, handsome Williams never married and he later exhibited some rather strange, paranoid behavior, it has been "established" that he was gay and severely conflicted by this. Instead of fact, we get the armchair psychoanalysts who just have "that feeling" that this was the way it was. No facts, no firsthand knowledge, just a feeling. Therefore, this speculation gets repeated as fact by "historians." I am not saying Williams wasn't gay; I am saying I do not know *for sure*. I have seen snide remarks like, "Wasn't he represented by Henry Willson??"

I was very surprised and happy to see that BearManor has published a biography, simply titled **Grant Williams**, by Giancarlo Stampalia. I can appreciate the research it took to compile this biography. Williams was a private, reclusive man and there are many contradictory statements made by the people who knew him. Among others, Stampalia interviewed Williams' secretary and his acting students and their comments are the highlights of this book.

I wish I could say I enjoyed the rest. Stampalia isn't a bad writer; he does, however, have a tendency to overwrite and use words the average person would find confusing; simplicity would have drawn in the reader better. When I started writing, I felt it was important to use "big words" or words not often used; it didn't take me long to realize this was unnecessary. A really annoying habit he has is needlessly capitalizing certain words. Where was the editor?

There are two chapters on *The Incredible Shrinking Man*. Some of it is quite good as the author compares the original story to the movie. But there's also a lot of mumbo-jumbo that will make your eyes glaze over. The rest of the film and episodic TV discussions are merely okay—a lot of weird exaggerations and analyses of Williams' performances. Stampalia's insult-laden write-ups on Williams' last two films, *Brain of Blood* (1971) and *Doomsday Machine* (1972), are simply awful, of no value whatsoever. But I respect the author's decision to include all of Williams' TV appearances—not an easy task, especially since many are from the 1950s.

We get it: Stampalia is "into" Williams. He's the greatest actor and the most divinely good-looking man to ever grace the screen (to the author). Anyone who spends a lot of time researching a single actor can understand where Stampalia is coming from: You need a certain obsessiveness to really concentrate on your subject. I do believe Stampalia goes overboard. He knows the size of Williams' childhood home, its exact location and his phone number—and that's just the start of the madness.

The worst case of the obsessiveness displayed here: Three pages are devoted to a scene in a movie where, for a few seconds, Williams runs his fingers through his hair. What does this gesture mean? What was Williams' thought process as he was planning it and doing it? What were the ramifications of that gesture? The author even brings up this gesture later.

Like it or not, fellow Universal contract player Rock Hudson was a caliber of star Williams never even slightly approached. To tear Rock down to strengthen your argument for Williams is unprofessional and off-base. Stampalia criticizes others for perceiving

Williams as "minor," and yet he calls Hudson a "minor talent." Rock was a good actor and no amount of sour grapes is going to change that. Arthur Kennedy and Ronald Colman are two other actors who come up short in the author's estimation when comparing them to Williams. Then we have *this*: Martha Hyer "does not seem to be trying very hard" in *Showdown at Abilene* (1956); Raymond Burr's portrayal of Perry Mason was made up of a "lazy, inexpressive deadpan and sluggish energy"; Willard Parker is not even mentioned as the star of *Lone Texan* (1959), I guess because Williams is *so* sensational in it and steals every scene; Elsa Martinelli "seems tone-deaf to both the style and the pace of what Williams is doing" in their scenes together in *Four Girls in Town* (1957); in fact, the whole *Four Girls in Town* cast, save Julie Adams and Williams, are "atrocious," according to the author.

Grant is a good actor, to be sure, but a little reality and common sense when dealing with his abilities would have been refreshing. The author can "see" Williams in *This Gun for Hire* (1942), in comedies with Doris Day and in Douglas Sirk melodramas instead of John Gavin and thinks he compares in style to Alan Ladd, Burt Lancaster and William Holden. He makes the comparison between Grant Williams and Lancaster more than once. I don't like mocking someone's love of an actor, but since Stampalia is putting this "out there," he must take responsibility for all this nonsense. He gives many excuses why Williams never became a big star and discusses this endlessly, but let's just get to the point: He lacked charisma and that ineffable "It" that all the greats have. I *do* think the author's statement that Williams shouldn't be considered a failure just because he didn't achieve A-list stardom is spot-on. An actor can be a success based on his abilities and/or longevity in the business.

I actually laughed out loud when Stampalia, listing what Williams had in common with composer Peter Tchaikovsky (whom he played on TV), stated. "Both were undervalued for their work during their lifetimes." Or this gem: "In an August 1961 profile of Williams, Columnist Eve Starr was explicitly appreciative of Wil-

liams' talent, stating, boldly, 'Williams is a talented man.'" So bold!
Eve Starr was such a rebel.

Stampalia's analysis of Williams' drunk scene on a *Hawaiian Eye*
episode is almost as bad as the "pushing away of the hair" debacle: "Williams' transformation into a drunk in five easy steps only
appears to be external; in fact, it comes from within, having been
prepared externally, and is a demonstration of both Method and
non–Method acting techniques, joined harmoniously together."
The author's contention that one particular episode of *Hawaiian
Eye* was better than the others was because it *might* have been
partly written (uncredited) by Williams is odd.

Particularly in the sections devoted to *Shrinking Man*, the author
argues with reviews. It gets very tiring, him continually claiming
the critics "just don't get it." In a baffling write-up about the music,
he even argues with what music expert David Schecter related
to him. If anything, I would side with Schecter, a historian who
knows more about music than anyone and writes in a style easily
accessible to the average reader. "The deuteragonist in the film's
leitmotif family is the Spider motif," Stampalia writes, "a brassy,
dissonant theme shrieked by a group of trumpets and trombones
accompanied by an ominous cymbal roll…" As clear as mud.

The copious footnotes are ridiculous and totally unnecessary—
and ramp up the word count. If Williams worked with someone
or, for Heaven's sake, was written up by a columnist, we get a brief
bio of them. If you are reading a book about Grant Williams, you
already know who Rosalind Russell is. Trust me. There's even a
footnote about the musical Russell starred in, *Wonderful Town*.
What a waste of space. Stampalia's note about another book is a
bit obnoxious, calling the volume ungrammatical and accusing it
of being hagiographic—that's the pot calling the kettle black.

Stampalia supplies great information about Williams and clears
up conflicting data, lies and exaggerations from publicity and elsewhere. (While adding his own exaggerations.) For years it was
believed Williams was an opera singer, but Stampalia proves this
notion wrong with solid facts and a rare photo of the "other Grant

Williams." He even tackles the subject of Williams' sexual orientation in a most respectful and insightful way. This is the biography's strongest selling point; unfortunately, you need to push your way through a lot of crap to get to this. If an editor had reined in the author, forcing him to concentrate on the essentials, and helped him write in a clearer manner, this would be a great book. Many of his quotes include redundant info and really needed to be tightened.

Quite a few of the photos are wonderful, but the screen grabs are horrendous and not really worth the "effort." One caption in particular is very curious: "Grant Williams and Coleen Gray in one of their hormonal scenes from *The Leech Woman*." Seriously.

Stampalia seems to be an intelligent, well-read person but he has regrettably allowed his subject to run roughshod all over him and cloud his better judgment. This would have been a better book if he had emotionally distanced himself from Williams and written it in a more subjective, straightforward manner.

Guest Parking 2: Ian Wolfe, Carl Laemmle Jr., Alan Napier, David Manners
by Rick Atkin

A few years ago, I was very hard on Rick Atkins' book *Guest Parking: Zita Johann*. I am happy to say that his follow-up, **Guest Parking 2: Ian Wolfe, Carl Laemmle Jr., Alan Napier, David Manners** (BearManor), is much better. I am not thrilled with the title because it suggests the book is about the hospitality service, but just to explain: "Guest Parking is a place in which life is precious yet temporary. When one stops to think about it, we really are only guests, alluding, of course, to our very temporal mortal existence here on earth."

Atkins records his friendships with Ian Wolfe (1896–1992), Carl Laemmle Jr. (1908–79), Alan Napier (1903-88) and David

Manners (1900–98); the author states that the stories are "true and written without guile"—an apt description. His writing style takes some getting used to, but in the end it's very sweet and admiring. It's still a little rough and rambling in spots but, considering some of the garbage I have been reading lately about Hollywood, this is a welcome respite and the perfect antidote to the trash. It also helps that this was better edited than his previous book, although there are several mistakes here and there (Elizabeth Taylor did not win an Oscar for *A Place in the Sun*, etc.), and the text needed to be trimmed at certain points and rearranged a bit (to put events in the proper order, especially in the Laemmle chapter). The film and stage lists, in particular, are poorly transcribed and could have taken up less space.

Each subject gets his own lengthy chapter made up of Atkins' personal letters and interviews, and career details culled elsewhere. The latter is less effective, but if you concentrate on the reminiscences of interviewees, you will be rewarded with some rare stories, insights and details about their private life you will not find elsewhere.

There are some charming moments, such as Ian Wolfe answering the door by stating, "Come in! Come in! It is so good to finally meet you. I'm the Big Bad Wolf!"

There is so much Laemmle history here that one wishes Atkins had just written a book solely about that clan. A lot of it is involved, but at least interesting, and because family members wrote to the author directly, it is all very personal stuff. Truth be told, Carl Jr. seems like odd man out in this book, since the other subjects are actors, but don't let that deter you. Atkins was thorough, even interviewing Earl Carroll girl Evelyn Moriarty, who had a relationship with Junior, and *Flash Gordon* star Buster Crabbe.

David Manners, who I know wrote and published poetry, proves to be a thoughtful letter writer and I enjoyed coming to know him through the missives he and the author sent back and forth.

Although Atkins writes like a fan, he had the good sense to put all this down for posterity. He is to be commended for that.

Some favorite quotes:

"I was pacing the floor and needed to go to the men's room. The place was so strange to me and I didn't know where to go. ...I said, 'Mr. Karloff, can you direct me to the men's room? Is there a toilet around here?' And with his face twisted to one side and one eye all faked, and his mouth twisted, Mr. Karloff said, 'The whole damn studio is a toilet.' And we both roared with laughter!"—Ian Wolfe, talking about *The Raven* (1935).

"You've tried to get me to remember that one. But I do not remember it, lad. Send me to the gallows!" —Ian Wolfe, about *Zombies on Broadway* (1945).

"My agent rang me one morning and said, 'I think you're going to be Batman's butler.'

"I said, 'What?'

"She said, 'Don't you read the comics?'

"I said, 'No. What is a Batman?'

"She said, 'You even get to drive the Batmobile.'

"I said, 'I don't want to drive the Batmobile. I've never heard of such rubbish. How do I know I want to be Batman's butler? What are you getting me into?'

"She said, 'Alan, if all goes well, it could be worth a hundred thousand dollars.'

"And I said, 'Oh ... of course I'm going be Batman's butler!'"—Alan Napier on getting the role of Alfred on TV's *Batman*.

"I lost all momentum in pictures and literally walked away from it. I don't like talking about this. It's from that other world. I'll succinct it to say, [Joan] swam against the current, metaphorically speaking. If that was her forte, so be it. It was not mine. And that, dear Rick, is the end of the story." —David Manners about the result of a "tiff" with Joan Crawford.

The photos are exceptional—candids, portraits (some excellent character shots), scene stills and family photos. I absolutely loved the one depicting Ian Wolfe and Nancy Kelly from the NBC radio series *The Wonderful Wizard of Oz* (1933-34).

While I had some issues with this one, I enjoyed most of it. True, it could be cluttered at times, but it is in many ways an important document, especially since Atkins' subjects have all passed. I cannot recall when Wolfe, Laemmle Jr., Napier and David Manners have been interviewed in such depth and with such an attention to their personalities and their every-day lives. Even with its faults, I found myself appreciating the effort it took to do this. I just wish the editing was stronger.

Hollywood Godfather: The Life and Crimes of Billy Wilkerson
by W.R. Wilkerson III

I am wondering how many people know who Billy Wilkerson (1890-1962) was. He was extremely influential: He founded and ran *The Hollywood Reporter*, started the Cafe Trocadero, Ciro's and other restaurants and nightspots; was involved with gangsters such as Johnny Rosselli and Bugsy Siegel; discovered Lana Turner; was a prime mover and shaker during the Blacklist years; was pals with Howard Hughes and J. Edgar Hoover ... and so much more. He was a man of extraordinary taste who was vindictive, had a gambling addiction and did some very bad things.

His son W.R. Wilkerson III has written the definitive book about him. A lot of the tales in **Hollywood Godfather: The Life and Crimes of Billy Wilkerson** (Chicago Review Press) are hard to believe, but Wilkerson III incorporates interviews he did with his father's secretary George Kennedy, his lawyer Greg Bautzer and others. It's a true insider's story.

Wilkerson III is a very meticulous writer, and it's a quick, captivating read. As hinted above, his father was not altogether a good guy, but Wilkerson III stays on an even course and lets the facts speak for themselves. He doesn't judge his father and doesn't make excuses.

There are surprising yarns concerning the Hollywood studio moguls. The section about Bugsy Siegel and the development of Las Vegas' Flamingo Hotel is something I never knew before. Ditto for its possible connection to Bugsy's murder.

There are enough anecdotes for five books, for cryin' out loud, and a surprise on every page. I found myself learning things I never thought I needed to learn! Not just about Wilkerson but Hollywood in general.

I think Wilkerson would have been proud of the job his son has done. It ain't pretty, but it's honest and riveting in spots. I enjoyed myself.

Hollywood Musicals You Missed: Seventy Noteworthy Films from the 1930s
by Edwin M. Bradley

McFarland has a new book out by one of my favorite authors, Edwin M. Bradley. He's an expert on early movie musicals, and he (pardon the pun) scores once again with **Hollywood Musicals You Missed: Seventy Noteworthy Films from the 1930s**. "Pre-World War II Hollywood musicals weren't only about Astaire and Rogers, Mickey and Judy, Busby Berkeley, Bing Crosby, or Shirley Temple," Bradley points out, and to prove it, he writes about *Broadway, Jazz Heaven, The Talk of Hollywood* (all 1929), *Captain of the Guard, Movietone Follies of 1930, Ladies in Love, Border Romance, Kathleen Mavourneen, Are You There?* (all 1930), *It's Great to Be Alive* (1933), *Harmony Lane* (1935)/*Swanee River* (1939), *Old Man Rhythm*/*To Beat the Band* (both 1935), *The Girl Said No* (1937), *Alexander's Ragtime Band* (1938), *The Star Maker, The Great Victor Herbert* (both 1939), *Pigskin Parade* (1936), *With Love and Kisses* (1936)/*Sing While You're Able* (1937)/*Thanks for Listening* (1937)/*Swing It Professor* (1937), *Mountain Music* (1937), *Kentucky Moonshine* (1938), *Down in "Arkansaw"* (1938)/

Jeepers Creepers (1939), *The Phantom Empire* (1935), *Palm Springs, Rhythm on the Range, The Devil on Horseback* (all 1936), *Harlem on the Prairie* (1937)/*Two Gun Man from Harlem* (1938)/*The Bronze Buckaroo* (1939)/*Harlem Rides the Range* (1939), *Rawhide, Cowboy from Brooklyn, The Terror of Tiny Town* (all 1938), *Ride 'Em Cowgirl* (1939)/*Water Rustlers* (1939)/*The Singing Cowgirl* (1939), *I Live for Love, Here's to Romance* (both 1935), *Give Us This Night, Fatal Lady, Follow Your Heart, Under Your Spell* (all 1936), *When You're in Love, Hitting a New High* (both 1937), *The Road to Reno, The Great Waltz* (both 1938), *The Big Broadcast of 1937* (1936)/*Hollywood Hotel* (1937), *Champagne Waltz* (1937), *Swing, Sister, Swing* (1938), *Going Places* (1938)/*Naughty but Nice* (1939), *Some Like It Hot, That's Right—You're Wrong* (both 1939), *Big Boy* (1930), *Too Much Harmony, The Way to Love* (both 1933), *Stingaree, 365 Nights in Hollywood* (both 1934), *In Person* (1935), *Sing and Be Happy, Something to Sing About, A Damsel in Distress* (all 1937) and *Let Freedom Ring/Broadway Serenade* (both 1939). Whew! Each film gets cast and crew listings, song lists, synopses and, most valuable, Bradley's informed commentary. Chapter titles are "Songs of the Dawn," "They Don't Write 'Em Like That Anymore" (songwriter biopics), "A Hillbilly-Sym-Funny," "Where the Tenors and the Baritones Play," "Invasion of the Opera Singers, or: End of an Aria," "The Teenagers Are Restless" and "Big Stars, Short Memories."

I know most of these movies, but I love reading Bradley's take on them and the chance to learn more. It was a pleasure to see a particular favorite of mine, *The Girl Said No* with Robert Armstrong and Irene Hervey, included here; also appreciated are the author's salutes to often-overlooked performers such as Noel Francis, El Brendel, Linda Ware, Pinky Tomlin, Dorothy Page, Smith Ballew, Herb Jeffries, Everett Marshall, Nino Martini, Jan Kiepura and Michael Bartlett. Usually when historians write about El Brendel, it's just to tell us how terrible he is. Bradley has a different, refreshing view.

I hope this review is music to the ears of serious fans of these movies, because I'm sure they'll eat this volume up. I know I did.

Hollywood's Made-to-Order Punks: The Dead End Kids, Little Tough Guys, East Side Kids and the Bowery Boys by Richard Roat/**Hollywood's Made-to-Order Punks Part 2: A Pictorial History of the Dead End Kids, Little Tough Guys, East Side Kids and the Bowery Boys** by Richard Roat/**From Broadway to the Bowery: A History and Filmography of the Dead End Kids, Little Tough Guys, East Side Kids and Bowery Boys Films, with Cast Biographies** by Leonard Getz

A book that had me reaching for the aspirin was **Hollywood's Made-to-Order Punks: The Dead End Kids, Little Tough Guys, East Side Kids and the Bowery Boys** by Richard Roat, with forewords by Mende Koenig and Brandy Gorcey-Ziesemer (BearManor). It's a complete mess. First of all, I would like to say that I am a fan of the Bowery Boys and their offshoot groups, and like all their movies. This book promised "detailed cast biographies and filmographies" with "information you won't find elsewhere." The author knew and became friends with most of these guys and "now he spills the beans about the whole friggin' bunch…"

Give me a friggin' break.

The book is separated in two sections, biographies and the films. First, the "revealing" bios. For the record, these are the actors highlighted: Bernard Punsly, Billy Halop, Bobby Jordan, Gabriel Dell, Huntz Hall, Leo Gorcey, Bernard Gorcey, Dick Chandlee, Mende Koenig, Hally Chester, Stanley Clements, Buddy Gorman, David Gorcey, Charles Duncan, Harris Berger, David Durand, Donald Haines, Eugene Francis, Frankie Burke, Billy Benedict, Benjamin "Bennie" Bartlett, Frankie Thomas, James McCallion, John Duncan, Ernest Frederick Morrison (Sunshine Sammy), Bobby Stone, Norman Abbott, Eddie LeRoy, William (Bill) Lawrence, Sam &

Jack Edwards, Mickey Martin & Wesley Giraud, Charles Peck, Ronald Sinclair, Ward Wood, Kenneth Howell, George Offerman, Jackie Searl, Gil Stratton, and William Tracy, plus lost players Eddie Brian, Jimmy Strand, Eddie Mills, William Frambes, Bill Channey, Bill Bates, Leo Borden, Al Stone, Jimmy Murphy and Lester Jay.

Impressive sounding, isn't it? And it is, to tackle all these actors. Some of the bios have good information, but much of it is poorly presented and written. The author's style is awkward-sounding at best.

His correspondence with some of the guys occasionally comes up with an interesting tidbit here and there. Too often, however, they turn out like the entry on Eddie LeRoy: "Once we started talking, we couldn't stop," Roat writes…and that's about it. Nothing is revealed except they had breakfast together and Roat gave him an address and phone number for someone. Boring. And not useful. It seems ridiculous that their meeting is even mentioned, unless Roat just wanted to brag that he had personal contract with LeRoy. The same with John Duncan: "We talked for two hours… and have remained good friends to this day." Annnnnnnnd?? And, nothing else. This happens a lot. Too many things are implied, not enough revealed. If he knew these guys as well as he says he did, well, I absolutely expect much more than what was delivered. Even when he does tell us what they said, it is often paraphrased—and not very well. He seems more concerned telling us that he got an autographed photo from them. A sure sign that this is written by a fan, not a writer.

I was greatly disappointed in the entry on Donald Haines. Recently, I was researching Haines for something I was writing. Unfortunately, having read this book, I knew that Roat didn't have much to say. Granted, info on Haines is hard to come by, but still, there is no excuse for this: "He was later killed in action, and he was listed as missing in action. His body was never found; there is no date of death. Just the year 1942." I did find a death date: February 20, 1943, which is on Haines' headstone. I wrote the following: "As part of the 93rd Fighter Squadron, the 23-year-old was killed in action in North Africa. In 1949, it was reported that Donald's body was repatriated to the United States. Military services were conducted at Pierce Bros.' Beverly Hills Chapel and he was interred in Inglewood Park Cemetery." That last bit of info was obtained through the *Los Angeles Times*—a source obviously not consulted by Roat.

As I read this, I had the feeling that Roat relied on light sources and didn't venture into anything deep—no newspaper articles and interviews. For instance, Sam Edwards. Tom and Jim Goldrup's interview with Sam appears in BearManor's *The Encyclopedia of Feature Players, Vol. 1 (Peter Adams through Terry Frost)*. So why wasn't this interview consulted? I would think Roat would seek out any and all info where he could. I guess not.

At least there is some good in this section and it's nice to see all these boys highlighted, with profile photos to match.

But, then we get to the films...ugh. I have a question: Why was this part of the book even included? Anyone? Anyone? Remember the volume *The Films of the Bowery Boys* by David Hayes and Brent Walker? If Roat thinks he can compare with that book, he is sadly mistaken. If this book only had the bio section, I would highly recommend it, large, bulbous warts and all, but...my God, this film section is just a waste. A mind-numbing waste of time and space. And I am trying to be nice.

Each film gets studio, release date and a review from *Variety*. Some of the bigger films—*Crime School, Angels with Dirty Faces, They Made Me a Criminal*, etc.—get a note section, again awkwardly written, and a lot of it was stuff I didn't care about, to be perfectly honest.

But, basically, the only text is from *Variety*. I have to question this off-the-wall decision to only relate what *Variety* thought of the films. Why *Variety*? Why for every movie? Reviewers never particularly liked the boys' hijinks—what enlightening insights could we possibly get from reading these reviews? The Bowery

Boys' films were for the fans. We need reviews from the author—a fan who appreciates the movies—not some highbrow critic.

The photos are great and the book's saving grace. I wish Roat had a more readable, compact style and was better able to organize facts to make each bio easier to read and interesting. Many of these guys had tragic lives and I felt no involvement as I read about their troubles. The movie section is worse and of no interest whatsoever. There's just nothing there of value. At least there are some tidbits in the actor entries. Oh, I am sure Bowery Boys fans will like this but, to me, this is very slapdash and could have been much better.

Roat also has another volume out: **Hollywood's Made-to-Order Punks Part 2: A Pictorial History of the Dead End Kids, Little Tough Guys, East Side Kids and the Bowery Boys** (Bear-Manor), essentially a collection of hundreds of photos from the movies. A good bet for fans, this is a nice picture book.

For good commentary about the Dead End Kids-Little Tough Guys-East Side Kids-Bowery Boys films, I strongly suggest the very worthy **From Broadway to the Bowery: A History and Filmography of the Dead End Kids, Little Tough Guys, East Side Kids and Bowery Boys Films, with Cast Biographies** by Leonard Getz, foreword by Leo Gorcey, Jr. (McFarland). Pretty much the same format as the above volume, but done superbly by the always-reliable layout staff at McFarland.

While Getz does not cover the same number of actors as Roat, he does comprehensively provide details on the major players, with the added bonus of a tribute from a friend or family member for each. Getz is a good writer and the editing is tighter. Not only that, but the film section is miles above the previous book. Not only do we get cast and crew, but the author supplies the plot with critiques and notes for each. Photos are also excellent throughout.

I know these two books are competing for the same audience. Both have strong points. I would hate to totally dismiss Roat's book, because I think there's a lot of good stuff there, just not done properly. The better book, in my opinion, is Getz. If you can ignore the poor writing and sometimes lack of common sense in Roat's book, you will be rewarded by a few nice stories and info on lesser-known members. The photos in both books are superb.

Houses of Noir: Dark Visions from Thirteen Film Studios
by Ronald Schwartz

At first, **Houses of Noir: Dark Visions from Thirteen Film Studios** by Ronald Schwartz (McFarland) looks to be an essential addition to any noir lover's bookshelf: "The author examines the best noir from each studio and includes each studio's history, a meticulous plot outline and information on the careers of each studio's star roster. He also comments on producers, directors, screenwriters, cameramen, composers, art and set directors and presents stills that represent the noir style. The book also has a discussion of independent productions and the second best film noirs of major and minor studios." Each film/studio gets their own chapter: *The Gangster* (1947, Allied Artists), *Gilda* (1946, Columbia), *Hollow Triumph* aka *The Scar* (1948, Eagle-Lion), *The Asphalt Jungle* (1950, MGM), *I Wouldn't Be in Your Shoes* (1948, Monogram), *Double Indemnity* (1944, Paramount), *Detour* (1945, PRC), *House by the River* (1950, Republic), *Out of the Past* (1947, RKO), *Laura* (1944, Fox), *Too Late for Tears* (1949, UA), *The Killers* (1946, Universal), and *Possessed* (1947, Warners).

Let's start with "meticulous plot outlines," since his entries are basically just that: long, agonizing plot retellings, containing spoilers. This would be boring anyway, but here it's made even worse by Schwartz's inability to distinguish between useless and interesting points. His writing is disjointed, making the stories of these classic films sound illogical and downright surreal. The incorporation of film dialogue just makes things worse and I just shook my head at passages like this one (from *The Gangster*):

Jimmy and Shubunka keep on talking in the booth as night falls. The sun sets, the shadows darken, become longer, and Jimmy confides to Shubunka: "You only need one person near and dear to you!" The camera then cuts to Nancy's apartment and Shubunka enters their bedroom and watches her sleeping. She awakens to the news that he went uptown and brought her something—a new mink coat! Confiding to her maid Essie how beautiful it is, Nancy tells Shubunka, "I hate you, I could kill you. I really don't want a Broadway show." He answers, "I really can't believe I have you."

And *I* can't believe I read this.

There's a lot of repetition. For example, in talking about *The Gangster*, he mentions twice that the "new cashier" Hazel was played by Shelley Winters.

Barry Sullivan did not star in *Framed* (1947), Glenn Ford did; Barry was third-billed. Did Sullivan really play Loretta Young's "duplicitous husband" in *Cause for Alarm!* (1951)? He was pretty loony in that, but made no bones about being paranoid.

About John Ireland: "After making *All the Kings Men* (1949) with Broderick Crawford for Columbia, his career rolled downhill after some disastrous marriages." This is a very simplistic view of Ireland. Also, Ireland was married only three times: Elaine Sheldon (1940–49), actress Joanne Dru (1949–56) and Daphne Myrick Cameron (from 1962 until his 1992 death). Plus, why no mention that Ireland got an Oscar nomination for *All the Kings Men*? There are many factors why certain actors never get the breaks, but Ireland's problem was hardly due to his marriages.

"Charles McGraw died abruptly in 1980 in a household accident." Vague writing irritates me. McGraw fell through his glass shower door, severed an artery in his arm and bled to death. (For the whole story, as well as a good read, get Alan K. Rode's McFarland book *Charles McGraw: Biography of a Film Noir Tough Guy*.)

In *Detour*, Schwartz claims that the Charles Haskell character dies from a stroke, but we are never sure what was wrong with him before he hit his head on the rock as he fell from the automobile. Weirdly, he calls the actor who played Haskell, Edmund MacDonald, "portly."

Detour, again: "Vera tries to come on to Al sexually but he refuses her advances because he doesn't like being a prisoner." Huh?

Tom Neal did not graduate from Harvard Law School; he studied at Northwestern University. He also did not marry Barbara Payton after her divorce from Franchot Tone.

Port of New York was Eagle-Lion, not United Artists.

"PRC was one of the most respected makers of Hollywood B-movies on what was known as Hollywood's 'Poverty Row.'" The laughter you hear is mine. Although I personally like PRC, it was considered the lowest of the B studios and was referred to as "Pretty Rotten Crap." Later, however, in the *Detour* chapter, Schwartz claims that the studio's main product were "all very forgettable titles."

Raw Deal (1948): "A gangster seeking revenge falls in love with two women."

The Long Goodbye (1973) was not Sterling Hayden's last film and it is highly debatable if that was the first color neo-noir. Misleading is Schwartz's claim that Hayden "usually played action heroes in the forties." He only made six films prior to *The Asphalt Jungle*, his most prolific period coming in the '50s.

Jean Hagen and Louis Calhern were known mostly for their comedies? Marilyn Monroe a "noir icon"?

Pushover was not Kim Novak's first film.

Apology for Murder (1945) was not a "virtual re-make" of *Double Indemnity*...it was a rip-off. PRC was going to call the film *Single Indemnity*, but Paramount lawyers stepped in. (See another, better McFarland book, *Savage Detours: The Life and Work of Ann Savage* by Lisa Morton and Kent Adamson.)

The author claims that Edgar Ulmer only made two film noirs, *Detour* and *Murder is My Beat*, totally overlooking *Strange Illusion*

(1945), *The Strange Woman* (1946) and *Ruthless* (1948); some even put *Bluebeard* (1944) in the quasi-noir category.

House by the River: "Jane Wyatt looks too good and innocent to understand her husband's carousing and weakness for loose women and cheap perfume. His nightly jaunts out on the town for sex and drink should have disturbed her earlier on." Wyatt has complete faith in her husband and is unaware of his dark side. While listing Wyatt's noir roles, he omits her against-type performance in *The Man Who Cheated Himself* (1950).

Against All Odds, the remake of *Out of the Past*, was 1984 not '94.

Rhonda Fleming was "hounded by Joseph Cotten and Wendell Corey" in *The Killer Is Loose* (1956)?? She was hounded by Corey, yes, but Cotten plays her husband.

It's very obvious to me that the author is not too familiar with the actors in the films he is writing about. He says that Lee Bowman played the "guy who doesn't get the girl in Rita Hayworth Technicolor musicals like *Cover Girl* (1944) and *Tonight and Every Night* (1945)." Bowman starred with Hayworth in the latter. And: "His best dramatic role was as singer Lillian Roth's husband in the almost-noir *Smash-up, the Story of a Woman* (1947) which starred Susan Hayward..." Lillian Roth was not in the movie and Hayward did not play Roth. *I'll Cry Tomorrow* (1955) was the Hayward-starring Roth biopic. *Smash-up* is considered the story of Dixie Lee and Bing Crosby.

Richard Webb "spent most of his career playing good guys in television films." That just doesn't make sense. He played Captain Midnight on television from 1954 to '56 and did only three TV movies.

The Blue Gardenia is "about a woman (Anne Baxter) who loses consciousness during an affair with Raymond Burr and finds him dead in the morning." Would it be asking too much to actually *watch* the film or find a reliable synopsis?

Dana Andrews "reprises the role of Detective Mark McPherson" from *Laura* (1944) in *Where the Sidewalk Ends*. No, he does not, he portrays Detective Mark Dixon. Schwartz mentions this bit of misinformation twice.

The Dark Corner (1946) was not one of Lucille Ball's "first non-musical-comedic roles." And she was not in a triangle with Mark Stevens and Clifton Webb in that film. By the way, Webb did not spend the rest of his Fox years in Mr. Belvedere comedies.

Lady on a Train (1945) is not Deanna Durbin's first film noir. She made *Christmas Holiday* (1944) before that.

Too Late for Tears (1949) was not producer Hunt Stromberg's last; he made *Between Midnight and Dawn* (1950) and *Mask of the Avenger* (1951) after that.

Virginia Christine was "not a femme fatale"? Give me a break. Watch her in *The Inner Circle* (1946). Yet, he says that Joan Crawford "usually" played femme fatales in the 1930s.

Filmakers was *not* "a group of actors, directors and writers who released their product through RKO." It was an independent film company headed by Ida Lupino and Collier Young. And it is spelled Filmakers, not Filmmakers.

The writing, oh Lord, the writing: Awkward and run-on sentences, misplaced commas, missing words, repetition, inappropriate words, and incomprehensible lines. There are long passages that would read better if they were trimmed, for example the part in the *Hollow Triumph* chapter talking about the photo negative/scar mix-up. Schwartz mentions it again later in the chapter, with the same exclamation-laden, breathless, I-can't-believe-it style.

And, I mean, seriously, how do you explain these sentences:

"In this scene, Muller, dressed in a suit and tries to convince Bennett to stay."

About *Gilda*: "Rita Hayworth was no stranger to the film noir style. *Gilda* was her first film in that genre ..."

A couple of pages later, same film: "Hungarian director Charles Vidor, no stranger to the noir style, made the pre-noir *Blind Alley* (1939) for Columbia (which was remade in 1948 as *The Dark Past*), as well as the Technicolor musical *Cover Girl* with Rita Hayworth before he decided to direct her in his best noir film, *Gilda*." (*Whew* all in one sentence!)

"His use of the key light as Rita sings 'Put the Blame on Mame' is also **extraordinary**. [Rudolph] Maté later graduated from cameraman to director, making the **extraordinary** *D.O.A.* (1949) in which Edmond O'Brien gives his most **extraordinary** performance." Someone, please, get this man a thesaurus.

"Muller asks Evelyn reluctantly until he talks to his brother in his office."

"*The Asphalt Jungle* is still one of the best 'heist film noirs' ever made and is only rivaled by Stanley Kubrick's *The Killing* (1956) and Jules Dassin's *Rififi* (1954), some critics insist that *Asphalt Jungle* is the quintessential noir heist film."

About Don Castle (another deep breath): "Beginning his career at MGM, he was immediately typecast as a juvenile in *Love Finds Andy Hardy* (1938) and later as an action hero in minor roles in *Wake Island* (1942) but became a Monogram star in *The Guilty* and *The Invisible Wall* (both 1947) and *Who Killed Doc Robbin?* [which is not a Monogram but a Hal Roach film] and *I Wouldn't Be in Your Shoes* (both 1948), his best film." And, no, Castle did not play multiple roles in *Wake Island*.

Suspense (1946): "Promoter Barry Sullivan falls out of love with ice skater Belita and tries to kill her by loosening a sword in a hoop. However, she avoids the hoop, the most dangerous part of her act, and survives."

Out of the Past: "He nods and so returns to Jim's car and they drive out of town."

Double Indemnity: (pg. 64) "Edward G. Robinson considered his role 'supporting' rather than a 'starring' one. (He had always been given top billing since *Little Caesar* [1930] and would not accept anything less.)" On pg. 65, the author claims that Robinson took the part because he wanted to "ease into character roles."

He calls Barbara Stanwyck and Fred MacMurray in that movie "the adulteress and the fornicator." And lest we misinterpret MacMurray and Robinson's characters' closeness and their use of

"I love you, too," the author says, "You really cannot decode this line and others like it as 'homo-erotic,' just the nature of closeness between men." Oh, good, I was worried there for a moment. Also, remember Robinson's "little man inside" that helps him figure out if a claim is legit or fake? The author says that's "probably his 'intuition.'" Maybe. We aren't sure.

Ann Savage was a "talented actress, but not as pretty as Barbara Stanwyck." Okay. *sigh*

At one point, the author is talking about how the title song of *Laura*, written by David Raksin, came about. For some reason, Schwartz feels the need to interject: "When asked by the composer which was my favorite Raksin score, I replied, 'Forever Amber,' the 1947 film adaptation of a scandalous novel of the mid-forties by Kathleen Windsor." Thanks for sharing ... but who cares?

Cinematographer Woody Bredell "only" worked on 75 movies in his career. And how many books has the author written?

Here are some comments that just...irritated me:

Don Castle: "A limited talent as an actor, he died without much publicity in 1966."

Director William Nigh was "a capable B artist, making few memorable films but keeping his cast on target..."

"*I Wouldn't Be in Your Shoes* belongs in the category of Monogram's B films but it surprises us with its competently told story and a plot that unfolds with deftness."

As an "added bonus," each film gets two "special photos" that "informs" the noir style. Or, it is my guess, they were the only photos the author could come up with. What they merely do is take up space as he reiterates what he said before. Why do I want him to describe a still I can plainly look at myself? This adds nothing to the book. At one point he tells us to take note of a painting behind the main characters in the photo, but the painting is blurry and he never tells us why we should be taking note of it.

I noticed that twice he referenced writer Michael L. Stephens, who authored two very bad, error-filled books, *Film Noir: A Comprehensive, Illustrated Reference to Movies, Terms and Persons* and

Gangster Films: A Comprehensive, Illustrated Reference to People, Films and Terms. (See my first volume of book reviews, *Let Me Tell You How I Really Feel*, for my reviews of them.) I guess, considering the mistakes here in *Houses of Noir*, that is very appropriate.

This meandering book should be avoided. The cover, however, is quite fabulous: a moody, foggy shot from *Detour* of Tom Neal and Claudia Drake. Otherwise, this is a misfire.

Ida Lupino: Beyond the Camera: 100th Birthday Special Edition
by Mary Ann Anderson with Ida Lupino

In 2011, *Ida Lupino: Beyond the Camera* by Mary Ann Anderson with Ida Lupino was published by BearManor. I attempted to read it then but its disjointed narrative put me off. Now in 2018, we have a new edition, **Ida Lupino: Beyond the Camera: 100th Birthday Special Edition** (BearManor). I thought, perhaps, this would be an improvement. I was wrong.

Anderson, the daughter of actress Emily McLaughlin, was Lupino's business manager and caregiver in her later years. This alone should have made this interesting and essential reading but Anderson is not a writer—not by a long shot. The fact that she trashes William Donati's well-researched and -written Lupino biography bothered me and seemed to be more jealousy than a real assessment.

The book includes many lines spoken by Ida to Anderson. But some of Lupino's quotes are just not necessary and should have been either cut or at least trimmed. In the middle of talking about a movie, Lupino describes a photo!

Ida starred with Robert Ryan in *Beware, My Lovely* (1952) for Filmakers. "I am discussing the intensity of this scene with director Harry Horner. I am reacting to the approaching footsteps after a day of terror in the house." These quotes, obviously in reference to photos Lupino was looking at, are dropped willy-nilly into the text.

Here's another: "'I appeared in *The Sea Wolf* and *Out of the Fog* for Warner Bros., both First National Pictures. My expression in this photo is strictly acting! I am rehearsing a scene with John Garfield, while visitor Jack Haley listens with his eyes closed,' Ida laughs." For some reason this quote starts off a chapter and refers to an unidentified photo above it (it should have been the caption). By the way, the eyes-closed actor is not Jack Haley but Jack La Rue. I don't think anyone ever confused those two actors before!

The above is just one instance where Anderson should have corrected Lupino's faulty memory: "I appeared in *The Sea Wolf* with Edward G. Robinson for Twentieth Century–Fox." This is where Anderson should have said, "No, you appeared in that 1941 movie at Warner Bros." instead of just carelessly including that line.

About the movie *Hollywood Canteen* (1944), Ida "informatively" notes, "This film's setting is the Hollywood Canteen..." Stop the presses! Help me here, I'm not exactly clear on what character Lupino plays in *Devotion* (1946): "*Devotion*, Curtis Bernhardt's expressive lumbering film about the Bronte family. I portray Emily Bronte, and I enjoyed working again with Olivia de Havilland, who portrays Charlotte. I play a good woman in this for a change, Emily Bronte."

Anderson should have discussed the movies to fortify Lupino's quotes about them instead of just having Ida say useless things like "I played [so-and-so] in this movie"—and that's it. What Anderson does write is very simplistic and should have been tightened considerably.

I was confused by this Lupino quote: "In 1935, I appeared as the 'Heart of Interest' of Harold Lloyd in *The Milky Way*. This was my first big-screen chance, and I starred opposite this fine comedian in the Paramount Production of this popular play." First of all, the film was 1936, second the character's name was "Polly Pringle" (I have no idea what a "Heart of Interest" is) and—this is important—Lupino did not ultimately play the role because she became ill and was replaced by Dorothy Wilson!

More confusion: At one point, Anderson said Lupino walked out on her Paramount contract and quotes Ida as saying she kept alive doing radio. Then there is mention of other studios' pictures. But then, when discussing *The Light That Failed* (1939), Lupino explains, "Bill Wellman was looking through the book at Paramount, noticed my picture and called me in to read for *The Light That Failed* with Ronnie Colman. I was desperate by then. The studio had planned to drop my option when it came due." Then after that: "He brought me back to Paramount at three times my former salary and got me a dressing room on the first floor."

"Ida had 'not wanted' to become an actress; composing and writing were her main interests." Why is "not wanted" in quotes? Is this an out-of-nowhere reference to her movie *Not Wanted* (1949) that we are all supposed to get?

The Light That Failed is a 1939 movie not 1932.

Thank Your Lucky Stars was Warner Bros., not RKO.

"Warren Beatty contacted me about a project for Ida. He had produced a movie of the week starring Katherine [*sic*] Hepburn and wanted to use Ida in a new project." This so-called Movie of the Week was a major motion picture called *Love Affair* (1994), which Beatty starred in and produced.

"Ida's tremendous one word, 'Free,' in the closing moments of this film [*High Sierra*] stands alone in the lexicon of cinema in the 1940s." Um, okay.

Do I believe Ann Sheridan changed her name from Clara Lou to Ann at Ida's suggestion? No. Or that *Deep Valley* (1947) was similar in plot to *High Sierra* (1941) before Lupino had them change the whole screenplay? No. Or director Lupino's comment about having trouble with Ronald Reagan on a set and telling her crew, "God help us all if Ron is ever elected president of the United States!" Yeah, no.

There is an interesting backstory about *Lust for Gold* (1949), based on Barry Storm's *Thunder God's Gold*, but you won't find it here. Anderson says the film is autobiographical, but Storm sued Columbia for libel, stating that he was falsely portrayed in the movie.

Harry Cohn is referred to as the "Columbian head," which sounds like…something else.

Anderson claims that the plot of 1953's *The Hitch-Hiker* "was based on the story *Out of the Past*, written by screenwriter Daniel Mainwaring, who was blacklisted at the time and did not receive screen credit. Ida took this and did a complete re-write." Anderson is confused. Yes, Mainwaring wrote the screenplay (from his novel *Build My Gallows High*) for the movie *Out of the Past* (1947), but his story for *The Hitch-Hiker* had no connection to it.

I am not denying that Lupino was a groundbreaking female director. But despite what Anderson claims, there were other female directors besides Dorothy Arzner and Lupino. To name just three: Alice Guy-Blaché, Dorothy Davenport and Lois Weber.

In the text, Lupino twice mentions keeping alive doing radio on "*Silver Theater* with Boyer on his show,"—whatever that means— and "with Tyrone Power and C.B. DeMille on his *Lux Theatre*." Trouble is, she cannot decide whether this was during her time at Paramount or during her years with Warner Bros.

There is a lot of repetition. The worst instance comes with her three mentions of the TV anthology series *Four Star Playhouse*. The first time is a mess and really tells us nothing. It starts off with the author writing, "This show featured four rotating stars, Charles Boyer, David Niven and Dick Powell," not even bothering to add Lupino as the fourth star until five paragraphs later. The rest of the info about the show is inconsequential.

Second remark, further on in the book: "Ida embarked on a new career in the dramatic anthology program *Four Star Playhouse*. Ida teamed up with David Niven, Dick Powell, and Charles Boyer, becoming the fourth star featured in its productions."

Third comment, even further on: "While pondering yet another divorce, Ida and partners David Niven, Dick Powell and Charles Boyer formed *Four Star Playhouse*. …I was impressed with the quality of Four Star Productions, and, on December 31, 1953, I made my debut on the small screen in 'House for Sale.' I portrayed a woman who encounters a psychopathic killer. I continued on, becoming their fourth star."

The book tries to stay in chronological order but strays frequently. All of a sudden, we get to the movie *The Hard Way* (1943) and the chapter starts with a slight credit list—a style not previously used. Then, under "Plot" is this: "A question was once asked in a very old book. Occasionally someone tries to answer that question; but if anyone has found the answer, he hasn't said so. The question reads: For what shall it profit a man if he gain the whole world and lose his own soul? Only one answer can be found in the ruthless of heart. Defeat!" What the hell is this supposed to tell us?? This nonsense is inexplicably followed by: "Helen Chernen wasn't thinking of the Bible when she and her sister, Katherine, stood in front of the shop window, staring at the white graduation dress displayed there. The only question in Helen's mind was how she was going to get that dress for her little sister. Katherine wanted it so much. Graduation from high school is an important event for a young girl, especially in Greenhill, Pennsylvania, where the grime and squalor and everyday poverty make every day life a pretty dismal affair." This is the end of any so-called plot retelling. Good riddance. The *Hard Way* "discussion" is helped immeasurably by a quote from its director, Vincent Sherman.

A lot just baffled me. "Ida: 'She was electric,' says Sally Forrest, whom I'd discovered and directed in three pictures, including *Not Wanted*." Just makes no sense. This is followed by a quote that I know is from Sally. Where is the editor?

"I co-authored with Paul Jarrico *Not Wanted*. This film tells the story, powerfully, frankly, in all its pathetic detail, through the eyes and tears of one girl, willful and beautiful."

Redundant: "Ida and Howard [Duff] starred together in the CBS comedy *Mr. Adams and Eve* (1957-58), portraying two movie stars who are married to each other. *Mr. Adams and Eve* is the everyday story of a movie-star couple living in Beverly Hills."

About *The Hitch-Hiker*: "This film noir was directed by Ida Lupino, who was dressed in dungarees, sneakers and a check flannel shirt, topped with a baseball cap and tied-back hair." Thank you, Mary Ann Anderson, for contributing a truly pointless remark.

Does Anderson actually believe that Lupino played "one-dimensional characters" during her career? Maybe in the 1930s, but she quickly showed her mettle by portraying a variety of roles.

Oh, the spelling is atrocious: Ivor Novella (should be Novello), Jesse L. Laske (Lasky), Vivian Leigh (Vivien), Isobel Elson (Elsom), Monty Wooley (Woolley), Sidney Greenstreet (Sydney), Roual Walsh (Raoul), Richard Wydmark (Widmark), Cormel Wilde (Cornel), Woman's Prison (Women's), Trelawney of the Well (Trelawny of the Wells), Jack Lemon (Lemmon), Katherine Hepburn (Katharine), etc. Did you know director Nicholas Ray has a Mexican cousin named Nichlos Reye? Neither did Ray.

Not everything is truly awful. I enjoyed the foreword, penned by Ida herself, in which she describes how she became interested in directing and what it was like helming her first feature. Anderson incorporates many of Lupino's memories of her childhood and what it was like working in England, in Hollywood movies and in television. The beginning section should have included a discussion of father Stanley Lupino and his career but for some reason Anderson put that near the end of Ida's life.

What this book needed was a strong editor to fix the multiple mistakes ("Its concern was a society woman...") and someone to take Lupino's stories and make them mean something. The beginning passages about her early life are by far the best thing about this volume. The story of Mae Clarke at the Motion Picture Home accusing Ida of stealing her false teeth is very funny.

The photos are excellent, although most are not identified. My favorite is the candid of Alan Hale Jr. carrying her in the water during the filming of *Gilligan's Island*.

Anderson describes her friendship with Lupino, which started in 1983. It isn't a pretty picture: "Ida had a lot to be depressed about—her three failed marriages, her waning career, her fading looks, money worries, and her wrecked house." I wish these stories were better told.

I think Anderson indulged Ida too much over third husband Howard Duff, whom Ida called "queer as muck." There is far too much bitterness, jokes at his expense and even a questionable story relating to Duff and their daughter's boyfriend. I am not saying Duff was perfect but too many times there are jabs that just didn't need to be here.

"These tabloids never get anything right," quipped Ida. "They never get my birth year correct, 1918, or my age correct. I am not eighty-seven years old! They can't even write!" Neither can Mary Ann Anderson, although she means well. "Ida was a grand storyteller, often revealing quite incredible ideas and scenarios," Anderson writes, but there is only scant evidence of that in this book. If you love Ida Lupino, by all means get this for the few good scraps you will find. However, this is not my idea of a birthday present.

Indestructible Man
by Tom Weaver

Three years after the publication of Tom Weaver's first *Scripts from the Crypt* book, *The Hideous Sun Demon*, the second in the series finally limped past the finish line: **Indestructible Man** (BearManor), a look-back at that lovably looney, painfully poverty-stricken 1956 science fiction–crime hybrid. A perennial on various Creature Features and Chiller Theaters back in Baby Boomers' TV-watching prime, it stars Lon Chaney as "Butcher" Benton, a convicted armored car robber; on San Quentin's Death Row, he swears to wreak vengeance on his fellow crooks who double-crossed him and put him on the fast-track to the gas chamber. Fortunately for the Butcher, the screenwriters are on his side: After the execution, his carcass winds up in the secret lab of a cancer researcher who performs a weird experiment which restores the spark of life—and also makes his skin like steel. Killing the researcher and his assistant is the Butcher's warm-up act before he sets out on the trail of his former confederates in crime.

Weaver is the Stanley and Livingstone of junk-film fact-finders so this book contains, in addition to the script, an armored carload of informational odds and ends. The everything-but-the-kitchen-sink lineup starts with an intro by indie filmmaker Fred Olen Ray, a long-time *Indestructible Man* fan who once planned a remake; several pages of bio on its producer-director Jack Pollexfen (by Weaver); the story of the making of the movie and a list of many of the script-to-screen changes (Weaver); David Schecter analyzing the music of Albert Glasser; Dr. Robert J. Kiss on the movie's theatrical release history; "Recommended Additional Viewing" (Weaver's mini-reviews of three back-from-the-dead movies he bets you've never seen: 1932's *6 Hours to Live*, 1946's *Decoy* and 1947's *The Gas House Kids in Hollywood*); and the pressbook. There's even a chapter about Pollexfen by the man who was his caregiver toward the end of Pollexfen's life; one incident he describes is the saddest thing you'll read this week or maybe this month. The book's last entry is the story of a real-life killer, Class of 1947, San Quentin gas chamber-bound, who tried to convince the warden to let Dr. Robert Cornish claim his body and resurrect him! Weaver opines that this incident may have been the inspiration for the Chaney movie.

The documentation of the making of *Indestructible Man* is enlivened by quotes from producer-director Pollexfen, screenwriters Vy Russell and Sue Bradford and actors Casey Adams, Ross Elliott and Robert Shayne. Weaver writes in his accustomed style: fact-filled, snarky-funny, but sometimes a bit snarky-disrespectful (for instance, he writes that actress Peggy Maley, a Lana Turner type in the 1940s, was "a bit past her 'sell-by' date" by 1956). Even some of the movie's characters find themselves on the wrong end of his poison pen, like Casey Adams' clueless police detective-hero "who couldn't find a pair of pajamas in a bowl of soup." Weaver's best piece of *Indestructible Man* trivia is that it uses a good bit of stock footage from the 1948 crime drama *He Walked by Night*—and that *Indestructible*'s storm drain climax features enough *He Walked* long shots that we're probably seeing quite a bit of that movie's stars, Richard Basehart, Scott Brady and Roy Roberts.

Indestructible Man's poster appears on the book's cover, and the back cover features original artwork by Marty Baumann, who (in the acknowledgments) Weaver lists as Marty "The Butcher" Baumann—hardy har har.

Jayne Mansfield: The Girl Couldn't Help It by Eve Golden/ Anna Held and the Birth of Ziegfeld's Broadway by Eve Golden/The Brief, Madcap Life of Kay Kendall by Eve Golden

Eve Golden is an author well-known to *Classic Images* readers; her articles have graced these pages since 1991. She is undoubtedly one of the best biographers out there. Her books are hallmarks of outstanding, thorough research and her writing is sharp, fun and filled with common sense. University Press of Kentucky has published Golden's newest, **Jayne Mansfield: The Girl Couldn't Help It**.

I've never been a big fan of the two films that made Jayne Mansfield (1933-67) a star and icon, *The Girl Can't Help It* (1956) and *Will Success Spoil Rock Hunter?* (1957). To me, she seemed too obvious in those films, trying too hard to be the ultimate sex symbol. However, I have enjoyed her performances in *Female Jungle* (1955) and *The Burglar* (1957), but these movies are not considered "Jayne Mansfield films" and are not emblematic of her screen image. Maybe that's why I like them.

There have been numerous books on Mansfield, all pretty much superficially the same, in my opinion, covering the same ground. Most writers have presented her rather shabbily, treating her as a joke and ignoring most of her films. Jayne usually comes across as a publicity seeker, because that's what is written about her. I don't have to tell anyone here: Eve Golden is not your typical writer. She has previously taken oft-covered subjects and made them her own. This is what she's done here.

In Golden's capable hands, Mansfield becomes a multi-dimensional person—never just a joke with a big bosom. The research is scrupulous and meticulous, showing us Jayne's complex nature in startling detail. She's not perfect, of course, and Golden describes her affairs and mistakes, while also making her sympathetic. You can't help but like Mansfield despite all her problems and her lapses of judgment. Jayne was generally an upbeat, positive person, despite what was going on in her life, and this will draw in the readers and make them empathize with her. One of Jayne's mistakes was boyfriend attorney Samuel S. Brody (who died in the car crash with her). The whole section about their alleged abusive relationship upset me greatly, but the author manages to handle this part with great care.

Golden doesn't forget the movies. Naturally, *The Girl Can't Help It* and *Will Success Spoil Rock Hunter?* are featured, but so, too, are *Female Jungle* and *The Burglar*, plus *Pete Kelly's Blues, Illegal, Hell on Frisco Bay* (all 1955), *The Wayward Bus, Kiss Them for Me* (both 1957), *The Sheriff of Fractured Jaw* (1958), *Playgirl After Dark, It Takes a Thief, The Loves of Hercules* (all 1960), *The George Raft Story* (1961), *It Happened in Athens* (1962), *Heimweh nach St. Pauli, Promises.....Promises!* (both 1963), *Panic Button, When Strangers Meet, L'amore primitivo* (all 1964), *The Fat Spy, Las Vegas Hillbillys, Single Room Furnished* (all 1966) and *A Guide for the Married* Man (1967); and also, her TV appearances. Golden's keen humor serves her well when handling the films and TV. Even when the movie is bad—or maybe because they are bad!—you want to seek them out. What is evident is Jayne's unfulfilled potential. Her film career could have been so much better if she hadn't relied so heavily on publicity.

Jayne's husbands, Paul Mansfield, Mickey Hargitay and Matt Cimber (who's interviewed), are all treated in a fair manner and we get a lot of fascinating personal info about them. I never knew what a rollercoaster the Hargitay marriage was.

Also interviewed was entertainer Nelson Sardelli, whose relationship with Jayne was complicated (to say the least). Golden writes at length about Jayne's five children, particularly Jayne Marie Mansfield and Emmy-winning actress Mariska Hargitay (*Law & Order: Special Victims Unit*). Jayne Marie's life was not an easy one, but I like the way Golden writes about her—not as a victim, but as a good-natured survivor.

This is a definitive, stylish biography, separating fact from fiction, presenting the good with the bad. There has been quite a lot of fiction attached to Mansfield, and *Jayne Mansfield: The Girl Couldn't Help* is here to sort it all out. Golden's commentaries on other writers' comments are terrific and show off her good judgment when dealing with her bio subjects. We are extremely lucky to have a historian of Golden's caliber writing biographies today.

There have been other Mansfield books, but none like this one. Golden's even-handed, sensible approach to Jayne's often-convoluted life pegs *Jayne Mansfield: The Girl Couldn't Help It* as a great star bio.

University of Kentucky has also reissued two of Eve's older books in softcover: *Anna Held and the Birth of Ziegfeld's Broadway* and *The Brief, Madcap Life of Kay Kendall*. I have read the latter (an excellent book), but never had the pleasure of reading Anna Held—until now.

Anna Held and the Birth of Ziegfeld's Broadway is a knockout of a book. If the only thing you know about Anna Held (1872-1918) was Luise Rainer's Oscar-winning portrayal in *The Great Ziegfeld* (1936), welcome to the club! Except for her relationship with Florenz Ziegfeld, I knew nothing—and if I continued to think of Rainer, I would still know nothing. Held was so much more than what was shown on screen. What a fascinating lady she turned out to be, especially with Eve's way with the narrative. Golden paints a lively picture of pre–World War I show business revues and vaudeville and the beginning of Ziegfeld's *Follies*. How many of us knew how much Held had a hand in his stage revues?

Writing intelligently and vibrantly about hundred-year-old stage shows requires a great deal of talent. Personally, I would be unable to make that era come alive. But for Eve Golden, it is a piece of cake. I savored every word she wrote and wish I could have seen *A Parisian Model* (1906) and *Miss Innocence* (1908), among others, as they happened. The way Golden describes Held's vivacious stage personality, with her flirty eyes and mannerisms, really takes you to the front row, as if you are watching Held now.

Held's daughter Lianne (with Maximo Carrera) is a major player in the book. She wrote extensively about her mother—and not with the truth in mind. In some of my favorite passages, Golden fact-checks Lianne and discusses her less-than-stellar stage career. As with her Mansfield book, Eve sets the record straight and clears up factual errors and often-told legends. Golden is at her best discussing Held's marriage (1897–1913) and professional relationship with showman Florenz Ziegfeld, and how his extramarital affair with actress Lillian Lorraine affected Held. Held's unstinting, commendable efforts during World War I to entertain the troops was another fascinating aspect.

Fantastically enjoyable, well written and researched, *Anna Held and the Birth of Ziegfeld's Broadway* brings back an actress who deserves to be remembered.

Eve Golden seems to have a knack for writing about people I have no clue about. Which is good, because I learn much from her books. I've seen Kay Kendall in, maybe, two films, but she never made an impression on me. Of course, I knew she had died tragically young (age 32 of myelocytic leukemia), and of Rex Harrison's "gallant" mission to make her last years happy through marriage to him. Well, after Eve's sensational biography **The Brief, Madcap Life of Kay Kendall**, I will never again take the actress for granted.

Golden's task was a tricky one. How do you handle a British-born actress whose film roles (26, many times in small parts; she's best known for her only U.S. film, *Les Girls* with Gene Kelly) were wholly unworthy of her? You tackle Kay's colorful private life, which isn't as easy as it sounds; but the author succeeds with enormous savvy, thoroughly capturing Kendall's energy, style, attitude and wild sense of humor, aided by a wealth of interviews with friends and co-stars, not to mention priceless assistance from Kay's sister, Kim Kendall. The whole book exudes a wonderful spirit of fun, but when the time comes, Golden writes compassionately, with enormous understanding, about Kendall's terminal illness.

Everyone seemed to love Kay and her sense of the absurd. Her friend, actor Dirk Bogarde, remembered how "we made ourselves ill with laughter." One story involved her taking a bath, while Rex Harrison and playwright William Douglas Home were in another room. When the telephone rang, Kay was expected to answer it. This she did completely nude (except for a towel on her head), right in front of Home. She accepted a dinner invitation from the British Ambassador on the phone, then, waving goodbye to the stunned playwright, "sashayed back into the bathroom." Home would later marvel, "The most splendid girl in the world."

There are plenty of stories similarly lively, and Golden gives us a real feeling of what Kay was like—while also making her likable. She could be crazy (pretending to be lost, kidnapped or, worse yet, considering her eventual outcome, dead, just to play a joke on a friend), insecure (especially about her famous nose) and outspoken. In the last regard, Kay would sometimes taunt Rex Harrison in public: "Sexy Rexy! Who said you were sexy?!" she screamed at one party. As Golden notes, "Those who had felt the sharp edge of Harrison's temper through the years were delighted, and Kay gained many admirers for this alone." In her wonderful acerbic way, she would tell friends, "He's twenty years older than I am, and he's got a concave chest and he's going bald," even though she did love him. Harrison's son Noel explains: "Kay was exuberant, generous, and good with my father. She would slap him down when he got uppity, calling him 'You stupid, long-nosed English actor.' They were equals. She brought out the lighthearted side of him." Which, if you knew Harrison, was a major feat, since he wasn't known for his sense of humor. Golden pulls no punches when it comes to him, giving a realistic assessment of his possible motives (many thought he used his doomed relationship with Kay, for whom he left actress Lilli Palmer, as a way of atonement; everyone blamed him for Carole Landis' 1948 suicide).

It really gets under your skin when you learn that he divulged the gravity of Kay's illness to only a select group of people, which did not include Kay or her family. Kim Kendall, by all accounts, has every right to call Harrison "the bastard of all time," as, even when Kay was slipping away, he denied Kim a final talk with her sister, telling her she was perfectly fine. Kay's death—minutes after Kim hung up thinking she was okay—was, to say the least, a surprise to her family, and extremely cruel.

Golden does a marvelous job of juggling the lightness of Kay's life and the terrible reality of her death; no author could have succeeded so well. Golden's style is just right for her subject, her narrative jumps off the page. After this, I plan on paying more attention to Kay Kendall. It's about time.

Jeffrey Hunter: The Film, Television, Radio and Stage Performances
by Paul Green

I was very happy to dig into **Jeffrey Hunter: The Film, Television, Radio and Stage Performances** by Paul Green, with a foreword by Robert Wagner (McFarland). Hunter (1926-69) has always been unjustly overlooked and it's nice to see him get some attention. Often dismissed because of his stunning good looks, he was a more than capable actor, a fact not lost on director John Ford, who cast him in *The Searchers* (1956), *The Last Hurrah* (1958) and *Sergeant Rutledge* (1960). I learned from this volume that Ford also sought Hunter for *Cheyenne Autumn* (1964), which would have been a good break for him considering some of the stuff he was doing at that time. I always felt Hunter was good at playing unstable characters; I especially recall an excellent *Combat!* episode he did in 1962. My favorite Hunter performance is a good example of his ability to play a mentally disturbed personality: *Brainstorm* (1965), portraying a man who feigns insanity to kill his lover's husband. Classic *noir* twists result.

Each chapter takes a film (or two) and discusses it at length, integrating the story of Hunter's life at the time with this work. Green is a good writer and is very interesting when he has something to say, such as in the sections about *The Searchers* and *King of Kings* (1961). For the former, he compares the original story with the screenplay to good effect. His other chapters are mostly very solid but he has an irritating tendency to rely on newspaper reviews to fill up space. I see no point in quoting Bosley Crowther, a critic who seemed to dislike most of the movies he reviewed. This offers us no insight into the films, about their intent, and the makings of the productions.

A weird moment occurs in the discussion about *A Witch Without a Broom* (1967), a low-budget affair filmed in Madrid by producer Sidney Pink. The latter is quoted as saying that the film would have been a "major hit with an actor like Cary Grant in the lead… Jeff Hunter did a good job, but he was no comedian in the fine timing that mark people like Cary Grant and Melvyn Douglas." When I first read that, I couldn't believe it. Pink was lucky his weak production had a game performer like Hunter in the lead. Grant would never have touched such an exploitation potboiler as *A Witch Without a Broom*. Yet, Green just lets the remark go, says nothing, not challenging the absurdity of it. There are a few missed opportunities like this one that go without comment from the author.

There's a lot of neat background for Hunter's movies, nice since some of his movies, especially the foreign ones, are obscure. Green's lengthy plot summaries are ponderous and, in my opinion, just too long. But when Green talks about the controversy in casting Hunter as Jesus in *King of Kings* and why he didn't join the cast of *Star Trek* after filming the initial pilot, he is in peak form as a writer and an astute critical commentator. There's also welcome attention drawn to Hunter's TV guest shots and his short-lived series *Temple Houston.*

There is a wealth of new information here, too. Green interviewed Hunter's first wife, actress Barbara Rush, quite a coup since she is rarely (if ever) interviewed. Other interviews, including those with Robert Wagner, Phyllis Diller (*The Private Navy of Sgt. O'Farrell* [1968]), Peggy King and childhood and college friends, give us insight into Hunter the man and how he approached his life and work. I was a bit disappointed with Wagner; to me at least, he sounded as if he was holding back, just trying to be nice. The two had a rivalry when they were both under contract to 20th Century-Fox.

This well-written volume is a necessity for Hunter's fans.

Joan Crawford: Hollywood Martyr
by David Bret

Joan Crawford is one of the most maligned stars of Hollywood's golden age. Many horrible things have been written about her— some true, most not. I didn't think it could get any worse, but I didn't reckon on David Bret, who sees Miss Crawford as an easy mark for his mud-slinging and a perfect excuse to indulge in gay fantasy lit in his "biography" **Joan Crawford: Hollywood Martyr.**

Others have reminded me that Bret is a "best-selling author" and that he gets good reviews from such respectable outlets as Publishers Weekly ("Fans who crave a lively insider view will most appreciate this bio"). Many love trash and don't care if it is true or not. Bret, with the help of clueless reviewers, panders to these readers. Being a "best-selling author" doesn't necessarily mean you are a good one. In my opinion, Bret is barely functioning on an acceptable level. His prose is quite juvenile as he breathlessly tells us who he thinks is gay or bisexual in Hollywood. Tangents are his specialty.

Joan Crawford: Hollywood Martyr is touted as "the first fully uncensored biography" of the star. Poor Joan. Instead of getting a comprehensive portrait of an obviously complicated woman, we get a bitchy, "sex-starved bird of prey" and egomaniac. According to Bret, "Aspects of Joan Crawford's extraordinary, complex psyche were incorporated into many of her films, within which the actress and character became as one, but such was the naivety of America during the Depression, few made the connection." Yes, her films' screenwriters based all her characters on her personally. Sure. (Sigh.) Talk about naivety. And Americans are naïve because they can't draw comparisons between an actress *they don't know person-ally*, and her movie characters? Well, that's just stupid on stilts.

He continues with his main objective, calling Crawford a "gay icon par excellence": "Few people [knew] of her fondness for gay and bisexual men.... Three of her husbands slotted into this category, as did many of her lovers, including Clark Gable." In Bret-speak, this means that if they slightly knew or worked with Crawford, they are, no doubt, gay or bisexual. That also means they are fair game in Bret's grimy agenda, as he speculates on the size of their private area (predictably, every man is "phenomenally endowed") and about how many people they've done the horizon-tal hustle with.

Granted, Bret seems to love Crawford as an actress, but he con-veys this by recounting the plots of allllll her movies. Page upon page of detailed plots. No worthwhile backstage stories, mind you, just tiresome, plodding, not-very-well-written synopses.

Bret blames Crawford's daughter Christina for sullying her repu-tation, but what exactly is he doing? He is taking what little dignity Crawford had left and stomping on it. I am certainly not a fan of Christina Crawford's writing and some of her accusations against her mother seem exaggerated, but what Bret does to Christina here is very shameful. *Mommie Dearest*, says Bret, is a "cruel, heartless testament" and Christina is "consumed by hatred" and her book should be "taken with a large pinch of salt." He defends Joan's parenting skills by writing, "Joan is known to have spanked her children or locked them in the closet for answering back—a common practice of the day." I honestly doubt locking kids in closets was a common practice. "She had adopted a child—one who would ultimately fling her every last kindness back in her face, with unspeakable vengeance, and posthumously leave Joan's reputation in tatters." Well, that's the pot calling the kettle black (again).

The book's raunchy tone starts at the beginning. Writing about a teenage Joan, he calls her "plump and ungainly with huge buck teeth, and that it was widely known that she had crabs due to her hatred of bathing, did nothing to deter would-be suitors in search of what appears to have been an easy lay." You know, if it weren't for low class, some books would have none at all.

The famous rumor that a young Crawford starred in stag films is here presented as fact although there is no proof. Crawford's mother is also labeled a tramp and said to have "resorted to prostitution, allegedly to make ends meet."

Joan just can't win. When a guy doesn't have sex with her and is just friends, he is "almost certainly gay." This includes her first beau, Ray Thayer Sterling. Another is the book's big "gay" shocker (there's one in all of Bret's books): Jack Oakie, another early Crawford pal.

Like her mother, Crawford was also allegedly a prostitute. Without sources, Bret reveals why this is so: "Many years later, Joan Crawford's police file would conveniently vanish from the Detroit vaults after she had convened a meeting with J. Edgar Hoover of the FBI—and threatened to expose him as a cross-dresser unless he agreed to remove the evidence that she had once been a hooker." On Planet Bret, Hoover's supposed cross-dressing is something many people knew about and always held over him.

After claiming that Crawford got a chorus girl job by servicing a producer, Bret has the nerve to question "unreliable sources" who say she missed most of the show's performances because she was being "treated for venereal disease."

There's a lot of nonsense, smut, bitterness and mistakes in *Joan Crawford: Hollywood Martyr*, so let's just dive in and look at a sampling of them.

Mario Caracciolo (later Carillo) is called "a hunky Italian in his mid-thirties who was also Valentino's lover and personal fitness adviser." I have no idea if Mario was Valentino's lover (and neither does Bret), but they were friends. Director John Ford said Caracciolo was a "captain in the Italian Army, but he wanted to be an actor. Valentino became famous and got rid of him right away."

As with most of Bret's books, there is an obsession with Valentino, since the "author" seems to think Rudy had sex with every male star in Hollywood history up until his death. Gary Cooper is linked to him here and, although it has been disproved, Ramon Novarro. The lie that Rudy gave Ramon an anatomically correct sculpture of his "manhood" is repeated and made even more absurd. Bret alleges that "Novarro's later lover," French dancer Pierre Bernay, told him in 1999 about it and how the sculpture was the "same one he was later choked to death with." It's been an established fact for many, many years that Ramon did not die in this manner. For a well-researched biography about Ramon, I strongly urge readers to get André Soares' *Beyond Paradise: The Life of Ramon Novarro*, which has been reprinted in softcover by University Press of Mississippi.

The choking-by-penis-sculpture rumor was started in *Hollywood Babylon* by Bret's guru, Kenneth Anger. It's almost as if the "author" thinks he needs to take up Anger's mantle. Bret calls *Hollywood Babylon* "unputdownable" and at one point writes, "As Kenneth Anger eloquently observed in *Hollywood Babylon II*..." Eloquent is not the word I would use. Bret quotes and mimics Anger quite a lot here. Anger's comment about Will Hays ("prim-faced, bat-eared, mealy-mouthed political chiseler") is so beloved by Bret that this is his third book in which he uses it.

Anger's stories have since been revealed to be false but that does not stop the oblivious Bret from repeating them as fact. Two notable examples: how he treats Marie Provost and poor Paul Bern.

Using almost the same line he used in his Jean Harlow book, Bret says that Provost's corpse was "part-devoured by her pet Chihuahua … [The] coroner's department recorded the death as the worst case of malnutrition it had ever seen." He doesn't mention if the malnutrition was Marie's or the dog's. (Sorry.)

Bret takes from Anger (and adds his own disgusting spins) when he writes about Paul Bern (1889-1932), who was married to Jean Harlow. Bern, a man much liked in Hollywood, is treated none too flatteringly, called "sophisticated, intellectual but unattractive." He "loved nothing more than listening to other people's problems—though not always helping them to solve them, or face up to his own…" Of course, Bret writes that he was gay and of course we get the usual nonsense: "[After] his death it would be revealed somewhat ungallantly that on account of his grossly underdeveloped genitals, he had been incapable of consummating any relationship." Notice the clumsy pairing here of the two conflicting words "grossly" and "underdeveloped." If you care, that's called an oxymoron. A talented writer would not have muddied his statement by coupling a word suggesting great size with a word meaning small.

There have been good books about Bern and his mysterious murder, including *Deadly Illusions: Jean Harlow and the Murder of Paul Bern* by Samuel Marx and even E.J. Fleming's *Paul Bern: The Life and Famous Death of the MGM Director and Husband of Harlow.* Even with these potential sources (not used), Bret gets the details of Bern's death wrong, mentioning that his naked body "drenched in Harlow's favourite Mitsuko perfume, had been found face-down on his bathroom floor, a gunshot wound to the head and a .38 pistol still in his hand." Bern was found in front of his closet, not face down, and there was no gun in sight.

Bret doesn't leave it at that. Oh, no, that would be too easy. He alleges that Bern was unable to have sex "on account of the severe genital abnormality he had hoped the sexually torrid Jean Harlow might have been able to cure (though he was physically attracted only to men). Bern had taken his frustration out on his bride and severely beaten her with a cane on their wedding night." None of this is true and of course Bret offers no sources. The so-called beating is also blamed for Harlow's untimely 1937 death.

It gets worse, far worse: "It emerged from the subsequent investigation that he had bought a huge ejaculating dildo … strapped this on and walked into Harlow's bedroom. Whether he had attempted to use this on her is not known—only that she had shrieked with laughter and, after leaving a note apologising for the abject 'humiliation,' Bern had shot himself." Shrieking with laughter would not be a woman's first reaction to the contraption Bret so vividly and gleefully describes. Shock would be more like it.

Even though Crawford was simply friends with Bern, she called Harlow the "trollop" who took him away from her.

Another Bern friend, actress Barbara La Marr, was not called by just one newspaper headline "The Girl Who Was Too Beautiful."

Bret's brief mention of Jackie Coogan starts with his film debut in *Skinner's Baby* and then suddenly jumps to his role opposite Crawford in 1925's *Old Clothes*. In between those two films, Coogan became a star in Chaplin's *The Kid* (1921) and headlined such productions as *Peck's Bad Boy* (1921), *Oliver Twist* (1922), *Circus Days* (1923) and *A Boy of Flanders* (1924).

Bret says that Tim McCoy only made a dozen films. Try 93 movies, Einstein. According to this book, Crawford said that McCoy, with whom she worked in *Winners of the Wilderness* (1927), had "the fastest draw, sure, and the weapon's got staying power and sure as hell don't fire blanks!" Who did she say this to?? And McCoy supposedly was also "servicing Pauline Starke" at the same time.

Apparently, Bret has a bone to pick with Loretta Young, so therefore Crawford despises her as well, calling her Gretch the Wretch numerous times. It's become common practice to attack "Saint Loretta" and her Catholic faith and to point out that she "certainly was not fond of practicing what she preached." She must be the biggest tramp in Hollywood. I am truly getting sick of this character assassination. Bret crudely adds that by the time Spencer Tracy started his affair with Crawford, he had "been through" Loretta.

Other recipients of hateful remarks are Mary Pickford (at one time Joan's mother-in-law), Bette Davis, Norma Shearer and John Gilbert. According to Bret, everyone in Hollywood "regarded Mary Pickford as a huge joke" and there's a lot about her being snooty and treating Joan like dirt.

His whole re-imaging of John Gilbert, professionally and personally, his stardom and his downfall, is all off-base. Do yourself a favor and get Eve Golden's *John Gilbert: The Last of the Silent Film Stars* (University Press of Kentucky) for the real story.

"Reputedly out of respect for Irving Thalberg, [Norma] Shearer never remarried." So, I guess Bret never got the invite to her 1942 wedding to ski instructor Martin Arrouge; they remained wed until her death in 1983. Bret also claims that *Photoplay* threatened to expose Norma's dressing room visits to Mickey Rooney. As if. There is absolutely no evidence that anyone knew of their trysts before Mickey's 1991 autobiography *Life Is Too Short*.

By the same token, Jeff Chandler's "fondness for cross-dressing" was not in supermarket tabloids in the 1970s. This was "revealed" (and then recanted) by Esther Williams in 1999's *The Million Dollar Mermaid: An Autobiography*.

Crawford was friendly with Fay Bainter until Bainter won an Oscar supporting Bette Davis in *Jezebel* (1938). Seriously?

Barbara Payton is always a sitting duck as well, since she became a prostitute. But, regardless of what Bret says here, she didn't start her film career that way and didn't end her life in the same circumstances. For a balanced, sympathetic view of Payton, I direct you to BearManor's *Kiss Tomorrow Goodbye: The Barbara Payton Story (Second Edition)* by John O'Dowd. On a side note, Bret writes about Tom Neal's death: "He would be found dead in bed—the unsubstantiated cause being heart failure, though there were many who believed that one of the many wronged suitors or husbands he had clashed with had caught up with him." No, I doubt any responsible historian would claim that's what happened.

One of Joan's husbands, Franchot Tone, is given the whole Bret treatment. The "author" claims Clark Gable called Tone a "goddam fairy." There are loathsome details about Tone's private area and some nasty comments on Bette Davis', referred to here as a "poison-trap." Ick, ick, ick!! Bret repeats the false story that Crawford paid Tone's medical bills at the end of his life and here says she also supported him when he was in "dire straits" in 1945.

Poor Ross Alexander is back and in a relationship with Tone, although he soon left Franchot when he "fell" for Errol Flynn on the set of *Captain Blood*. The story of Ross and Errol on the set of *Captain Blood* is a favorite of Bret's and it's pathetic how many times he can mention Ross' "exuberant armpits" and the ludicrous story of Flynn threatening Michael Curtiz with a razor to the throat if he removed "one hair of his lover's magnificent oxters." By the way, in case any of my gentle readers have forgotten, this is a Joan Crawford bio I'm reviewing here. Sometimes as I waded through all these nauseating tangents, I forgot who the book was supposed to be about.

Although he had no personal dealings with Crawford, Ross is extensively written about. Bret claims that Ross did not kill himself because he was haunted by his second wife's suicide. No, it was brought on by "crass hypocrisy, double standards and greed." The "evidence" is located in diaries and letters that were removed by Jack Warner from Alexander's house. Since there has never, ever been any mention of such documents, you have to wonder how Bret knew of their existence. Ross had affairs (it says here, so it must be untrue) with Flynn, Tone, Rod La Rocque and a "young drifter," which sent him over the edge. The latter was called a "hobo" in Lawrence Quirk's highly questionable Bette Davis biography. Bret used that book as his main source but embellished the rest. That Bette Davis would call Ross a "queer" to a member of the press is unlikely. Nor would Bette curse to reporters. And if she did, they never would print it. The same goes for the accusation that Don Barry made "a few comments in public" that Crawford was "easy meat."

After Ross' funeral, Errol Flynn and Franchot Tone spent the night together "in memory of the lover they shared." Ha ha.

As I pointed out in a previous review, Ronald Reagan was not one of the reasons Ross killed himself; Reagan was not yet signed by WB when Ross was alive. This does not faze Bret who says that for the rest of Flynn and Tone's lives, "they detested Bette Davis and Ronald Reagan and held them responsible for Ross' death." Despite Davis and Reagan's "homophobic rantings," to Flynn's knowledge they "both had engaged in a number of gay affairs." And who, pray tell, did Flynn say that to?? Oh, that's right—nothing here is sourced.

Bret wrote a book about Clark Gable, so naturally there's loads of stuff here about him since he and Crawford paired numerous times on screen and had an off-screen romance. He pegs Gable as "the archetypal repressed bisexual" who was involved with "three of the twentieth century's acknowledged 'fag-hags'—Crawford, Carole Lombard and Marilyn Monroe." Since when was Gable involved with Monroe?

Of course, we get the standard spiel about Gable's "acute halitosis and decaying teeth" and obsession with cleanliness. "Gable never took baths because, he declared, this would mean sitting in water he had contaminated." This supposedly inspired Crawford's lifelong clean-freak tendencies. Before that, Bret excitedly writes, she "had not been overly fastidious with personal hygiene (she arrived in Hollywood with crabs!)..."

Gable "loaned his meaty charms" to "influential bisexual reporter" Ben Maddox in "exchange for a high-profile interview." (Maddox is also romantically connected with Robert Taylor, Tyrone Power and Errol Flynn. And, no, there is no truth to the rumor that his business card said, "Influential Bisexual Reporter.") Gable is also having sex in outside "shrubbery" with "whoever might have taken his fancy, male or female." Bret repeats the rumor that William Haines also had sex with Gable. This bit of info is blamed for why George Cukor was fired from *Gone with the Wind*. For years, gossips have all agreed that Gable had Cukor fired because he "knew" of Gable's gay past. Now, Bret adds to that, saying that Gable was paranoid because Haines visited the set and was seen laughing with Cukor and he worried that he would "spill the tea" for the director. By the way, in case any of my gentle readers have forgotten a second time, this is a Joan Crawford bio I'm reviewing here.

Regarding William Haines, a Crawford pal: I seriously doubt that *Photoplay* would run a "thinly disguised attack" on Haines' sexuality. They just didn't do that back then. Issue and page number, Mr. Bret (we all know you're reading this).

Bret refers to the movie *Tell It to the Marines* and its "not-so-subtle gay subplot," quoting his idol Kenneth Anger: "Sergeant Lon Chaney and New Recruit [William] Haines have what can only be described as an odd love-hate sado-masochistic love-affair." This segues into a story about Crawford joining Haines, who had his pick of "scores of on-leave sailors," in downtown Los Angeles' Pershing Square, "a notorious gay pick-up area." Also: "Ironically, his final film was titled *The Marines Are Coming* (1934)!"

That last comment is just one more vile example of the dirty-minded Bret taking perfectly innocent movie titles and making them obscene. As with Bret's Gable book, he picks out Rod La Rocque's film titles as being "screamers": *The Coming of Amos* ("an inappropriate title for an actor who was sexually interested only in other men"), *What's Wrong with the Women?, Let Us Be Gay, The Gay Bandit* and *Hi, Gaucho!* Regarding Jackie Cooper's sexual relationship with Crawford, as revealed in Cooper's autobiography, Bret makes the title of his serial (not film) *Scouts to the Rescue* (1939) sound dirty.

He also views a scene in *Strange Cargo* (1940) as homoerotic where Clark Gable "almost kisses Ian Hunter on the mouth."

Harry Warner "only just realised that every man within Joan's inner circle was either gay or bisexual." Yet, Bret knew all along! For those keeping score at home, here are just some of the actors and actresses "outed" by the "author": William Bakewell, Barbara Stanwyck, Dolores del Rio, Janet Gaynor, Rod La Rocque, Mary Martin, Fay Wray, Mary Astor, Dolores Costello, Francis Lederer,

Edith Head, Marjorie Main, Robert Taylor and Gilmor Brown (it was a "well-known fact" they had an "open, year-long relationship"), Ricardo Cortez (Crawford was "aggravated to learn [he] licked the other side of the stamp"), Johnny Mack Brown and Nils Asther (who were "much more interested in each other than they were in her"), Cary Grant (once found with a "sailor in a department-store men's room"), Esther Ralston, Claudette Colbert, Lucille Ball(!), Ruth Chatterton, Merle Oberon and Katharine Hepburn (the last seven supposedly had affairs with director Dorothy Arzner, a very busy gal), "former child star" Gene Raymond and Charles "Buddy" Rogers (caught in bed together by Mary Pickford), John Carroll, Phillip Terry (with Robert Taylor and numerous others), Conrad Veidt, Jeff Chandler ("fresh from his involvement with Rock Hudson" when he hooked up with Crawford), Scott Brady and Ben Cooper (during *Johnny Guitar*), ad absurdum.

Rod La Rocque, he alleges, retired from acting because he was "tired of the threats of press exposure."

Bret claims that *Screenland* magazine called Robert Taylor and George Raft "Gillette blades which cut both ways"—"in other words, men willing to have sex with other men providing these were paying for the privilege." Yeah, that's right, that's what a fan magazine was going for. Maybe in a parallel universe, but not on this Earth. Issue and page number, please, Mr. Bret! *Classic Images* readers will be looking to the next letters column for this additional information.

When Crawford was divorcing Douglas Fairbanks, Jr., she said he made "unflattering—in other words homophobic—comments about some of her male friends." Where is the proof that Fairbanks said anything remotely homophobic about her friends?

And do you know that Robert Taylor's chest was so hairy because of the hormone injections MGM gave him to "control" his gayness? (For the record, Taylor wasn't as hirsute as Bret thinks he is. I make a point of knowing these things.)

Bette Davis "didn't know" her longtime love George Brent was gay. At a fundraiser, Bette came with Brent, while Crawford came with five escorts, "all of whom were gay and one went home with Brent."

Bret is fond of labeling actors he finds attractive. "Flapper-queen" Francis X. Bushman, Jr., is "a strapping young actor of androgynous beauty." John Garfield also is androgynous looking. Francis Lederer is "ethereal-looking," as is Zachary Scott. About the latter, Bret quotes Paul Roen's "authoritative" book *High Camp*, "His aura of swishy mellifluousness could, in a more enlightened era, have made him a paragon of androgynous chic."

Jean Dixon in *Sadie McKee* (1934) is called "that delightfully homely Jewish actress, who in her first scenes here is a dead ringer for the Miss Tony Curtis of *Some Like It Hot*."

More body hair worship: The Hays Office and Bret had a "problem" with "Mr. [Lester] Vail's flagrant display of under-arm hair" in *Dance, Fools, Dance* (1931). But were they exuberant armpits?

Some weirdness connected to Ricardo Cortez. First, he was in the 1931 *Maltese Falcon*, not the 1941 version. (Yeah, I really want to learn closely guarded Hollywood secrets from a guy who doesn't know that Humphrey Bogart starred in the 1941 *Maltese Falcon*.) In the early '30s, it was common knowledge that Cortez was not the Latin Lover he was touted as in the silent era. Bret claims that his marriage to Alma Rubens was "lavender" and that he had an affair with Loretta Young (who was actually wary of him because of his nasty reputation). Bret says that Rubens tried to knife a gas station attendant, but it was actually a doctor she attempted to stab. In case you've forgotten a third time, I'm writing about a Joan Crawford bio here.

"More Than You Know," written by Vincent Youmans with lyrics by Billy Rose and Edward Eliscu, was introduced in the 1929 Broadway musical *Great Day* where it was sung by Mayo Methot. Bret says it was written for Fanny Brice and "later revived" by Barbra Streisand in *Funny Lady*. "More Than You Know" had a long history, it's a standard, and didn't need to be "revived."

Just a few instances of misspellings: Katherine Cornell (should be Katharine), Frederic March (Fredric), Jimmi Fidler (Jimmie), and Stephen Spielberg (Steven). Yet again, Bret has been matched with an editor and a proofreader who share his same weak grasp of Hollywood history *and* spelling.

Billie Burke did not play the Blue Fairy in *The Wizard of Oz* (1939); she was Glinda the Good Witch. He is mistaking *Oz* for Walt Disney's animated *Pinocchio* (1940), where Evelyn Venable voiced the Blue Fairy.

Kent Douglass aka Douglass Montgomery, who appeared with Crawford in *Paid* (1930), is described by Bret as a "big blond Canadian" who would "score his biggest success with *The Cat and the Canary* (1939)." The Los Angeles-born Douglass had a supporting part in *Canary*, which was such a "success" for him that he never made another Hollywood film!

His list of MGM stars when Crawford was under contract (up to 1943) and who were getting better roles than she, includes Betty Grable, Irene Dunne and Ava Gardner. Grable was at Fox and Dunne at Universal and Columbia, and Gardner didn't start getting good roles at Metro until '47.

Errol Flynn was not the only Warner Bros. star to stand up to Jack Warner. What about James Cagney, Ann Dvorak, Kay Francis, Bette Davis, Ann Sheridan, Olivia de Havilland *et al.*?

Glenn Ford did not have a bit part in *Babies for Sale* (1940)—he had the lead.

John Garfield's mock violin-playing in *Humoresque* (1946) is "so spot-on that it is impossible not to believe him an authentic virtuoso violinist." It is known by everyone, except this "author," that Garfield never played the violin in the film. Out of view, one violinist acted as his right arm, another the left, creating the illusion that Garfield was playing. Editor Rudi Fehr has been quoted several times in books about this. Real books. Good books. Not books like this.

Garfield was not unemployed two years before his 1952 death. He was seen in the movies *Under My Skin, The Breaking Point* (both 1950), and *He Ran All the Way* (1951) and did theatre.

Boy, this book is teaching us so much about Joan Crawford!

Valley of the Dolls' Helen Lawson was not based on Crawford, nor did Bette Davis turn down the movie part because of this. It was based largely on Ethel Merman. It's also very wrong to call Lawson the novel's "alcoholic, neurotic heroine."

Jack Carson was very well-liked in Hollywood and to say his character in *It's a Great Feeling* (1949) was based on his true character is absurd. Bret says the movie was cast with "Carson-unfriendly directors." You don't get writing like this in other Hollywood biographies! Well, not in *good* ones.

Kent Smith did not screen-debut in *Cat People* (1942). Previously, he did *The Garden Murder Case* (1936) and *Back Door to Heaven* (1939). Ruth Donnelly retired to write hit songs? She recorded an album of songs she wrote, called *Souvenirs*, but to say she wrote hit songs is a stretch.

Rossano Brazzi didn't come to Hollywood in 1945 to star in *Little Women*. That movie was filmed in 1948 and released the following year. (Plus, he wasn't the star!)

Resenting that Crawford was dubbed in *Torch Song* (1953), Bret takes a couple of potshots at "the now forgotten India Adams." On the song "Two-Faced Woman," in which Crawford appears in blackface, Adams sounds "more like a poor man's Marilyn Monroe than any Ebony Venus." Miss Adams, an excellent singer, at the time of this review was still performing and going strong. She passed away in 2020.

Although he did not know them personally, Bret says that Clark Gable was "educationally challenged" and Marilyn Monroe was "not the brightest of individuals." He simply cannot resist scarring us all by claiming that Marilyn never wore underwear, even during her monthly period.

A persistent theme in Bret's books is that his subjects like it rough. I will not get into most of what he says about Crawford (it's pretty horrifying), except that he alleges that "Joan felt no shame at showing friends and fans her latest black eye or bruise, or her swollen wrists where her lover had pinned her down while forcing himself upon her." She made her lovers beg for her favors and delighted in humiliating them (again no details here). Supposedly, she made Phil Terry put the toothpaste on her toothbrush as a way of putting him in his place. You're so cruel, Joan!

This is not even remotely the insider view Publishers Weekly claimed it is. It's creepy fan-fiction which joyously details the "trail of broken hearts and abortions" Crawford "left in her wake" and the people she knew or maybe knew. It's quite a loathsome, catty book. My fear, as with similar volumes of this sort, is that it will be referenced by other writers as the truth. The best thing you can say about this book is that it lacks credibility. Sadly, however, the credulity of some readers and writers will ensure that it is used as a reference.

So, if someone offers to give you a copy of this book, tell 'em, "Please, no, *don't*. I read about it in *Classic Images*!"

Laird Cregar: A Hollywood Tragedy
by Gregory William Mank

I know I am not the only one who has been fascinated by Laird Cregar (1913-44), an actor whose life and career were tragically cut short by his compulsion to lose weight. An extremely effective character actor, he also excelled in his featured part in *I Wake Up Screaming* (1941) and his intense lead performances in *The Lodger* (1944) and *Hangover Square* (1945). Years ago, I did some research on him but came up with very little. What I did find was suspect, at best, because Cregar was often economical with the truth about his background.

Finally, we have a biography of Cregar that clears up the many errors and adds immeasurably to our knowledge: **Laird Cregar: A Hollywood Tragedy** by Gregory William Mank (McFarland). To say that Mank did an extraordinary amount of research would be an understatement. His interview with Cregar's niece is an invaluable peek into the actor's personal life. I found her quotes were my favorites in the book.

Mank admits that he has long had an obsession with Laird and has collected extensively on him. Fans couldn't ask for a better writer to tell his story. I felt that he masterfully handled the subject of Cregar's sexual orientation and without judgment. Usually, writers paint Cregar as a tormented, lost soul, so it is good to have a balanced view of him here. The actor's dissatisfaction and frustration with his career trajectory is a running theme and I could not help feeling sorry for him and the way he was typecast. Mank also expertly weaved in columnists' comments about Cregar's weight— something that would not fly today—to show how all this might have affected him.

The book is at its best when it concentrates on Cregar's complicated personality and on the Making Of details of his movies. Mank supplies a lot of interesting inside information on the production of the films, especially about Cregar's last hurrah, *Hangover Square*. (Mank was lucky enough to interview *Hangover* leading lady Faye Marlowe.)

The filmography at the end is a bit cluttered with facts we do not need and short cast bios. You pick up a Laird Cregar book, you don't want to read about John Payne's life. Also, I have noticed in this (and in Mank's past books) that he enjoys padding them with material that is overly sexual. Double-entendres abound in his world. He reads perversion into plot points and storylines where I don't believe there is any. All highlights for him have something sexual about them. I shook my head in dismay at how he described the *Blood and Sand* (1941) plot—I certainly have never taken *that* away from watching it. He even sees the title *I Wake Up Screaming* as sexual. And I certainly could have done without hearing that John Barrymore's "wang" was a "world-beater." And Mank's opinion that Sydney Greenstreet's best moment in *The Maltese Falcon* was giving Elisha Cook, Jr., a "subtle but sassy pat on his ass." (Yes, you read that correctly.)

The author's digressions distract from his basic story. Just because Cregar worked with Paul Muni doesn't mean we need to hear a totally unrelated story from the 1950s about chorus girls flashing him on stage. This has nothing to do with Cregar. Same with the whole chapter on actor David Bacon and his murder. While Bacon was friends with Laird, we did not need as much as we got about him. It was just an excuse to talk about the sordid details of the case and Bacon's homosexuality. Trimming this superfluous text would have greatly helped the flow of the narrative.

The photos are superb, many rare shots. In many ways I liked this book tremendously. I especially admired the format used to tell his story. I just feel that Greg Mank needs to get over his fixation on sex and stick to his subject. When he does that, his writing is gold. I recommend this book but be prepared for the red-light district detours.

Leonard Maltin's 2015 Movie Guide: The Modern Era

By now everyone has heard that, after 45 years, Leonard Maltin will no longer be putting out his yearly movie guide. His latest, **Leonard Maltin's 2015 Movie Guide: The Modern Era** (Penguin Books), is his adieu. This is blamed on poor sales due to "easy, free accessibility" of the Internet. Think about it: for nearly half a century, readers supported the *Guides*, but today everyone seems to expect the information packed into Leonard's tome (over 1500 pages) should be given free of charge. According to CNN's inane claim, the Movie Guide "isn't as necessary when IMDb and Wikipedia (not to mention countless blogs) are at your fingertips." From this statement we can conclude that a lot of people don't care where they get their information, as long as it's free. Whether good, bad or indifferent, information is all the same, these benighted souls believe. You have no idea how many times I've heard people ask where they can get this or that book, or a movie, for free. Never mind that it's available for sale in countless places—that's not good enough. "[W]hen a growing number of people believe that everything should be free, it's impossible to support a reference book that requires a staff of contributors and editors," Leonard writes.

But is getting movie information free really worth it? I say no. IMDb is a major power but, let's face it, it is hardly reliable. Any halfwit, it seems, can go there and add the most absurd misinformation. Too many times I've seen a movie listed with credits that belong to another movie. Sometimes the same actor is given separate entries, or worse yet, credits for two different actors are blended into one entry. And, drum roll—those idiotic IMDb reviews. "The book's loyal followers know that we strive to offer something one can't easily find online: curated information that is accurate and user-friendly, along with our own reviews and ratings," Leonard writes in his guide. Amen, brother.

User-friendly is not a word I would use to describe IMDb reviews. They are good only if you like poor grammar, spelling errors, haphazard capitalization of words, and total lack of critical skill. Here are some examples:

"I was pleasantly surprized with this one it is pretty good and has some suspense. It's not Shakespeare, but its not bad!"

"Crash Corrigan was an able-seaman in the Oscar-winning 1935 production of 'Mutiny On The Bounty.' I suspect those outrageous underpants of his were the cause of the rebellion amongst so many desperate and deprived shipmates!"

"I wish the movie had some memorable feature, something to distinguish it from other crime features of the period. But it doesn't. The undercover plot is borrowed from a hundred scarier crime dramas of the time."

"*Brothers of the West* is one of a bazillion B-westerns that were made in the 1930s. However, among these, it's certainly one of the lesser films as it's made by a lower than usual budgeted small studio and the quality is correspondingly low. Plus, to be quite blunt,

Tom Tyler has the personality of a bag of lint compared to most other cowboy stars."

"This was an extremely well written screenplay for an 'indie'."

"This is a minor entry in the Vincent Price catalogue but even so he's on good form. Just as well as the supporting cast is forgettable."

"The movements between segments of the movie were abrupt but everything else I liked a lot."

"Rosalind Russell plays Louise Randall Pierson (someone I've never heard of, but is based on her autobiography)."

"I turned this on almost reluctantly. Nothing else was on."

"If you are a fan of old films simply for the sake of their age, then this might be a film you would enjoy. Most others would not be impressed with this film."

"The movie's highlight scene occurs when the Nazis decide to use force on the reluctant [Dean] Jagger. He's shown, stripped to the waist, bound to his printing press, while Sidney Blackmer—yes, Sidney Blackmer—beats him 21 times across the back with a nasty-looking length of rubber hose. This being 1940s Hollywood, the hose is never shown actually striking Jagger's back and Jagger's reaction shots—he's only photographed from the shoulders up—merely show him to be mildly distressed, as if he ate something that didn't quite agree with him."

I could go on, but this is getting very upsetting. Sometimes I feel as if I'm one of the few who notices how bad these reviews can be. As I've written before, this menace is growing and books are starting to quote these dopey "Internet reviews." Oh, sure, I would rather take JoflexR34, BrocoLee8, Whipsaw, CottageCheeze3, Pizzaman765 and RazzzberryJuice76 opinions over Leonard and his staff. Not. Many of the IMDb "reviewers" can't spell, disparage most of the films, and don't seem to understand anything. Worse yet, some don't even watch the whole movie, and often are confused by the plot. Progress in film scholarship seems like an obsolete concept.

Whenever I am writing something, I can always turn to Leonard's guide for a correct spelling or a concise review. Always reliable. But I guess quality isn't worth much these days.

Also sad is the idea that everyone wants this stuff for free. As a fellow writer said, "Writers like me (and thousands of others) who won't do a halfway job of writing a book—who have to buy a lot of research material and DVDs of movies and TV shows to watch, and who need to travel (airfare, cabs, hotel) to the places and the people that can help—it's starting to spell the end of us. If most fans of the subjects of our books won't read 'em unless they're free, then we're digging our own financial graves (and making fools of ourselves) by writing them." I hope that's not true. Seriously. I hope that Leonard does not decide to stop writing books completely. We need him.

In any case, I don't believe that the web puts everything at our fingertips. What if the Internet goes down, or there's a power outage—what then? In the dark, with my flashlight, I can use a book to look up something. You don't have that option with the Internet.

In the past, reliable information illuminated our lives. Today, the lights are going out all over.

A Life of Barbara Stanwyck: Steel True, 1907-1940
by Victoria Wilson

Since Barbara Stanwyck's death in 1990, her reputation has risen considerably. For some years, Bette Davis, Katharine Hepburn and Joan Crawford, along with Marilyn Monroe, Judy Garland, Mae West and a very few other Golden Age icons, have been hailed as among the most enduring actresses of that fabled era. This was in great part because they were such over-the-top personalities with exaggerated features, mannerisms and voices that were so duplicated by impressionists and drag queens. In time, they began to seem like living cartoons. On the other hand, no one ever "did"

Barbara Stanwyck, and she never became a parody of herself. Instead, over time, more and more writers have taken second and third looks at her work and realized the extent of her remarkable talent. No gimmicks, no imitable mannerisms, just a raw talent and awesome range few other actresses could match.

Victoria Wilson is the latest to add to our understanding of Stanwyck. She has taken 15 years to complete only Volume 1 of a two-volume project, **A Life of Barbara Stanwyck: Steel True, 1907-1940** (Simon & Schuster). Of all the books published on Stanwyck thus far, this is the topper. It covers her life and work up to 1940 in (too) exhaustive detail and has more information than any other source to date, thanks in no small part to the many interviews Wilson conducted with surviving friends and family. She is currently completing Volume 2, beginning with her glory years in the 1940s. I only hope it won't be another 15-year wait.

Don't let the length faze you. The actual text ends on page 860, followed by 180 pages of stage-film-radio chronologies, notes, acknowledgments, selected bibliography and the index. This is one hefty book, and at 3¾ pounds, it's not too comfortable to hold or to carry to the beach. But beyond that, for long-time Stanwyck admirers (like me), as well as those coming late to the party, this is the go-to book on Stanwyck's complicated life and times.

Every one of her stage and screen appearances is covered in minute detail, and there is more information on her childhood and her siblings than has ever been gathered elsewhere. Ditto for her many years of hoofing in cheap cabarets and Broadway revues, and her emergence as a serious actress. Her tempestuous seven-year marriage to Frank Fay, which first got her to Hollywood, and then her coupling with Robert Taylor, are covered at length. Of particular interest is her decision, from the very beginning of her movie career, to never sign an exclusive seven-year contract with any studio. All the ensuing complications resulting from that decision are given extensive and illuminating coverage.

This is not to say there aren't a few minuses.

Discussing Stanwyck's role in *The Purchase Price* (1932), Wilson correctly mentions on page 303, "Barbara was given her first number to sing on-screen." But on page 548, talking about *Banjo on My Knee* (1936), she notes that in this film, "Barbara had to sing for the first time on camera." Oops.

There's a glamorous Stanwyck portrait titled "Photograph: George Hurrell, circa 1934" which was actually taken by Hurrell in 1942 while she was filming *The Gay Sisters*.

There are 274 photos strewn throughout the text. The quality of reproduction is quite poor, and most are too small or blurry. This is a pity since many of the photos, especially from Stanwyck's early years, have never been published before. In addition, far too many photos aren't of Barbara at all, just random shots of coworkers/ friends/other performers/directors/writers/houses/buildings, etc.

I'm personally not partial to movie star bios that go into full-tilt summaries of every plot twist and detail of every movie they ever made, and that does occur in this volume. For those unfamiliar with Stanwyck's movies, this may be useful, but the rest of us might do well to just roll our eyeballs downward and jump ahead to the plot summaries' conclusions.

But Wilson's biggest misstep is one that's way too common among writers: She fell in love with her research. This starts on page 2 with a complete history of Stanwyck's entire family lineage from as far back as 1740(!), and it's but a prelude to what's in store for the reader. The Stanwyck saga is continuously interrupted by biographies of practically every producer, director, writer and actor she ever worked with (not to mention many she never worked with) for pages and pages at a time. Worse is the inclusion of lengthy historical dissertations on Prohibition, the stock market crash, unemployment, the Great Depression, President Roosevelt, trade unions, studio histories, the Production Code, Social Security, *ad nauseam*. I'll grant that placing Stanwyck's life and work in the world in which she lived is essential, but Wilson's frequent historical treatises arrest the flow of her book. These distractions amount to at least 200 pages of information that should have been severely trimmed or even excised from this already gigantic book. (This is most peculiar, considering that Victoria Wilson's day job is as vice-president and senior editor at Alfred A. Knopf publishers.)

This book has so much extraneous matter that it sometimes seems Barbara Stanwyck is playing a cameo role in her own biography. But at its best, the book is amazingly informative and insightful. All in all, this biography has been well worth the long wait. Here's hoping some of these flaws will be missing in Volume 2, and that I live long enough to see it.

Life's Rough Roads: A Jewish Actor and a Catholic Nun Struggle for Happiness by Carol Jones

Recently I watched the Ida Lupino–directed *Outrage* (1950), about the rape of a woman (Mala Powers) and the turn her life takes afterwards. Not familiar with the actor portraying the rapist, Albert Mellen, I looked him up on IMDb: no birth or death dates, no place of birth, no biography, and only one credit, *Outrage*. I did a quick search in the newspaper archives and came up empty there as well.

A Google search of his name and the movie, however, took me to a book, **Life's Rough Roads: A Jewish Actor and a Catholic Nun Struggle for Happiness** by Carol Jones (CreateSpace). The description nearly knocked me over: "Albert Mellen, a Jewish actor, plays the part of a rapist in the 1950s movie *Outrage*.... His acting career ends when he is stricken with mental illness requiring years of treatment. Ann Tracy joins the convent at age fifteen and later discovers the desire for a different life." The couple, who married in the 1960s, told their life stories to Jones and the product was this book. Intrigued? You bet I was!

As a rule, I am wary of self-published books, because they're often sloppily done and poorly edited. This book is an exception, and to my surprise it was one of the most poignant books I have ever read. There was good reason why the Mellens put their trust in Carol Jones.

Their stories are told in alternating chapters until they come together near the end. Jones makes us understand Albert and Ann's struggles, fears and insecurities and we come to truly care about them. Both grow before our eyes as they overcome what life throws at them. Albert's stay in a mental hospital, his shock treatments, his relationship with his family, his struggle to think clearly are all vividly and sometimes harrowingly told. I cringed a few times as he went through periods of shock treatments. Ann was only a teenager when she chose to enter a convent, doing so for the wrong reasons. Her lingering doubts but acceptance of the nun's life is heart-wrenching and real, as is her decision to finally leave after almost 40 years. Both thought it impossible to ever attain true happiness.

Jones' style is quite affecting and her dialogue never seems phony. We fully become enmeshed into the narratives and root for them to find the contentment they are seeking. I became teary-eyed more than once.

This page-turner was a real surprise and I thoroughly enjoyed it. Who knew that a simple search on IMDb would bring me one of the best books of the year? Carol Jones is really a talented writer.

Madeline Kahn: Being the Music, A Life
by William V. Madison

There are few books that actually take my breath away when I open the package. **Madeline Kahn: Being the Music, A Life** by William V. Madison (University Press of Mississippi) is one such volume. It was a total surprise; I had no idea this was even in the works. Kahn (1942-99) is a favorite of mine and I know a lot of classic movie fans enjoy her work as well. An impeccable actress and singer, she is best known for her movies with Mel Brooks (*Blaz-*

ing Saddles, Young Frankenstein, High Anxiety, History of the World: Part I) and Peter Bogdanovich (*What's Up, Doc?, Paper Moon, At Long Last Love*). She was twice nominated for Oscars, for *Blazing Saddles* and *Paper Moon. The Adventure of Sherlock Holmes' Smarter Brother* has always been among my personal favorites because it showed off her range as a singer.

She has long been deserving of a biography, and I am happy to report that Madison does Kahn full justice. He did incredible, in-depth research, interviewing family and co-workers. I was impressed that almost every moment of her life was accompanied by a quote from someone who was there to witness it. The same goes for the movies, theater and TV shows she appeared in. The section about the Broadway show *On the Twentieth Century*, a musical production fraught with problems and whispers about Kahn's possible drug use, is handled superbly and from all angles; the author really goes into detail about what was going on backstage and fully addresses the scandal.

I had once begun research on a Madeline Kahn article of my own and came across some references to her mother's domineering nature. The author discusses this extensively; I had no idea what an erratic, manipulative woman her mother was, and the hold she had over Madeline.

Madison was lucky to have had access to Kahn's journal and letters. His take on her personality, insecurities about her looks, weight and acting and singing abilities, and how she approached her work and the people in her life, is amazing and will be an eye-opener to her fans who only really know her from some of her raunchier work with Mel Brooks.

I was just a teenager when her TV series *Oh Madeline* (1983-84) aired, but I loved it and watched every episode. Little did I know the behind-the-scenes drama attached to it. While I don't agree with the author's assessment of the program, he is very persuasive and explains himself well.

After the *On the Twentieth Century* fiasco, Madeline's career was hit or miss. Madison captures her frustrations as she navigated rough career seas and tried to find work, accepting just about anything, whether it suited her or not. Her Tony-winning performance in *The Sisters Rosensweig* helped her regain her standing, although she was most proud of her last film, *Judy Berlin* (1999).

An excellent writer, Madison puts a lot into each page. His style is lively, thoughtful and intelligent, and he has a firm grasp on his complex subject. Very interesting, sad in spots, and always entertaining and enlightening, I recommend this candid, comprehensive biography.

The Magnificent Max Baer: The Life of the Heavyweight Champion and Film Star
by Colleen Aycock with David W. Wallace

In the 21st century, boxer Max Baer's reputation has taken a beating. If you've ever watched Ron Howard's *Cinderella Man* (2005), a feel-good biopic on boxer James J. Braddock, you would think that Baer (1909–59) was a snarling, bloodthirsty beast. That's certainly how Craig Bierko played him. To add drama and suspense to their story, screenwriters Cliff Hollingsworth and Akiva Goldsman made Baer into a monster. They ignore some real-life drama surrounding the 1935 Baer-Braddock match in favor of making Baer a savage. Hollingsworth and Goldsman were obviously taking their lead from *The Harder They Fall* (1956), in which Buddy Brannen (convincingly portrayed by Baer) makes mincemeat of boxer Toro Moreno (played by Mike Lane). This depiction of Baer in *Cinderella Man* is grossly unfair. His son Max Baer Jr. has given many interviews in which he defended his father's reputation.

An even better defense of Baer Sr. can be found in **The Magnificent Max Baer: The Life of the Heavyweight Champion and Film Star** by Colleen Aycock with David W. Wallace (McFarland)—one of the best books I have read in a long time. A member of the International Boxing Research Organization and the New

Mexico Boxing Hall of Fame, Aycock has written about boxing for numerous publications. Her connection to Baer comes from her father, Norman "Ike" Aycock, one of Baer's sparring partners. "Ike" told his daughter stories about Baer.

This is no sugarcoated biography, but we get a clear picture of who Max Baer was—and he was not a nasty guy. To the contrary, he was well-liked, glamorous and jovial. If we are to believe *Cinderella Man*, Baer proudly boasted that he killed a man in the ring. In reality, Frankie Campbell's death in the ring haunted Baer for the rest of his life and changed the way he approached boxing. He was not a heartless man. Aycock does a remarkable job making Baer come alive on the page; Baer's entertaining comments really enliven the text. He was a jokester, in and out of the ring, but was serious when he had to be. Max's reaction to Campbell's death was heartbreaking.

There is a tremendous amount of boxing history and the author details the dirty deals and frustrations which affected boxers' careers. We get nice little side info on Baer's opponents, managers and promoters. I learned so much from this book. I am a casual boxing fan but I am interested in people such as Baer, Gene Tunney, James J. Corbett, Maxie Rosenbloom, etc. (Another good McFarland book: *James J. Corbett: A Biography of the Heavyweight Boxing Champion and Popular Theater Headliner* by Armond Fields.)

Aycock's writing is concise and always interesting. A great part of this book is devoted to her descriptions of the fights—she puts you in ringside seats for the slugfests and you can vividly picture battles involving Baer, his brother Buddy, Braddock, Primo Carnera, Joe Louis, Max Schmeling, etc. Punch by punch, it's a real sockeroo. The author has a knack for this kind of slam-bang writing.

Also covered are Max's movie appearances, including *The Prizefighter and the Lady* (1933), *The Navy Comes Through*, *The McGuerins from Brooklyn* (both 1942), *Ladies' Day*, *Buckskin Frontier* (both 1943), *Africa Screams* (1949), *Skipalong Rosenbloom* (1951), *The Harder They Fall* (1956) and *Utah Blaine* (1957). Considering all the work the author put into the main biography, I was hoping for deeper coverage of each movie. There are also a few mistakes, like misidentifying Lupe Velez as Patsy Kelly in a photo (a first!). But the author is a boxing person not a film historian. The photos throughout the book are excellent.

Aycock may have miffed on movie coverage but this book is still a gem, hard to put down. Everything you wanted to know about Max Baer—the good, the bad and the ugly—is here. I am glad this book is out there to refute *Cinderella Man*. It's too easy to believe the worst about someone. This book goes a long way in showing what a down-to-earth, easygoing guy Max Baer was. And it's so much more.

The Many Faces of Nehemiah by Nehemiah Persoff

Nehemiah Persoff's (1919-2022) long-awaited autobiography, **The Many Faces of Nehemiah**, is only 196 pages. This is a man who lived to the age of 102, acted on screen from 1948 to 2003, with more than 200 credits to his name—and this does not include his stage work.

This book has gotten some wonderful reviews. Hoping for the best, I started to read this slim volume. It was okay, until I got to the part where he drowned kittens in a bathtub. The sickening reason? Preparing for a stage role where he kills someone, he thought it necessity to know how it felt to actually kill. In excruciating, disgusting detail, Nehemiah described how he did it, what the kittens were doing as he did it, and how the dismayed mother cat reacted to not finding her babies.

Well, that did it. I threw that book as far as I could.

This unpleasant person's book ought to have come with a warning label. What a vile individual, to have done that in the first place, and then to put the tale of his crime in print believing that it would entertain readers. It'll be a good long time (if ever) before I watch any show with Nehemiah Persoff in the cast.

Marilyn Monroe, Her Shoe and Me: A Story of Unbelievable Truth
by Howard G. Allen

I have read some crazy books in my time—remember Wampa 12's *The Film Noir Bible: When White People Had the Blues*? Well, **Marilyn Monroe, Her Shoe and Me: A Story of Unbelievable Truth** by Howard G. Allen (Xlibris) ranks right up there. No, it is not about the author's foot fetish, although there sure could be books devoted to that. Allen's focus is the week in 1960 he spent with Marilyn and her then-husband Arthur Miller. A friend of Allen's arranged the visit because Allen wanted to become an actor and Marilyn was going to show him around New York City and, I guess, talk to him about acting.

It's difficult to enjoy *Her Shoe and Me* for the simple reason that it is poorly written. Allen, although a professional writer (according to Allen), knows little about sentence structure, spelling, punctuation and a hundred other things an author should know. He has trouble distinguishing between "ask" and "asked," for instance. One consistent problem is punctuation in dialogue, e.g.: "Of course Dr. Colin said! Howard I am so pleased to meet you..." Or this one: "Dr. Colin tried to get me to enroll right away saying 'That it is good for a student to study and work at the same time, that it would give me incentive, initiative.'" He never closes up quotes and it looks dang weird.

Stilted? My God, many of the sentences don't make sense or are just inappropriate:

"I plundered through my cerebrum as to what my future should be. Like a mad man in a desert searching for water because I felt that I was dying of thirst for a direction, my mind frantically searching my cerebrum for an answer."

"He said, 'I have some good news for you. Do you know who Arthur Miller is?' 'Do you mean the playwright I ask.' 'Yes he said.' 'Of course I said. I have read every play that he has ever written.' 'Do you know who Marilyn Monroe is?' he ask. I said 'Of course, who doesn't know who Marilyn Monroe is. She is married to Arthur Miller I said, is she not? She is my all time favorite actress.'"

"I didn't ask him anymore questions, we then had petty conversation about the weather and etc."

"Drink twist every man and woman to a certain degree and in my opinion no one should drink alcoholic beverages because drink does indeed twist the personality." (At this point, I'm starting to wonder if drink twisted the punctuation.)

"When we got to Lexington Avenue she told me that 'This is Lexington Avenue.' When we reached Park Avenue she said 'This is the famous Park Avenue where the wealth of the world lives.' Upon approaching Madison she said 'This is Madison Avenue where all of the publicity of every medium is sent out to the world.' When we reached Fifth Avenue she said…" What do you think she said, dear reader??

"… 'Miss Monroe I have your favorite booth for you, the quite little booth in the corner.'"

"Marilyn said 'Patients is not one of my virtues.'"

Throughout his book, Allen can't make up his mind about how old he was at the time—and he mentions it a lot. Is he 20? Or months away from 20? The jury is still out. On one page he bought a suit for the journey to New York and then called the train station; the next page, he bought a suit and then went back to his apartment and called Marilyn. He didn't buy two suits; he just apparently forgot that he wrote about it already. There is a lot of repetition. Allen needed an editor because of the number of times he repeats things.

And are we to believe that he remembered every line of dialogue everyone said to him almost 60 years ago? Believe me, if Arthur Miller talked the way Allen has him talking in this book, he would never have sold a play. Miller comes across as a mannered fool, as does Marilyn. We have some inane exchanges between Marilyn and Allen about what kind of sandwiches he wanted to eat. Was the visit this boring? His recollections while visiting Marilyn are about him sleeping, eating, showering, etc. Nothing earthshaking…until…

The crazy part. The first half of the book is fairly harmless. Hard to read, but harmless. The section about meeting Lawrence Tierney is nuts, but it pales compared to the moment when Allen and Marilyn sit in Central Park and she reveals to him that she is a psychic. It goes on from there into some bizarre territories. The author alleges that Marilyn told him that after she eventually dies, she would be reincarnated into the body of his future daughter Laura (to be born in 1967). Then Allen claims that *he* is psychic, although he never mentioned it before he met Marilyn.

The ramblings that follow are ridiculous and very sad. As he was in the middle of writing this book, his daughter died. "I blame her death on the GODS or some discarnate that wanted her to come to the other shore to be with them. I feel it to be murder on their part. Those asshole GODS or DISCARNATES whoever they were that drew her to the other side were totally responsible for her death and I curse them to the core of my soul even if it is GOD HIMSELF." Alrighty, then. Then he blames her death on the Ramone's Dee Dee Ramone (Allen spells the first name Dee, Dee). Why, you ask? Well, of course, the Gods were Ramone fans and when Dee Dee said he missed Laura, they reunited them. Allen wants to go to the netherworld and kick their asses and describes how he will do it. The Gods have a vendetta against him because he was a king in another life. Oy gevalt!

Allen also goes on for an uncomfortable amount of time about wanting to die because he loves and misses his daughter. This book was ostensibly about Marilyn Monroe but turns into a depressing therapy session. He doesn't even relate half the week with Marilyn! He says he simply cannot go on with the story. Look, I feel bad for Howard Allen and the fact that his daughter passed away but why subject innocent bystanders to all the angst? And repetitive angst, at that. How do we even know he met Marilyn? There are no pictures of him with Marilyn or Arthur Miller. If you had a once-in-a-lifetime visit with Marilyn Monroe, wouldn't you get a picture taken with her? The only photos in the book are some creepy shots of his daughter, including one in a bikini. (I'll say nothing about that.)

If you are a Marilyn completist, then by all means waste your money. Marilyn should have thrown the shoe at him.

Mean...Moody...Magnificent!: Jane Russell and the Marketing of a Hollywood Legend
by Christina Rice

My practice has been to read a book, make notes, write the review and then set the volume aside to make way for a new one. There's little time to revisit a tome, or even think about it after finishing with it. **Mean...Moody...Magnificent!: Jane Russell and the Marketing of a Hollywood Legend** by Christina Rice (University Press of Kentucky) was totally different: I read this biography three times! I can't say it's because Jane Russell (1921-2011) is one of my favorite actresses—she's not. I do, however, adore her in most of her movies (except *Young Widow*), and I love her singing ("You Kill Me" from *Macao* is an unheralded gem). I read this three times because Christina is a damn fine writer, truly in the top five of great biographers. University Press of Kentucky also published her sensational *Ann Dvorak: Hollywood's Forgotten Rebel* (see review above).

Russell is one of the best-known actresses in Hollywood history. Some of that popularity is based on the major films she has done, notably *The Outlaw, The Paleface* with Bob Hope, *Gentlemen Prefer Blondes* with Marilyn Monroe and her films with Robert Mitchum. She is also known for the publicity surrounding her debut film, *The Outlaw*, produced and directed by Howard Hughes.

Anybody who has read Jane's 1980s memoir, *My Path and My Detours: An Autobiography*, or any of her later interviews, would know of the baggage she brings to a biographer. After reading *Mean...Moody...Magnificent!*, I realize there's so much more; it's little wonder no one has previously tackled a Russell bio. First of all, she had a complex personality, one with baffling contradictions. Also, you cannot tell her story without diving deep into what went into promoting her in *The Outlaw*. Hughes and Russell Birdwell's publicity campaign was marketing genius (although it often caused Jane distress).

Christina has undertaken the unenviable job of explaining Russell and does so in a pithy, reasonable, fair and fascinating manner. While I've enjoyed Russell's movies through the years, I always felt she was not a person I would particularly like personally. The author has changed that, explaining why Russell did or said certain things, while commenting on conflicting statements and actions, and shining light on her good work with the World Adoption International Fund (WAIF). Incidentally, the section about WAIF could, in a lesser writer's hands, have been quite convoluted since there are some political aspects; the author clearly and concisely describes everything.

I enjoyed the way the movies were handled. Many writers feel the need to run down an actor's "lesser" films while hyping the established classics. Christina provides a balanced view of all of Russell's movies—the good points as well as the bad. Mercifully, she does not go on and on (and on) with plot descriptions. That aspect often ruins books. You know an author understands their subject when they do not utilize plot synopses as a crutch and/or page-filler.

The research is excellent. I was particularly impressed by her history of *The Outlaw* and the publicity behind it, which is one of the book's main selling points. Anyone looking for information will not be disappointed with what the author has uncovered. It's an interesting look at how publicity was handled back in the 1940s, especially when going against the Production Code Administration. The PCA's objections to *The Outlaw* and Russell's bosom are other fascinating aspects of the book, giving us a peek at 1940s morality. Rice's history of the PCA is extremely well-written and thorough, and helps us understand why Hughes and *The Outlaw* pushed the envelope.

Two other selling points: Howard Hughes and Marilyn Monroe. I have read several biographies on both and many times authors treat them disrespectfully. We often get the same thing: Hughes was crazy and reclusive; Marilyn was always late, unhappy and insecure. While Christina mentions all this (how could she not?), she adds much, much more. I don't think I have ever before read a more sympathetic understanding of Hughes. The part where he invited Russell over to sign a contract on Christmas because he didn't want to be alone—that "got" me. The way Rice detailed Hughes and Russell's relationship makes it clear why they were associated with each other for so long. Marilyn, too, is treated honestly and even-handedly.

A quick note about Russell's first husband, football player and pseudo-actor Bob Waterfield. Personally, I always thought he came across as a jerk. My hat's off to Rice for restraining herself. While she describes his questionable actions, she doesn't malign him; she lets us judge for ourselves.

Christina is a cut above other film historians based on her research, attitude and outstanding, easy-to-read writing style. I've read many biographies and this is by far one of the best. I learned a lot from it, was engaged in the emotional relationship between Russell and her husbands as well as the problems that befell her, and enjoyed the movie info. I feel the title is perfect for the subject since Jane Russell was mean (at times), moody (definitely) and magnificent (always)—and it's also a recognizable slogan from *The Outlaw*.

A better book on Jane Russell will never be published. Christina Rice has nailed it.

Michael Curtiz: A Life in Film
by Alan K. Rode

I have previously read only one book about Michael Curtiz, James C. Robertson's *The* Casablanca *Man: The Career of Michael Curtiz* (1994). It was called a "major reassessment" of the generally neglected director's career, but I was underwhelmed by the result and felt I knew less about Curtiz than when I started. Consider just some of the films he helmed: *The Cabin in the Cotton, Doctor X* (both 1932), *Mystery of the Wax Museum, The Kennel Murder Case* (both 1933), *Black Fury, Captain Blood* (both 1935), *Kid Galahad* (1937), *The Adventures of Robin Hood, Four Daughters, Angels with Dirty Faces* (all 1938), *Dodge City, The Private Lives of Elizabeth and Essex* (both 1939), *Santa Fe Trail, The Sea Hawk* (both 1940), *The Sea Wolf* (1941), *Casablanca, Yankee Doodle Dandy* (both 1942), *Mildred Pierce* (1945), *Night and Day* (1946), *Life with Father* (1947), *Romance on the High Seas* (1948), *The Breaking Point* (1950), *White Christmas* (1954), *We're No Angels* (1955), *King Creole* (1958), *The Comancheros* (1961), etc. Curtiz might not be regarded as an auteur filmmaker, but who cares? I always thought that theory, as popularized by Andrew Sarris, harmful as it created the wrong impression that wonderful directors such as Michael Curtiz were somehow not as talented as, say, Hitchcock, because there was no discernible theme running through their movies. Curtiz could be relied on to consistently give us entertaining films.

Alan K. Rode has given Curtiz his due in **Michael Curtiz: A Life in Film** (University Press of Kentucky). I rarely have read a more interesting, thoroughly researched study of a director. At more than 700 pages, this is worth the price tag. Never once does the author get bogged down by his meticulous research. Rode is such a good writer that his narrative flows and makes all the information easy to digest in a very readable style.

Before Hungarian-born Curtiz arrived in Hollywood, he worked in the theater and in films in his native country. I was almost dreading this early part of the story. Like perhaps 99 percent of film fans (I may be low-balling the number), I am unfamiliar with this aspect of his career and I have never seen any of these movies. To my surprise, and to Rode's credit, I found this section fascinating. It's a brisk, interesting and enlightening read. It perfectly set up Curtiz's Hollywood career. Rode did a lot of impressive research in Hungary and was able to fix other authors' many mistakes, including the date of Curtiz's birth. He also deals with the erroneous "fact" that Curtiz was married to actress Lili Damita. (IMDb still has them listed as man and wife. It took Wikipedia a while after the publication of this book to fix the error.)

Each of Curtiz's films is given an extensive production history. I always complain when authors rely simply on plot descriptions to fill up space. Not Rode. With the help of an excellent knowledge of players, personally conducted interviews, studio production reports and a keen eye for criticism and the source material, the author provides us a complete picture of each film. I was often amazed at some of the behind-the-scenes problems, in particular on *Night and Day* and *Life with Father*. (Jimmy Lydon supplies a hilarious remembrance about the latter that involves Curtiz's explosive temper.) A story related by Stuart Whitman about *Francis of Assisi* (1961), one of Curtiz's last films, is not only bizarre but heartbreaking.

By most accounts, Curtiz was not an easy man to work with but the author doesn't demonize him *or* condone his questionable actions. Often, I have read accounts of the director's cruel treatment of horses, as related in many books and even autobiographies, and the deaths involved in the flood scenes in *Noah's Ark* (1928). Armed with production reports, Rode does not let the myths continue, but sets the record straight. It's nice to know that the author was not content to blindly repeat stories but to find out what really happened—no matter how long ago it supposedly occurred. In one instance, Rode relates what Errol Flynn wrote in his autobiography, but instead of letting that (now-established) "fact" stand, he proves it wrong. So many other writers would have taken the easy way out and taken Flynn's word for it.

Curtiz's personal life was also a bit complicated. I had no idea about any of his troubles with his daughter Kitty, his affairs or his multiple illegitimate children. Rode did a great job uncovering all this and telling it all in a straightforward manner.

Even when Rode deals with pretty sordid stuff (the *Confidential!* magazine allegations in the 1950s), he doesn't embellish or resort to the David Bret brand of smut. Alan is a classy biographer. He has written a terrific biography that should be a model for all film historians. His impeccable research is coupled with fine knowledge and writing ability. He really sets the bar high.

My Life and the Final Days of Hollywood
by Claude Jarman Jr.

Many books can fall between the cracks because they're self-published or published by an obscure company. One such is Claude Jarman Jr.'s 2018 autobiography **My Life and the Final Days of Hollywood** (Covenant Books). Jarman is best known for his performance as Jody Baxter in *The Yearling* (1946), which won him a special Academy Award. Other films in his brief career: *High Barbaree* (1947), *The Sun Comes Up, Roughshod, Intruder in the Dust* (all 1949), *The Outriders, Rio Grande* (both 1950), *Inside Straight* (1951), *Hangman's Knot* (1952), *Fair Wind to Java* (1953), *The Great Locomotive Chase* (1956) and the TV miniseries *Centennial* (1979).

Jarman describes what it was like being transplanted from his Nashville home to Hollywood. The section where he recalls the train trip to California is charming in its detail and paints a picture of the times. Unlike many of his peers, Jarman had a stable homelife. It was that, plus leaving Hollywood when he did, which played a big part in him leading a good life without bitterness and addictions. His family instilled in him good values. Reading about his experiences as an MGM contract player and a freelancer, I found myself liking Jarman very much.

The Yearling and *Intruder in the Dust*, which are considered his best films, are given substantial space. Both were directed by Clarence Brown, and Jarman's memories of him are warm and insightful. My favorite: Jarman's comments about *Roughshod.* I am glad he had sweet things to say about Gloria Grahame. In contrast to the "motherly" Gloria was the "piece of work" (but very funny) Myrna Dell. (And her 2003 letter to him, recounted in the book, is hilarious.) He doesn't have much to say about *The Sun Comes Up* (except how bad it is), but there is one harrowing story attached to that film: Lassie bit Jarman's face!

After his acting career ended, Jarman was executive director of the San Francisco Film Festival. There's quite a bit about how he managed that and about some of the celebrities he wrangled for the fest. A big surprise (for me, anyway) was learning that he was executive producer of the concert film *Fillmore* (1972). That was an interesting interlude.

The writing is mostly excellent except for some repetition—points are stressed more than once, especially later in the narrative. I didn't like the vague title. The title should have emphasized Jarman, and should not have implied that this was a history lesson about the fall of Hollywood. In a way, Jarman tries to make part of the book just that, about the fall of Hollywood, but his story is the meat of the narrative. Perhaps this is why this book was overlooked when it came out. Otherwise, an extremely worthwhile read. The photos are amazing. My favorite is the cute one from *Roughshod* with Jarman, Jeff Donnell, Myrna Dell and Gloria Grahame.

The Odyssey and the Idiocy, Marriage to an Actor, A Memoir
by Candace Hilligoss

It takes a special kind of actress to be remembered for her only starring role more than 50 years after the film's release. Candace Hilligoss is such an actress. In the horror cult classic *Carnival of Souls* (1962), she played church organist Mary Henry, the only survivor of a car crash off a bridge and into a river. Now she finds herself stalked by a ghoulish, white-faced man (creepily played by Herk Harvey, the film's producer-director–co-writer) and drawn to an eerie abandoned lakeside pavilion. Many of Hilligoss' scenes rely on her facial expressions and she gives a restrained performance and imbues her character with a striking melancholy. *Carnival of Souls* is definitely not camp, and this is largely because of Hilligoss. Funnily enough, after watching the movie at the time, her agent decided not to represent her anymore because he thought she was "too weird" and he had "a reputation to protect." One of Hilligoss' strong points as an actress is her uniqueness.

I have always been intrigued by Hilligoss, as I knew very little about her. Unfortunately, her credits are minimal; her only other substantial movie part came in *The Curse of the Living Corpse* (1964), which was Roy Scheider's film debut, and she did some television. Most of her work has been on the stage.

That's why I was eager to read her autobiography, **The Odyssey and the Idiocy, Marriage to an Actor, A Memoir**. I was a little wary, however: It's close to 300 pages, and I thought, "What could she possibly write about with so few movies on her résumé?" Was I ever wrong!

Throughout the book, Hilligoss chooses to call her ex-husband "Richard Forest," which is not his real name. "I changed it," she says, "not to protect him, but because he doesn't deserve this much free publicity." Out of respect for Hilligoss, I shall also call him Forest in this review. (He was an actor; nosy parkers can find his real name via the Internet Movie Database and Wikipedia.)

She gave up her career as an actress to take care of Forest and raise their two children, dealing with his serial infidelities along the way and helping to boost his fragile ego. After 20 years, Forest left her for a younger woman (who dressed a little like Pocahontas). "Hell hath no fury like a man who wishes to marry a girl half his age," she notes. And there is a lot of fury as the two go to court through the years battling over alimony, which he doesn't think she deserves.

Most of the book is devoted to her relationship and divorce from Forest—but don't let this deter you. I promise, you will find it as engrossing as I did, and marvel at the absurdities she had to deal with, not only from her husband but her own lawyers and the trial judges.

Hilligoss had no ghostwriter or collaborator, which makes her effort all the more remarkable. Her style is sharp, witty, laugh-out-loud funny many times, and heartbreaking. She is quite a storyteller.

She comes across as a very likable lady, someone you would really love to know. I have read other reviews of her book claiming she's bitter and saying that, after all these years, she should let it go. Easy to say. The smug "Forest" really put her through the wringer, both during and after the marriage. His suggestion that she become a nun, of all things, and "be useful" is infuriating, but she sees the humor in that too. He also thought she needed "psychological testing to find out what her true vocation should be." Her hilarious stories of her father's distrust of men who don't wear undershirts and her wild ride with a taxi driver who, to paraphrase Alan Jay Lerner, did not want to Get Her to the Church on Time to marry Forest can be seen as prophetic moments. (The taxi ride is my favorite section of the book. I was howling.) Hilligoss is a survivor, and her self-deprecating humor and gutsy approach got her over the (many) rough patches. Her clever, biting humor and honesty make her identifiable and real.

The narrative shifts between her court battles, her career and her married life. She had a varied background, studying acting at the American Theatre Wing and also with Sanford Meisner, and she was a Copa Girl at New York's Copacabana.

Hilligoss possesses a dry sense of humor and she has a way of phrasing things that puts a funny spin on them. She had been crowned Greenfield Garden Princess by the North Carolina Azalea Festival and went on tour with the 1960 winner, actress Linda Christian. Christian claimed she had been discovered by Errol Flynn while she attended medical school, to which Candace cracks, "Nothing she said to me during our trip ever gave evidence that she had attended any institute of higher learning." Regarding this trip, she relates a sweetly memorable account of her meeting with actor Paul Henreid.

When the occasion arises, there is poignancy. When one of her (many) lawyers asks her what she wants, Candace's response just broke my heart: "I want my youth back!" It's a killer moment and you sincerely feel for her.

There are too many good stories to summarize all of them here, but I will highlight a few of my favorites.

Writer Gertrude Walker getting on the stand to be Hilligoss' character witness is pure heaven. "I've done everything twice and hated it," Walker tells a star-struck judge who revels in her colorful stories of meetings with celebrities.

You have to feel sorry for Hilligoss on one of her post-divorce dates. As they are having dinner, the guy starts nibbling on her toes(!) and her reaction is totally priceless. I have tears in my eyes laughing as I write this. Also, her diving out of a car and rolling down a hill to escape an overly amorous date.

Then there is a getaway, a "break from the heat and hassle," supposedly a nice gesture by her husband, but just his way of getting her far away so he can play. Everything that could go wrong does, including quicksand on the beach, threatening high tides and bats.

I don't want to give anything away, but Hilligoss' childhood story of her tangle with a milking machine is freaky.

Her comments about people she worked with on stage are very revealing. I had no idea what a stinker Robert Webber was (he threw her in a swimming pool when she wouldn't fool around with him). Her story about Veronica Lake, who let Candace stay at a house she was renting, is one of the more balanced things I've read about Lake. Mostly, you hear how troubled Lake was, but Hilligoss' memories and insights give a different side to the actress, and it's a pleasure to read. "Veronica fell into my life for a few memorable moments like the sister I never had, the mother I lost in childhood, then just as quickly was gone." The stuff she learned about Lake's ex, André De Toth, is pretty horrifying.

One of the more disturbing stories has to do with Mel Brooks, a friend early in her career. Less disturbing, but still creepy, were her dealings with playwright Sidney Kingsley. Acting with Joseph Wiseman on stage in *Turn on the Night* (1961), which closed out of town, was another interesting experience.

Fans of *Carnival of Souls* will not be disappointed, as Hilligoss spends a whole chapter going behind the scenes. The filming was, at times, hazardous, and Herk Harvey even took out an insurance policy on his leading lady! She gives a nice nod to the underappreciated Harvey, calling *Carnival*, "a testament to how talent can compensate for the hurdles imposed on independently produced, low-budget films."

The book is nicely produced and the fabulous, clear photos are great: rare candids, newspaper clippings, scene stills, etc. My favorite scene from *Carnival of Souls* is captured where Hilligoss screams in terror in a doctor's office at the sight of the smiling Man (Harvey). Brilliance. There are also a few cute drawings by her late friend Garrett Lewis.

Early on, Gertrude Walker encouraged her to "take notes, write this court stuff down. The best revenge is to tell this story." Candace replied, "Oh, Gertrude, another boring tale about a middle-aged woman getting divorced. Who'd want to read it?" Boring tale? Hell, no. Thank goodness Hilligoss decided to take Walker's advice. I look forward to more books by her; she is a talented writer. Buy this book!

Olivia de Havilland: Lady Triumphant
by Victoria Amador

Olivia de Havilland: Lady Triumphant by Victoria Amador (University Press of Kentucky) started off winningly. Amador's introduction details the reasons she loves and appreciates de Havilland and related the personal connection she has with the actress. The two have had a long correspondence which took many years to advance into personal meetings. In fact, there were several aborted attempts by the author to get together with de Havilland. I thought it odd that de Havilland would delay the initial meeting so long, given the warmth of their interaction in letters, but I guess it is understandable, given Olivia's advanced (triple-digit!) age. Also, I sensed that Amador is more than a little obsessed with her subject, especially in regard to her looks and speaking voice.

The best feature of *Lady Triumphant* is the participation of de Havilland via letters and emails sent to the author. Olivia has never been happy with the errors that have crept into other writers' accounts of her life story. So, I guess, we can safely assume that Amador has gotten the basic biography correct, or at least to de Havilland's satisfaction. Olivia's quotes are the main attraction of this biography.

When I saw that de Havilland helped in such a profound way, I thought this would elevate the manuscript to a higher level than most. Unfortunately, *Lady Triumphant* left me with a feeling of unease, annoyance and wanting much more.

There is a lack of good primary research; Amador's sources are extremely limited in scope. There should have been more information culled from the archives of Warner Bros., where de Havilland was under contract for years. I was startled when Amador repeated a scandalous item from IMDb which started, "Interoffice memos clearly indicate that Olivia was not the first choice for the role of Marian" in 1938's *The Adventures of Robin Hood*. "The original actress, whose name is blacked out in each of [the] documents [archived at the USC Cinema Television Library], became pregnant out of wedlock, and could no longer accept the role." Instead of going to the original memo, the author accepts this as fact. Given the nature of these "memos," a real biographer would have checked to see if they were real. Truth be told, it really wasn't anything that should be quoted, but if you do want to go down that path, check the source before spreading something salacious like this.

On the same note, instead of going to the book *Curtis Bernhardt: A Directors Guild of America Oral History* (Scarecrow Press) to find out what the director thought of *My Love Came Back* (1940), Amador relies on a TCM online article.

Much of what Amador writes is self-indulgent and really of no interest. We get long, uncomfortably adoring descriptions of how Olivia looked on- and off-screen, how she formed her words, how she sounds, *ad nauseam*. No, I do not think Olivia (whose "cleavage is impressive") taking a bubble bath in *Princess O'Rourke* (1943) is the equivalent of an ingénue today doing a nude scene to "show the world she's become a woman." Eeeek.

The movies' plots are told in excruciating detail, to the point where I just didn't care about them. Waste of paper and ink.

And Amador's interpretations of the movies are, on occasion, off-kilter. I am thinking in particular of her assertion that the great romance in *Gone with the Wind* (1939) was between Rhett and Melanie. Now, you can make a case for anything, but this struck me as very fanciful and more than a little peculiar. Her reading of moments might be a little off, as well. Paul Henreid, while doing *Devotion* (1946), didn't really care for de Havilland (unpardonable!), so the author mentions an "unromantic" kiss between the two that looks as if Henreid "wants to shatter Olivia's mouth with his teeth." Amador, I think you are looking too closely at these movies…

Few actresses had the career de Havilland enjoyed: an eight-film partnership with Errol Flynn (*Captain Blood* [1935], *The Charge of the Light Brigade* [1936], *The Adventures of Robin Hood*, *Four's a Crowd* [both 1938], *Dodge City*, *The Private Lives of Elizabeth and Essex* [both 1939], *Santa Fe Trail* [1940] and *They Died with*

Their Boots On [1941]); a role in a movie many consider one of the greatest of all time [*Gone with the Wind*]; two Oscars (*To Each His Own* [1946] and *The Heiress* [1949]); and participation in quite a few more memorable movies. She was also a groundbreaker in her legal actions against Warner Bros. Yet through all this, Amador gripes about movies that she thinks were beneath Olivia, whom she insists should have gotten meaty, important dramatic parts in the 1930s. I love these writers who think their subject should jump right into superstardom without paying their dues. Even Bette Davis had to endure projects she didn't particularly like before she graduated to the stronger stuff. These discussions are a fruitless exercise, especially when you know your subject will eventually hit the big time (and the Oscars). Look: Many actresses found themselves playing second fiddle to leading men and were in B movies, that's just the way it was. Get over it!

Amador complains about co-stars to the extent that it made me sick. Poor Jeffrey Lynn and Sonny Tufts, two good leading men, are roasted by the author. On a lesser note, Patric Knowles (who had nice chemistry with Olivia) is supposedly just not good enough to play opposite her. Okay, you don't have to like them, but is this the place to broadcast your obviously strong dislike? Of course, Ronald Reagan is mentioned a bit negatively, although nowhere as bad as Lynn and Tufts, but I've come to expect that in books where someone (whether they admit it or not) cannot separate actors from their politics. On the other hand, when she called Dennis Morgan "luscious" and John Lund a "beefcake," I laughed out loud. I love Morgan and Lund, but this is a little extreme. (It reminded me of a comment I made about Warren Hull in *Killer Tomatoes: Fifteen Tough Film Dames*. It tickled my co-writer Ray Hagen so much, we kept it in, but now, in my maturity, I realize it was sorely out of place. But I am still glad it amused Ray.)

The author seems to have a thing for James Stewart and his one-time romantic relationship with de Havilland, as it is much discussed within the book. Wouldn't it have been wonderful if they did *The Man Who Knew Too Much* (1956) together? Oh, what were they thinking when they ran into each other at that event? How were they feeling? What emotional intensity was bubbling just below the surface? How can I keep myself from obsessing over this sentimental, romanticized view? There's quite a bit about de Havilland's romance with director John Huston, which was more serious, but the Stewart-de Havilland pairing is the one that really makes the author's heart go pitter-patter.

Kill me now.

This is the umpteenth book to retell two untruths about director Michael Curtiz: that he was married to actress Lili Damita and that he abused horses during the making of *The Charge of the Light Brigade*. Both of these were debunked in the University Press of Kentucky's splendid *Michael Curtiz: A Life in Film* by Alan K. Rode (see above).

The fact that the song "To Each His Own" was popular does not attest to the "power of the picture." It was a good song. Period. I love how the author says the song is of "the saccharine crooner variety." "Irony" is a word Amador uses a lot, whether it's appropriate or not, but in this case, it is very ironic that, with her occasionally saccharine writing style, she is making that point.

I just don't get it: Calling *My Love Came Back* (1940) "a black-and-white, 1930s *High School Musical* [2006]" is absurd and leads me to believe she did not see the film.

More head-scratching: When I think of de Havilland, do I really think of a "ninja Red Riding Hood"? Um, no. Not when un-medicated, anyway.

Why quote Ingrid Bergman saying that de Havilland won the Oscar for *The Snake Pit* (1948)? Amador knows this is not true, so why include it?

Amador, in a clear case of confusing fact and fiction, writes that Irwin Allen is "reminiscent in the trailer [for *The Swarm*] of Ed Wood" when "he calls out 'Cut! Sensational!'" She must be thinking of Johnny Depp in *Ed Wood* (1994), which by most accounts is not an actual representation of the real Wood.

Do we really need the superficial, cruel comparison of how de Havilland, David O. Selznick and Vivien Leigh looked at a 1961 screening of *Gone with the Wind*? Let's see how well the "chic and joyful" de Havilland would have looked if she walked a mile in Leigh's shoes.

Where does Amador get that *Not as a Stranger* (1955) made $50 million at the box office? The top domestic grosser of 1955, *Cinerama Holiday*, made $10 million. The top *six* domestic grossers of 1955, together, didn't add up to $50 million! (My info comes from *Variety*.)

The author also gives the impression that *Dodge City's* premiere in Kansas was just a screening with Errol Flynn and Ann Sheridan. Famously, that junket, which included many top Warner Bros. stars, was a major publicity event.

There's some repetition in the text. You said it once, you don't have to stay it twice or more. The author reiterates quite a few points and even jarringly uses the same quotes multiple times.

I don't think the author quite got a handle on de Havilland the person. De Havilland's complexities are many and instead of exploring some of the negative stories about her, Amador makes excuses and doesn't really seem to believe them. A person's faults make up who they are and make them interesting. No one is perfect. Her feud with her sister Joan Fontaine is discussed, sometimes objectively—sometimes not.

"Balancing my lifetime of fandom with the biographer's task of providing an accurate interpretation of her life and times was daunting," the author writes. "It is my hope that Olivia de Havilland and her many admirers will find this work an extravagant bouquet of roses, replete with beautiful scents and textures and colors—and the occasional thorn." Personally, since I like de Havilland as an actress and admire her gutsy resolve, I was disappointed by this book.

✷

One Man Crazy ...! The Life and Death of Colin Clive
by Gregory William Mank

It is surprising to find that there have been no full-length books on Colin Clive (1900-37), a British actor best known for portraying the title role in *Frankenstein* (1931). His manic intensity informed many of his screen and stage portrayals and it is a well-known fact that the high-strung Clive, who died at the young age of 37, led an unhappy life. His story has been placed in the capable and appreciative hands of Gregory William Mank, whose new book is the biography **One Man Crazy...! The Life and Death of Colin Clive** (Midnight Marquee Press).

Right off the bat, Mank says this is a "dark book," and he is right, of course. Clive's family included insanity and he had a serious problem with alcohol and a mass of insecurities. This is all discussed, as are the stage productions and movies in which Clive appeared. There is extensive coverage of *Frankenstein, Journey's End* (both stage and screen), *Christopher Strong, Bride of Frankenstein, Mad Love*, etc. It helps considerably that the author has interviewed past co-workers and acquaintances such as Lew Ayres, Charles Bennett, DeWitt Bodeen, Mae Clarke, Frances Drake, Marilyn Harris, Katharine Hepburn (a brief note), Rose Hobart, Valerie Hobson, Josephine Hutchinson, Elsa Lanchester, David Lewis, David Manners, Pauline Moore, Alan Napier and Stella Zucco. The latter contributes a fun moment when recalling an altercation between Tallulah Bankhead and Clive's second wife Jeanne de Casalis:

> Well, Tallulah and Jeanne got into a fight over Colin Clive—and I mean a fight [pantomiming fist-fighting]! They had to be separated! George [Zucco] did partly, and several of the guests helped him. I imagine Tallulah and Jeanne were fighting over who got to go home with Clive that night. I don't recall who won. I couldn't have cared less! [Laughs] Fancy two women fighting over Colin Clive! Why?

Speaking of Jeanne de Casalis, most of the pictures of her do not resemble the "drag queen" description the author gives of her. To me, she merely looks glamorous. Later, Mank calls her "attractive in her witchy way, playing with wicked comic timing. In Hollywood, Hal Roach might have cast her effectively as Stan Laurel's batty, oversexed sister—or wacky, transvestite brother." If that's how he sees it, fine; I don't.

The author is more taken with Clive's girlfriend near the end of his life, Iris Lancaster, whom he calls "an eyeful." Actually, I was also more interested in Lancaster than de Casalis—but for another reason: She was a B movie actress who appeared mainly in Westerns with John Wayne, Fred Scott, Jimmy Wakely, etc., and changed her name to Iris Clive in the 1940s. Mank includes some really good information about Iris, for which I am grateful. Despite the looks remarks, there is also a wealth of info on de Casalis and Clive's first wife, Evelyn Taylor. (The latter's demise was especially surprising and pretty horrible.)

Mank's research is most impressive and his writing excellent (I particularly enjoyed his recap of the plot for the stage version of *Journey's End*). And he paints a vivid picture of Universal's backlot. The editing was a bit rough at times but generally it does not interfere with the narrative.

I have come to expect all of Mank's books to include some very inappropriate remarks and asides that make so sense. This one is no different. He talks about "the beast with two backs"; "sloppy seconds"; remarking that the Oscar statuette has a "suggestive connotation: a naked man, stabbing a sword into a reel of film with five holes"; calling James Whale and Jean Harlow "the synthetic English aristocrat who held his penis like a gentleman, vs. the blonde bombshell who iced her nipples"; referencing Karloff's reputation as "a swordsman." The rumor, Mank writes: "Jimmy Whale cast Boris as the Monster due to tales about the actor's quite splendid natural endowment. 'Monster indeed!' Karloff might have laughed"; describing Peter Lorre in *Mad Love* as looking like "a kinky Humpty Dumpty"; and claiming that Dolores del Rio in 1935's *The Widow from Monte Carlo* "looks like she could snap her skeletal co-player in half with her thighs." (That last remark did make me chuckle.)

These and many other questionable, cringey comments are only a slight distraction, thank God. The heart of the book is in the intense picture the author paints of the complex Colin Clive. It is all supplemented by rare photographs and theatre items, the latter particularly interesting to see.

Peg Entwistle and the Hollywood Sign Suicide: A Biography
by James Zeruk, Jr

Peg Entwistle is a name film buffs and even non–movie fans know because she famously jumped off the Hollywoodland sign in 1932. But what do we really know about her? We have always been told she was a failed actress who ended her life because most of her footage in the movie *Thirteen Women* (1932) was cut and she was dropped by RKO. That's about it—and it is completely wrong.

A friend recently gave me a copy of McFarland's **Peg Entwistle and the Hollywood Sign Suicide: A Biography** by James Zeruk Jr., with a foreword by Eve Golden. What a revelation! How fascinating to finally learn about Entwistle's life, her horrible marriage to Robert Keith, her passion for acting and her successes and failures on the stage. The detailed chapters about *Thirteen Women* and the reasons her part was mostly deleted are handled well. It is a glimpse into how the censors worked and the attitudes that were prevalent in the 1930s.

Zeruk had help from Entwistle's family, who granted him interviews and furnished letters, photos and other material. He added to that impeccable research of his own from other sources. The way he meticulously weaves her compelling story around the facts is what makes Zeruk such a marvelous writer. I envy his ability to personalize her life story in a way that captivated me. I became so involved with Peg's ups and downs that by the time she made her trek up to the Hollywoodland sign, I felt a sense of melancholy. The author makes Peg Entwistle more than "The Hollywood Sign Girl"—she is a living, breathing, multifaceted person whose fragile emotions got the best of her. He dispels all the misinformation out there to give us the complete story and the real reasons she made that leap.

How I wish there were more dedicated writer-researchers such as James Zeruk Jr. His readable style alternates beautifully from serious to fanciful and back again, without it seeming odd or out of place. He has written a fabulous book that should be read by every movie and stage enthusiast. He makes all of it look easy but I am sure a lot of blood, sweat and tears went into compiling this amazing biography. I appreciate the time he took to understand Entwistle and bring out her true story.

Pine-Thomas Productions: A History and Filmography
by David C. Tucker

For years my go-to films have been those produced by Pine-Thomas. And why not? Their movies featured my beloved Richard Arlen, Robert Lowery, Jean Parker, Chester Morris, Philip Reed, Rhonda Fleming, Arlene Dahl, John Payne, etc. William H. Pine and William C. Thomas were nicknamed "The Two Dollar Bills" because they delivered a lot on a small budget. Action? You got it in spades with Pine-Thomas. "I can fly that crate with my two arms around a blonde," Arlen boasts in *Forced Landing* (1941).

So, I was very excited about the new volume **Pine-Thomas Productions: A History and Filmography** by David C. Tucker (McFarland). It bodes well for this book that its author is Tucker as his writing and research is always flawless. He does not disappoint.

The first section gives us a history of the Pine-Thomas partnership and the individual life stories of William H. Pine (1896-1955) and William C. Thomas (1903-84). Immeasurable help was given to Tucker by Bill Thomas' daughter Carol and his access to Thomas' unpublished memoir. Other aid comes from Bill Pine's family. It all adds up to a complete picture of what made these two men tick and how they did what they did on such tight budgets.

All of Pine-Thomas' films and shorts (including those made after Pine's death) are discussed at length, complete with credits, plots, reviews, etc. The films: *Power Dive, Forced Landing, Flying Blind, No Hands on the Clock* (all 1941), *Torpedo Boat, I Live on Danger, Wildcat, Wrecking Crew* (all 1942), *High Explosive, Aerial Gunner, Alaska Highway, Submarine Alert, Tornado, Minesweeper* (all 1943), *Timber Queen, The Navy Way, Gambler's Choice, Take It Big, Dark Mountain, One Body Too Many, Dangerous Passage, Double Exposure* (all 1944), *High Powered, Scared Stiff, Midnight Manhunt, Follow That Woman* (all 1945), *People Are Funny, Tokyo Rose, They Made Me a Killer, Hot Cargo, Big Town, Swamp Fire* (all 1946), *I Cover Big Town, Seven Were Saved, Fear in the Night, Danger Street, Jungle Flight, Adventure Island, Big Town After Dark* (all 1947), *Albuquerque, Caged Fury, Mr. Reckless, Speed to Spare, Big Town Scandal, Shaggy, Waterfront at Midnight, Disaster* (all 1948), *Dynamite, El Paso, Manhandled, Special Agent* (all 1949), *Captain China, The Eagle and the Hawk, The Lawless, Tripoli* (all 1950), *The Last Outpost, Passage West, Crosswinds* (all 1951), *Hong Kong, Caribbean, The Blazing Forest* (all 1952), *Tropic Zone, Jamaica Run, Sangaree, The Vanquished, Those Redheads from Seattle* (all 1953), *Run for Cover, Hell's Island, The Far Horizons, Lucy Gallant* (all 1955), *Nightmare* (1956), *The Big Caper, Bailout at 43,000* (both 1957), *Cat Murkil and the Silks* (1976) and *High Seas Hijack* (1977). The shorts: *A Letter from Bataan, We Refuse to Die, The Price of Victory* (all 1942), *The Aldrich Family Gets in the Scrap* and *Soldiers of the Soil* (both 1943).

Tucker treats the plot descriptions concisely and gives a clear picture of each production with some excellent background info. He is not afraid to quote a bad review here and there, but he respects B movies, which is a definite plus for the book. There's a fascinating backstory about the authorship issue surrounding *The Lawless* (1950) and Tucker skillfully compares *Fear in the Night* (1947) and its remake *Nightmare* (1956).

Interviewees include Bob Hanks, the son of Robert Lowery and Jean Parker, and the still-feisty Arlene Dahl, who appeared in three Pine-Thomas films in the 1950s. She supplied one of my favorite quotes in the book when she reminisced about John Payne, the Two Dollar Bills' leading man in 11 films: "He didn't believe in rehearsals. He was a one-shot actor. It was like working with a glass of water." (By the way, I love Payne.)

I really enjoy Tucker's writing style and the subtle humor he exhibits in the captions and the text (e.g., mentioning a "lavish" flashback a character has where he can remember "scenes he wasn't in" and his commentary on the "romantic" dialogue in *The Eagle and the Hawk*). About *Forced Landing:* "This film represents what's most likely a moviegoer's only opportunity to see one of the Gabor sisters [Eva] at the helm of a military plane under attack."

Appendices give biographical sketches on actors, directors, etc., who worked often for Pine-Thomas. There are more than 50 wonderful photos you won't see anywhere else. (One is misidentified: singer Bob Graham is ID'ed as Philip Reed from *People Are Funny*. How many would notice, though? I happen to be a fan of Graham's.)

If you love B movies, this is for you—on a subject not covered at any kind of length elsewhere. Tucker did an exceptional job of bringing the Two Dollar Bills to life and honoring their work.

Sluggy: Bogie's Other Baby: Mayo Methot—Star of Stage, Screen & Wife of Humphrey Bogart
by Roy W. Widing

In 2019, about two months after I submitted to McFarland the finished manuscript of *Hollywood's Hard-Luck Ladies: 23 Actresses*

Who Suffered Early Deaths, Accidents, Missteps, Illnesses and Tragedies, I noted the release of the book **Sluggy: Bogie's Other Baby: Mayo Methot—Star of Stage, Screen & Wife of Humphrey Bogart** by Roy W. Widing (Quality House). I was surprised because I had included in my book a chapter on Methot, and had no idea that anyone was writing a whole biography on her. I lamented that it might include revelations that I could have incorporated in the Methot chapter in my book. Oh well, I thought, I did the best I could and, besides, I only had x number of pages to tell the story of the third Mrs. Bogart.

Widing's research cannot be faulted. As a resident of Oregon, where Methot (1904-51) grew up, he had access to its historical society, to Mayo's personal papers, to local newspapers, and he had a familiarity with the areas she traveled. And the photographs? Good grief, he had photos of her early life I could have only dreamed about! The image of Mayo sitting on a piano while composer Vincent Youmans played, while lightly reproduced, is a wow. I was amazed, too, to see pix of Methot's first two husbands, John M. La Mond and Percy T. Morgan Jr. (as well as interesting personal info on them). Widing had noble intentions: to give Methot her due and to paint her as more than an alcoholic, violent spouse of a superstar actor-husband.

I happily learned a lot from *Sluggy: Bogie's Other Baby,* pre– and post–Bogie. Widing did an outstanding job giving details about Mayo's parents.

However, strong insights and first-rate points are occasionally hampered by repetition. The author's freewheeling writing style could have used an editor to tighten it up. Often, he just goes on and on, presenting us with the same ideas. Nowhere is this more evident than near the end where he goes on for pages about where (and how) Methot died. It could have been said in one simple, strong paragraph. Because Methot once appeared in a play as a woman who marries a widower, he quotes from some publicity piece her thoughts on marrying such a man. This has no bearing on her story, it's just padding. Widing should have been more judicious when putting his research findings on paper.

Hither and thither there are some odd remarks: After Methot underwent surgery for appendicitis, she did the play *The Medicine Man*. "It's an open question if Mayo had flashbacks of her surgery while performing in a play with a medical title."

"Given his former wife Mayo's childhood comparisons and similar early roles, it's ironic that graveside services for Percy [Morgan] were held in the same cemetery where child acting sensation Shirley Temple was also laid to rest." No one has ever compared Mayo Methot with Shirley Temple—ever.

Factual errors: Lauren Bacall's real name was Betty Joan Perske, not Lauren Bacal. Most sources (including IMDb) give Mayo credit for *Lilly Turner* (1933), but the actress playing the uncredited part of Gordon Westcott's wife is not Mayo. Of course, the spelling is Katharine, not Katherine, Hepburn. Bogart played Duke Mantee in *The Petrified Forest*, not Roy "Mad Dog" Earle, which was the name of his *High Sierra* character. Et cetera.

I got the sense that "The Movies" is not a subject on which the author is expert. He makes comments about "production values" from the early 1930s not being up to par with "the modern cinematic experience." His "helpful" history "lessons" on such things as the "de Havilland Law" (among others) are too simplistic—and also not correct. I would have welcomed more critiques of Mayo's movies, certainly a lot more on *Marked Woman* (1937). Incidentally, the mustachioed actor with Mayo and Bette Davis in the *Marked Woman* photo is Carlos San Martín, not Allen Jenkins. The author quotes various Bogart biographies, but head-scratchingly, not the best of the lot: A.M. Sperber and Eric Lax's *Bogart* (1997), which had substantial Methot coverage.

In the end, I enjoyed *Sluggy: Bogie's Other Baby* and I'm glad I read it. Methot certainly deserves a full-length biography, especially one which treats her honestly but sympathetically and with respect. No matter how rough the narrative, there's quite a lot to savor. Anything that adds to our understanding of this underappreciated actress should be cherished.

Still Here: The Madcap, Nervy, Singular Life of Elaine Stritch
by Alexandra Jacobs

I have mixed feelings about **Still Here: The Madcap, Nervy, Singular Life of Elaine Stritch** by Alexandra Jacobs (Farrar, Straus and Giroux). This was *The New Yorker's* favorite non-fiction book of 2019 and a *New York Times Book Review* Editors' Choice. I obtained a copy when it first came out but it took me many months to finish it.

I happen to love Elaine Stritch, an amazing performer and storyteller. Her autobiographical one-woman show *Elaine Stritch at Liberty* is extraordinary—funny and heartbreaking at the same time. Her life was a thorny one, to say the least.

Jacobs' book title promises a madcap and nervy life. Substitute "infuriating" for "nervy" and eliminate "madcap" and you'll have a more accurate description. I have heard some positive anecdotes about Stritch as well as horror stories. Everyone knew she was a pain in the ass. But her humor saved her.

Still Here: The Madcap, Nervy, Singular Life of Elaine Stritch is lacking that key ingredient. Instead of mingling Stritch's amazing humor with her trying personality, we have a mostly downbeat, negative narrative. We get hit over the head with a really unlikable, annoying Stritch who drinks too much and makes life miserable for everyone around her. There had to be more to her than that—and there was.

I really looked forward to this biography. I wanted to love it, at least like it. It instead exasperated me. Not only for the reason stated above, but because Jacobs omits much of Stritch's work. The author did a great deal of research and her writing is okay. But Stritch needed someone who truly understood her, who was able to convey her humor, and not just recount every awful thing she ever did to almost everyone with whom she came in contact. What made everyone love Elaine despite her personality?

If you want a recitation of the moments Stritch was drunk and mean, by all means buy this. I was disappointed because I wanted a book with a sardonic wit to match its subject. I wanted an even-handed biography that combined the good and bad in Stritch. For now, I will rewatch *Elaine Stritch at Liberty*.

Sweet Oddball: The Story of Alice Pearce
by Fredrick Tucker

The sublimely funny Alice Pearce was known for her role as the nosy Gladys Kravitz on TV's *Bewitched* (1964-66) (which earned her a posthumous Emmy) and for her supporting performance in the Broadway and film versions of *On the Town*. Pearce was only 48 when she died of ovarian cancer in 1966. As endearing as she was (and is), this talented lady has been pretty much overlooked in the years since. Not any longer!

Fredrick Tucker has written an exceptionally fine biography: **Sweet Oddball: The Story of Alice Pearce** (BearManor). This 400-plus-page volume is a remarkable look at Alice's life and career, never stinting on the details. Tucker started collecting and researching Pearce in the early 1970s, so he got to interview or receive letters from an impressive array of her colleagues and friends. His acknowledgments cover three and a half pages.

Tucker is quite a writer, painting a portrait of Alice at variance with her famous role as Gladys Kravitz. She was loved by all, born into affluent surroundings, traveling as a child, and graduating from Sarah Lawrence College in 1940 with a degree in drama. From there, she went into nightclub and stage work. This is all detailed alongside a marvelous selection of rare photos, many from the collection of her friend, actor-photographer Cris Alexander (who was on Broadway with her in *On the Town*). The images of her as a young girl are treasures and there are many glamour shots.

She might be called the "chinless wonder," and some might deem her homely, but as evidenced by several photos in this book, Pearce was beautiful. Of the photos later in her career, I adore the one of her and Phil Silvers (in drag) from *The New Phil Silvers Show* in 1964. And then there's the one with Laird Cregar from a 1944 Connecticut stage production of *The Man Who Came to Dinner*! Pearce played the part of Miss Preen, the character created on Broadway (and played in the 1942 movie) by Mary Wickes. An intriguing section deals with Wickes and her reaction to Pearce, and the idea that some find them similar.

A true testament to Tucker's skill as a biographer is how he deals with Pearce's illness and her brave determination to keep working. I will admit to getting a lump in my throat reading these passages. And then to see the pictures of her ravaged by sickness—poor Alice! Pearce's personal character is so gentle and sweet, but with a streak of eccentricity (and that adenoidal voice!) that you can't help but love her. The story of actor Wendell Corey confronting a nightclub patron who insulted Alice during one of her acts was one of my favorite parts of the book.

Sweet Oddball is given deluxe treatment by BearManor with a larger format (8 x 0.95 x 10 inches). It also has one of the cleanest texts, with no errors. Fredrick Tucker needs to write more books. Now. Today. His approach, his research and his writing talent demand it.

Tappin' at the Apollo: The African American Female Tap Dance Duo Salt and Pepper
by Cheryl M. Willis

McFarland has another book that might interest show business devotees: **Tappin' at the Apollo: The African American Female**

Tap Dance Duo Salt and Pepper by Cheryl M. Willis. This was a subject with which I was unfamiliar. I had seen a preview of it, and was knocked out by the rare photos and ads. I decided I needed to acquaint myself with Edwina "Salt" Evelyn and Jewel "Pepper" Welch, who danced around the country despite "racism, sexism and homophobia."

Willis presents an intriguing picture of what show business was like for these two ladies. This is helped immensely by the author's interviews with Salt and Pepper. However, the writing is at times uneven: Quotes needed to be proofread for clarity and tightened; there is some word repetition; and names are misspelled. Worse, Willis takes time out for numerous unnecessary asides about other performers and the history of chorus girls. This stuff belongs in another book. At one point, she describes two matchbooks she found on eBay. Seriously? An editor should have gone through this manuscript and done some *Scrappin'* at the Apollo.

By skimming through some off-topic sections and ignoring numerous errors, I did enjoy learning about Salt and Pepper, two overlooked performers of the 1940s.

Then & Now: A Memoir by Barbara Cook and Tom Santopietro/**The Night and the Music: Rosemary Clooney, Barbara Cook & Julie Wilson Inside the World of Cabaret** by Deborah Grace Winer

When Barbara Cook passed away on August 8, 2017, at the age of 89, we lost one of our greatest singers. Starting with the short-lived *Flahooley* (1951), she went on to become one of the leading Broadway ingénues in such musicals as *Plain and Fancy* (1955), *Candide* (1956), *The Music Man* (1957), *The Gay Life* (1961) and *She Loves Me* (1963), plus City Center revivals of *Carousel*, *Oklahoma!* and *The King and I*. She also did musicals and straight plays in stock.

While Leonard Bernstein's operetta *Candide* was not a hit, it gained legendary status and was a personal triumph for Cook; the song "Glitter and Be Gay" is considered one of her best. She originated the role of Marian the Librarian in Meredith Willson's *The Music Man*, opposite Robert Preston, and it won her a Tony. With her dazzling lyric soprano, Cook sang "Goodnight, My Someone," "My White Knight," "Will I Ever Tell You" and "Till There Was You."

In *She Loves Me*, another important Broadway show for Cook, she introduced another of her signature tunes, Sheldon Harnick and Jerry Bock's "Vanilla Ice Cream." The book by Joe Masteroff was adapted from Miklós László's 1937 play *Parfumerie*. *Classic Images* readers know it best from its film versions: *The Shop Around the Corner* (1940), *In the Good Old Summertime* (1949) and *You've Got Mail* (1998).

As the 1960s progressed, Cook began to experience problems in her personal life and it eventually led to divorce, alcoholism, food addiction, weight gain, depression and panic attacks. The early 1970s found her almost unemployable. With the help of pianist-composer-arranger Wally Harper, Cook resurfaced in cabaret and in a triumphant 1975 Carnegie Hall concert. Back on top, she had a whole new career as a concert artist and one of the best interpreters of the American Popular Songbook. She sang for four presidents at the White House; recorded numerous albums; blew everyone away in the famous 1985 concert version of Stephen Sondheim's *Follies*; won many awards; was Tony-nominated for the Broadway revue *Sondheim on Sondheim* (2010); and was one of the honorees at the 2011 Kennedy Center Honors. Through it all, Cook grew as a singer and managed to get better, her soprano lowering and growing richer as the years passed. Her ability to get to the heart of a song's lyrics has never been surpassed.

On December 18, 2017, there was a memorial tribute to Cook at Lincoln Center's Vivian Beaumont Theater. Renée Fleming, lyricist Sheldon Harnick, Kelli O'Hara, Audra McDonald, Vanessa

Williams, Norm Lewis, Frank Langella, John Pizzarelli and others spoke and/or performed.

I became a Barbara Cook fan late in the game. While growing up in the late 1970s and '80s, I was exposed to her mainly through records belonging to my mother: the Broadway cast albums of *The Music Man* and *She Loves Me* and an amazing *Show Boat* LP from a 1966 Lincoln Center production Cook did with Stephen Douglass. (This remains my favorite recording of the Jerome Kern–Oscar Hammerstein II show.) One of the first records I ever bought on my own was Cook's *The Disney Album*. My love of her singing built from there and I discovered so many more musical gems. For me, there are few things as beautiful as Cook doing "Magic Moment," "All the Things You Are" and "If Love Were All," or as thrilling as her "He Loves Me," "Them There Eyes" (with her kazoo solo), "A Wonderful Guy," "Don't Blame Me" and "Glad Rag Doll." She was consistently great, her versatility well-known.

I had only sketchily known the details of her tumultuous life, mostly from Deborah Grace Winer's book *The Night and the Music: Rosemary Clooney, Barbara Cook & Julie Wilson Inside the World of Cabaret* (1996); more about this later. In 2016, I was excited to see that Cook's autobiography, **Then & Now: A Memoir**, written with Tom Santopietro, was published by HarperCollins. It took a while, but now that the paperback has been issued, I have a copy.

It was worth the wait! Told in a highly readable, direct style, *Then & Now* is one of the most honest books out there. By turns heartbreaking and uplifting, it details Barbara's struggles without sinking in a morass of self-pity. She had a lot to deal with, even as a kid, events that planted seeds for later neuroses. When her 18-month-old sister died, their mother blamed six-year-old Barbara for her death as the younger sibling had gotten double pneumonia at the same time Barbara had whooping cough. When her parents divorced, her mother again blamed Barbara. These obviously painful events are told simply and with clarity by Cook. Her relationship with her mother was, to put it mildly, difficult. "My mother was two people," she wrote, "and I never knew which mother I was going to get, the good or the bad." She adored her father, but saw little of him. Barbara and her mother lived pretty much in poverty in Atlanta, a place Cook always professed to dislike. Her anxieties started at a young age and took her into adulthood, although she was able (more or less) to break free from her mother's grip in the late 1940s.

One wonderful memory from her childhood: the 1939 Atlanta premiere of *Gone with the Wind* and the parade of movie stars. (An addendum to this story is when Cook met Vivien Leigh at a 1963 party and told her how she saw her in 1939; Leigh froze and turned away from her—"I think I stupidly told her how old I was that night in Atlanta and she sure as hell didn't want to hear about that.")

Cook is very honest about herself (to the point of telling us some brutal, embarrassing moments) and the effect is that she makes herself very likable. She was a strong lady—she had to be to survive not only a tumultuous personal life but show business in general. This honesty extended to the others in her life. I love the moments when she calls certain performers pains in the ass, paranoid and "a little nuts," or when she tells stories about the likes of Ethel Merman (the turban anecdote is my favorite), Katharine Hepburn, Mike Nichols, Lillian Hellman, Elaine Stritch, Maureen Stapleton (hilarious), Ronald Reagan, Jo Van Fleet and Mary Martin. These are told sometimes with the salty language Cook became known for. (Her ex-husband did not like her to curse during the marriage and she confessed that when they divorced, she made up for lost time.) She also sprinkles the text with occasional (and charming) expressions like "Holy Hannah!"

Cook doesn't disappoint with behind-the-scenes details about *Candide*, *The Music Man*, *The Gay Life* and *She Loves Me*, even discussing in a delightful manner her acclaimed revival of *The King and I* with Farley Granger. Her audition for Bernstein for *Candide* is most interesting, as is the process she went through to learn the difficult aria "Glitter and Be Gay" and the trouble she initially had.

There was more trouble with her association with the "infamous and ill-fated" musical version of *Carrie* (1988), based on the Stephen King novel and the 1976 Brian De Palma movie. Cook played the mother and Linzi Hateley the title character. The production was fraught with problems. Cook wisely left the show in London before it opened and bombed in New York. (She knew it would be a disaster. When an interviewer asked about the efforts to improve the show, Cook remarked, "We're doing a lot of work but it's like rearranging the deck chairs on the *Titanic*." She also didn't understand why a gym teacher would be wearing high-heel pumps in front of a class.) This is the most I have read about *Carrie* and it's an eye-opener.

Cook is consistently funny; oftentimes subtly, as when she tells of a moment in *Candide* she considered strange: After the cast sang "Make Our Garden Grow," a "transcendent, even spiritual moment," at the finale, the director Hal Prince had a live cow come on stage and "die" at their feet. "I just can't figure that one out," Cook wrote.

When it was announced that she was to receive the Kennedy Center honors, she revealed that a friend forwarded her a tweet that read, "Who the fuck is Barbara Cook?" Her reply makes her even more endearing: "I liked that one because part of me was thinking, 'Who the fuck thinks Barbara Cook deserves to be a part of this amazing group of people?'"

The collapse of her personal and professional life is rough and it is hard not to feel enormous sympathy and respect for her. Cook was so broke that she actually shoplifted sandwich meat. She is not searching for approval by any means, but the forthright way she tells of her troubles is inspiring—and more than a little harrowing. Even when she mentions her Carnegie Hall triumph that put her back on the map, she finds fault in at least one of her performances. She strove to be better and always succeeded. As I like to say, the only singer to ever top a Barbara Cook rendition of a song was Barbara Cook herself.

She writes sweetly about her son Adam, with whom she was always close. Extremely poignant is her relationship with Wally Harper, her "musical savior" and closest friend. "Wally understood exactly how I sang, and our musical partnership evolved into a shorthand that was closer to musical telepathy." I love her comment that he would lick furniture when no one was looking just to make her laugh. He was also an extremely complicated man. While Cook conquered her alcoholism, he never did; her recounting of his later life is heartbreaking. They were devoted friends until his death in 2004.

"For a long time I wasn't fully aware of how much of my own life I put into interpreting lyrics, into communicating on a very personal level with the audience. ...I believe art that is authentic can be healing. I suppose that I've come to think of myself as a salesman, because I really do believe that what I have to say through my songs can help people."

This also applies to her memoir, which is a classic example of someone rising from the ashes to even bigger heights. It is superbly written and inspiring and if you're a fan of Cook's, you will love her even more when you know all she went through.

When Deborah Grace Winer's **The Night and the Music: Rosemary Clooney, Barbara Cook & Julie Wilson Inside the World of Cabaret** came out in 1996, I confess I bought it solely for Cook. It offered a portrait of her as a person I never saw elsewhere. It is the perfect complement to *Then & Now* because it includes different material and some very perceptive comments regarding all three ladies. ("There is a kind of raw empathy about Barbara, a poignancy in everything she does. Like Garland, she exudes a dual image, and it appeals to both sides of her audience's psyche—at once the veteran, nurturing, seen-it-all mother and the uncertain, hurting little girl.")

What Cook (1927-2017), Rosemary Clooney (1928-2002) and Julie Wilson (1924-2015) had in common were personal and professional rebirths long after their initial successes. Winer concentrates on these three artists (alternating chapters) and how they dealt with the rigors of performing in cabaret, focusing on the 1993-94 season. (A few others are touched upon, including Karen Akers, Barbara Carroll, Annie Ross, Andrea Marcovicci, reviewer Stephen Holden, Judy Argo, Mary Cleere Haran, Michael Feinstein, Linda Ronstadt and Ann Hampton Callaway.)

Along the way, we learn of the nightclubs' inner workings and how grueling it can be for singers. For many, it also wasn't very financially rewarding.

The author followed Clooney, Cook and Wilson to see how they coped with the everyday life of a singer. How they endure talkers in the audience (one Clooney story is excellent); trying to get lyrics correct with little or no rehearsal; getting paid (Wilson's experience is horrifying); the downside of doing benefits; run-ins with fans (the story of a fan's visit to Clooney's dressing room is disturbing); their time in therapy (Wilson's one time is a hoot); illness (Clooney in the emergency room all night as a woman strung out on crack sang "The Star Spangled Banner" hour after hour— "She was having a little trouble with the words, so I was kind of helping her out"); and unexpected weather that kept the patrons away. We learn that Clooney was addicted to Court TV and Cook was a wiz at the *New York Times* crossword. Wilson took nursing classes so she could care for her ailing mother.

I found it fascinating that when this book was being prepared, the Tonya Harding and O.J. Simpson scandals were in the news, and we get Clooney and Cook's reactions (respectively) to the cases. ("Barbara will get home in time to see Simpson taken into custody. And pick out what she's going to wear for tomorrow's performance.")

This, like *Then & Now*, showcases Cook's humor. I adore her comment about a tepid response she received from an audience: "I mean, you leave your liver out there on the stage... [The audience is] just kind of old. But on the other hand, I'm probably older than most of 'em—and if I can sing it, they can applaud." Admiring a wall clock Wally Harper received for his participation in the show *The Best Little Whorehouse Goes Public*, which shows a "scantily clad hooker," Cook remarks, "I think that's the most tasteless thing I've ever seen. Don't you love it?" They then look for a place to hang it in his apartment. Her work with Harper is also explored here, and how they run through songs (Cook never could read music). In one instance, she wants to sing "Sweet Dreams" (written by Amanda McBroom, the daughter of actor David Bruce). Harper thinks it's too depressing: "You'll have to pass out razor blades," he tells her.

If you are a fan of any of these ladies, I urge you to seek this out. Winer is an excellent storyteller (she also co-authored the wonderful *Sing Out, Louise!: 150 Stars of the Musical Theatre Remember 50 Years on Broadway*) and she really gets to the heart of her subjects so we feel we know them personally. Unlike Rosemary and Barbara, Wilson never wrote her autobiography, so this is especially important.

The sensational cover painting, by the author's sister Jessica Daryl Winer, is worthy of special note.

This Was Hollywood: Forgotten Stars and Stories
by Carla Valderrama

TCM has collaborated on the book **This Was Hollywood: Forgotten Stars and Stories** by Carla Valderrama (Running Press). First, the title: It's quite a stretch to say it contains all things forgotten. Rudolph Valentino, Rita Hayworth, John Garfield, Olivia de Havilland, Eleanor Powell, the Nicholas Brothers, Marni Nixon, Loretta Young, Paul Newman, etc., have "faded into obscurity"? I think not. To say that Loretta Young's love child with Clark Gable is a "little-known tale" is the height of absurdity. On the contrary, I wish so-called film historians would stop referring to it! I am tired of hearing about it every time Young is mentioned.

Susan Peters is one of the few performers featured who could be called forgotten. I found it irresponsible of the author, however, to imply that an early appendectomy could have been an abortion and that, possibly, Peters' husband Richard Quine might have been to blame for Peters' shooting accident. Putting those ideas out into the marketplace may lead others to report them as fact, even though it is just the author fantasizing. Could those things possibly have happened? Well, yes. And Sal Mineo could have possibly tampered with the brakes on James Dean's car, and Carole Lombard possibly could have put the pilot in a figure-four leglock before the fatal plane crash. Please! Save nonsense like this for books of fiction.

I didn't expect it, but it would have been nice if Valderrama had checked out my Susan Peters chapter in *Hollywood's Hard-Luck Ladies* (McFarland). Or even better: In her chapter about Cora Sue Collins, she could have given Darin Barnes and Darrell Rooney credit for their interview with Cora Sue in the Winter 2018/19 *Films of the Golden Age*—instead of claiming that the stories in her interview have never been told before. Complete BS. I often notice the absence of *Classic Images* and *FGA* from bibliographies. This is exasperating because we often print interviews that should be referenced.

The chapter on Paul Newman and his first film, *The Silver Chalice* (1954), was my least favorite. We all know that Newman hated the movie and famously took out an ad apologizing for it. It would have been nice if the author had shown the movie's good and bad sides. Instead, in a fawning attempt to agree with that "god" Newman, she goes all-out to trash it, calling it "hilariously bad" and a "nightmare."

Years ago, both Virginia Mayo and Michael Pate (both in the movie) complained to me about Newman and his treatment of *The Silver Chalice*; they felt he insulted the other actors by putting out that ad. Just because he was bad and miscast, Mayo told me, didn't mean everyone else was. Pate was angrier and called Newman a pompous ass. In 1978, Martin Scorsese, a fan of the film, mentioned that he hired Boris Leven to design *New York, New York* (1977) because Leven worked on *The Silver Chalice*.

One thing I will gladly say is that this book is visually stunning. The color and black-and-white photos are amazing, and the page design is fun, vivid and clever. It's Carla Valderrama's first book and she's a pretty fair writer when she concentrates seriously, but not so much in her lighter moments. She needs to show less bias and to keep the fantasizing to a minimum (translation: "Don't fantasize!").

The Thrills Gone By: The Kay Aldridge Story
by Jim Manago

Initially, I was eager to read a whole book devoted to actress-model Kay Aldridge (1917-95). From beginning to end, however, **The Thrills Gone By: The Kay Aldridge Story** by Jim Manago (BearManor) is a disappointment.

A lot of research went into this volume. The author was lucky to be given access to scrapbook materials and letters, supplied by one of Kay's daughters, who also provided insights into her mother's personality (nothing too probing, though). With all this going for him, Manago should have pulled together a better book for Kay's admirers.

A fan isn't necessarily a good person to write a book on one of their favorites. In most cases, he needs a strong editor, one who can guide him to put his story into a correct chronology, stay in that order, and flesh it out.

The main problem here is that the author doesn't seem to know how to organize a story properly. He wants to quote every available source on Aldridge, even if that means repeating himself frequently. In the middle of talking about *Perils of Nyoka* (1942), he quotes a columnist writing about that serial. That's fine, but he keeps quoting the rest of that article, discussing Kay's upbringing, and then he corrects the misinformation therein. No, no, no! First of all, reprinting some other writer's misinformation and then correcting it can be cumbersome, and if you do it, you need to, for instance, place misinformation on her childhood within your coverage of her childhood and not in the discussion of a film. This mistake gives the book an air of repetition, and even worse, a disorganized, chaotic feel. After a while, the reader begins dreading the detours and tangents to come, like a lost motorist who realizes that his wrong turns keep taking him right back where he was before.

His book starts off terribly. His explanation of how he is going to present her name within the book is best put in the intro, but he places it in the main text, just before she is born! Strangely, he decided to refer to her throughout as K.A. (There are a lot of abbreviations in the book. The author would have done better to just put certain info in an endnote section instead of adding more mess to his narrative.)

I'm not sure the author knows what is and is not useful biographical material. He goes on for at least a page about a nail polish ad she did, about what the ad said, etc. He also transcribes Kay's "dating tips." I can understand talking about her ad campaigns, but this was too much. Also, he uses reviews of films in which she only had bits! Or he quotes reviews that tell us nothing other than that she is in the cast. Later, with not much to tell us, he writes down TV listings of her movies. For some reason, he also felt the need to describe practically every single picture of Kay that ever appeared in a newspaper. Cut this—it means nothing. Too much wasted space and padding. More waste: Recounting a marriage report at length and then having Kay's daughter correct it. Just give us the true story up front and be done with it. A childhood friend of Kay's offers some valuable observations but then Kay's daughter comes in after to correct the ages of the two girls. Why make the friend look stupid? You could have edited the quote. I just found all this unnecessary and it was very trying to read. My eyes glazed over more than a few times and I just wanted the book to end. I like Kay Aldridge and want to know more about her, but not from a book like this. True, there is some good information here, but irritating writing smothers it.

The reader would have been better served by a cleaner style and a lot of tightening. There seems to be no editing here and there are quite a few non-sentences and misplaced commas (or no commas). There are numerous mistakes. *Louisiana Purchase* was released by Paramount, not Warner Brothers, and there are name misspellings (e.g., Jeanette McDonald, Scarlet O'Hara). One jumbled sentence makes it seem as if Gary Cooper starred in *Yesterday's Heroes*. I love the weird comment that *Navy Blues* and *You're in the Army Now* are the same movie.

Manago has a wrong-headed approach. He repeats several times that Kay is forgotten, but it is absurd to say this in a book appealing to the select group of people who remember and care about her. Would someone writing a book on the recondite details of molecular theory for a readership of physicists keep belaboring the point that the general public knows little and cares less about the subject? Of course not. Most potential buyers for this volume know who Kay Aldridge is and to them she is not forgotten. Worst of all, he says that Kay was not a good actress. That may or may not be true, but she is still remembered by serial fans, so she had to have something to remain a favorite of the sort of people who might want to read this book. He's also a bit demeaning to serials in general. Once more, he is thoughtlessly alienating the people likely to be interested in his book.

Overall, I do not feel that Manago does Kay justice. As a Kay Aldridge fan, I found much to dislike here—the author even had the nerve to criticize Merrill T. McCord's 1979 book *Perils of Kay Aldridge*. I do not have that earlier book, but my familiarity with the general high quality of Mr. McCord's research and writing leads me to say that Mr. Manago could learn much from Mr. McCord, if he took the time.

Tin Pan Alley Girl: A Biography of Ann Ronell by Tighe E. Zimmers/**On the Sunny Side of the Street: The Life and Lyrics of Dorothy Fields** by Deborah Grace Winer

Tin Pan Alley Girl: A Biography of Ann Ronell by Tighe E. Zimmers (McFarland) is about a songwriter you might not know by name but you should know her work: "Rain on the Roof," "Willow Weep for Me," "Who's Afraid of the Big Bad Wolf?," etc.

I find Ronell a novel and intriguing subject for a biography, and was very much looking forward to reading about her. Zimmers does not disappoint and uncovered some interesting stories, particularly Ronell's participation in the screen versions of *The Gypsy Baron* (not made) and *One Touch of Venus* and her battles against Walt Disney over her maybe-maybe not co-authorship of "Who's Afraid of the Big Bad Wolf?" from the Oscar-winning cartoon *Three Little Pigs* (1933). (Frank Churchill is the main composer attached to the song, with Ronell given an "additional lyrics" credit.) The author had access to Ronell's papers, a valuable resource.

Ronell seemed to get tangled into a bunch of lawsuits and comes across as a bit cranky, but it adds drama to the book. Her relationship with her husband, producer Lester Cowan, is discussed, and I couldn't help noticing that she threw away her peak years on him and his needs.

Despite the author's elevated view of Ms. Ronell's successes, she did not have a large number of hits. This is no reflection on Ronell or her talent. Zimmers falls into the category of authors who feel they have to tear others down to make their subject look better. Their subjects' talent and successes should stand on their own. It's easy to fall into this trap and, as an author myself, I had to overcome this in my early writings. Ronell was a versatile songwriter and handled different styles, all expertly, and she was unique—and should be treated that way.

Ronell was Oscar-nominated for Best Music, Original Song for "Linda" from *The Story of G.I. Joe* (1945). It's a lovely song but, like it or not, Jack Lawrence's hit song of the same name from 1946 (inspired by then-infant Linda McCartney) was a bigger hit and is better remembered. Musically, it can't compare to Ronell's song, but that's life. Pretending otherwise is pointless.

Parts of the book are written for those who understand music, but the general musical fan will not be able to follow the complicated descriptions. Only a few lyrics are reprinted. While this is a shortcoming, it is understandable because of music rights. But this leads to Zimmers analyzing the songs and this gets sticky for the layman.

The biographical narrative is out of order, which results in some repetition. Anna Maria Alberghetti shouldn't be talked about in the section covering the 1930s.

The 40-plus photos are wonderful, a standout being Ronell on the *One Touch of Venus* set with Ava Gardner and Olga San Juan.

If this book was better-organized and the text tightened, it would have been exceptional. There's a lot of gold here which makes it ultimately worthwhile. I learned a great deal about someone who should be remembered. When was the last time *you* read about Ronell??

Zimmers pretty much brushes off Dorothy Fields, a librettist and lyricist who had more recognizable songs than Ann Ronell: "The Way You Look Tonight" (Oscar winner), "On the Sunny Side of the Street," "April Snow," "Make the Man Love Me," "Don't Blame Me," "A Fine Romance," "I Can't Give You Anything But Love," "I'm in the Mood for Love," "You Couldn't Be Cuter," "Big Spender," "Exactly Like You," "Close As Pages in a Book," "I Won't Dance," "Stars in My Eyes," "I Feel a Song Comin' On," "Lovely to Look At," "Pick Yourself Up," "Remind Me," "April Fooled Me," "Bojangles of Harlem," "Thank You for a Lovely Evening," "If My Friends Could See Me Now," "Blue Again," "I Dream Too Much," "Diga Diga Doo," "Serenade for a Wealthy Widow," "I Must Have That Man" and many more. Her major collaborators include Jimmy McHugh, Jerome Kern and Cy Coleman. She came from a show business family: Her father was vaudevillian Lew Fields and her brothers, Joseph and Herbert, were also Broadway stalwarts as producers and writers. Does that make her better than Ronell? No, but to pretend that Ronell was *it* during the early days is unfair, to say the least, and short-sighted.

The best book about Fields is **On the Sunny Side of the Street: The Life and Lyrics of Dorothy Fields** by Deborah Grace Winer (Schirmer Trade Books). Winer is one of the better writers of musical books, and certainly my favorite, and I wish she had more books published. She is the author of *The Night and the Music: Rosemary Clooney, Barbara Cook & Julie Wilson Inside the World of Cabaret* (see above), as well as *Sing Out Louise!: 150 Stars of the Musical Theatre Remember 50 Years on Broadway* and *I Remember Too Much: Eighty-Nine Opera Stars Speak Candidly About Their Work, Their Lives, and Their Colleagues* (the last two with Dennis McGovern).

On the Sunny Side of the Street: The Life and Lyrics of Dorothy Fields is a fine mixture of biography and song discussion (the latter aimed towards the average music lover). The bio doesn't go too deep; for instance, the author mentions Dorothy being an alcoholic, but it is dropped casually into the text and left there without further comment.

Otherwise, the narrative is swift and engaging and goes by very quickly, very pleasantly. The author hits all the right notes and a lot of lyrics are reprinted, which enhances the discussion.

The production is extremely inventive, with loads of sidebars and photos. It's a nice-looking book. It's not a riveting biography by any means, but I learned the essentials about the songs I love and a few personal items about Fields. Some books are just enjoyable and don't have to be in-depth reads.

※

Turner Classic Movies Presents Leonard Maltin's Classic Movie Guide: From the Silent Era Through 1965: Third Edition

The latest **Turner Classic Movies Presents Leonard Maltin's Classic Movie Guide: From the Silent Era Through 1965: Third Edition** (Penguin) is out—the last edition was printed in 2010. Entirely separated from Maltin's other, discontinued *Movie Guide* (covering modern films), this classic volume will hopefully continue. Now that TCM has stamped their name on the title, I hope so, because we need this. You could present me with a thousand different websites with movie information and I would still trust Maltin head and shoulders above the rest; at least he consults film credits to get it right. (His quest to place a proper comma or exclamation point in the song title "Ah! Sweet Mystery of Life" is wonderful.) This is a valuable resource. It is the only reference I use to properly check actor names and film titles when I am in doubt. I see that Tom Weaver is now associated as one of the editors, and that bodes very well for this as a definitive book. Each edition keeps getting better, this guide boasting revised and updated reviews, expanded indexes, a list of personal recommendations, and more than 200 new entries. And there is a respect for film you won't find elsewhere (certainly not in many of the so-called IMDb "reviews"): "Part of the fun of being an old-movie buff is coming upon a hidden gem," writes Maltin, "a film that slipped through the cracks and didn't get the attention it deserved when it was new. I hope this book will lead you to some personal discoveries that you can share with like-minded friends." My kind of book.

Unsung Hollywood Musicals of the Golden Era: 50 Overlooked Films and Their Stars, 1929–1939 by Edwin M. Bradley/Marjorie White: Her Life and Work
by Gary Olszewski

Edwin M. Bradley's focus in **Unsung Hollywood Musicals of the Golden Era: 50 Overlooked Films and Their Stars, 1929–1939** (McFarland) is one that I wholeheartedly approve. "I have chosen to encompass (mainly) efforts by short-lived stars of (mainly) secondary musicals during the first decade or so of the genre," he writes. This is a path less traveled by historians and it is handled well by Bradley, an excellent writer and keen observer, who adds, "These 'lesser' folks, and their films, deserve to be rescued from obscurity, even if only in this account." The concentration is on "minor" musicals of Fox, Paramount, Universal and Poverty Row: *Weary River, Lucky Boy, The Battle of Paris* (all 1929), *Lord Byron of Broadway, Oh, Sailor, Behave!, Paradise Island, Queen High* (all 1930), *Hello, Everybody!, International House, Melody Cruise, Moonlight and Pretzels, I Am Suzanne!, The Phantom Broadcast, Dance, Girl, Dance, Rainbow Over Broadway, Broadway Thru a Keyhole, Myrt and Marge, Torch Singer* (all 1933), *Wake Up and Dream, Let's Fall in Love, Moulin Rouge, Bottoms Up, Music in the Air, Girl o' My Dreams, Down to Their Last Yacht, Harold Teen, Little Miss Marker, Shoot the Works, One Hour Late, Gift of Gab* (all 1934), *Love in Bloom, Under the Pampas Moon, The Shadow of Silk Lennox, Dizzy Dames, The Old Homestead, Lottery Lover, Paddy O'Day* (all 1935), *Banjo on My Knee, The Music Goes 'Round, Frankie and Johnnie, Stage Struck* (all 1936), *Talent Scout, Ready, Willing and Able, Music for Madame, Top of the Town, New Faces of 1937, The Hit Parade, Manhattan Merry-Go-Round* (all 1937), *Swing Your Lady* (1938), and *The Ice Follies of 1939* (1939).

Instead of names such as Bing Crosby, Fred Astaire, Alice Faye, Judy Garland, Jeanette MacDonald and Nelson Eddy *et al.*, Bradley's book serves up George Jessel, Charles Kaley, Charles King (the singer, not the Western bad guy), Stanley Smith, Russ

Columbo, Hal LeRoy, Dorothy Dell, Joe Morrison, Peggy Fears, Kate Smith, Harry Richman, Jeanne Madden, Lee Dixon, Nino Martini, Phil Harris, Lawrence Gray, Phil Regan, etc. My kind of book! Covered, too, are actors-turned-singers (e.g., Claudette Colbert) and there are nice sections about producer Lou Brock and Peggy Hopkins Joyce.

Bradley used a myriad of sources, particularly publications from the time when these films were new. Far from "fluff," they reflect how actors and movies were then perceived and puts everything in the context of the times. Just because we, in 2016, think a movie is minor, this doesn't necessarily mean it was in, say, 1933. I am thinking specifically of *Moonlight and Pretzels*. The same goes for actors and singers who were well-known then but whose stars have dimmed over time.

Each chapter gives cast-crew credits, short synopses, reviews and a behind-the-scenes look at the production and information about the players. Some films have more involved and interesting histories than others, notably *Broadway Thru a Keyhole, Melody Cruise, New Faces of 1937* and *Frankie and Johnnie*. I am more than happy with Bradley's thorough treatment here and I learned a lot. Where has Charles Kaley been all my life?? Bradley also gives his own assessments of the movies. I might not agree with his critique of *Top of the Town* and star Doris Nolan's performance, but I respect the way he explains himself.

There's also a lot of fun here. I literally laughed out loud—and read it to all who would listen—at his description of a 1994 UCLA screening of *Lucky Boy*: "Rose Marie was in attendance, sitting next to Ron Hutchinson of the Vitaphone Project. When the third rendition of 'My Mother's Eyes' began, she leaned over to Hutchinson and said, 'I can't take it another time,' and exited the theater." Two phrases I really liked: "*The Battle of Paris* wielded a 10-cent script by Gene Markey to go with its million-dollar names" and "...an obvious attempt by [Lou] Brock to out–Busby Warner Bros. master Berkeley." His description of character actor

Paul Hurst is spot-on: "The type of fellow who can get into a fight and then can't remember why."

It's a very enjoyable, informative read, with some terrific photos. This could very well be one of my favorite books about musicals. I really appreciated the effort and his redirection of the spotlight on lesser-known movies, actors and singers. Bradley knows his stuff. He is also the author of *The First Hollywood Musicals* and *The First Hollywood Sound Shorts, 1926-1931*, both available from McFarland.

One singer-actress who does not come up in Bradley's book is the wonderful Marjorie White (1904-35), memorable in supporting roles in the early musicals *Sunny Side Up* (1929) and *Just Imagine* (1930), and as the lead in *Happy Days* (1930) and *New Movietone Follies of 1930*. With Thelma White (no relation), she performed in vaudeville as the White Sisters.

Author Gary Olszewski claimed it took him seven years to research and write **Marjorie White: Her Life and Work** (Bear-Manor). There must have been an awful lot of breaks during these years for him to come up with the pittance we see here. At less than 100 pages, several of which are blank(!), it is more like a pamphlet, one that could practically fit in a #10 letter envelope. A friend called it "vaguely book-esque."

I knew I was in trouble when I read, "One could say that what Garbo was to drama, and Jean Harlow to sex appeal, Marjorie was to comic entertainment." Actually, Marjorie White is practically unknown except to diehard musical fans. There's a torrent of typos, too many caps, parentheses that never close, and rambling passages. But I don't think editors could have fixed this. Yes, they could have cleaned up the punctuation, spelling errors, and non-sentences, but I'm wondering if what this book needed was another writer entirely. Heck, it needed a writer, period. As well-meaning as Olszewski is, I wonder if he just doesn't understand how to tell a story or present information in an interesting way. Nothing jells. "This work results from the examination of newspaper articles, reviews of her work, and her partner Thelma White's book, *Thelma Who? Almost 100 Years in Show Biz*. So as not to infringe on any copyrights, and more importantly, not to insult her or Thelma's memory, anything I quote verbatim/directly I disclose, in full, the source, author and date (if known)." Isn't this called a bibliography?? Everyone does it, Gary, and you don't need to explain it as if you are blazing a new trail.

I still don't understand why it took him seven years to research this. Did he track her family's history back to the Middle Ages, and then withhold all that information from us? I once researched White for three days—and I found more material than Olszewski includes here. He fails to mention so many interesting tidbits, reviews, etc., pertaining to her. I am very detail-oriented when I write and research, and this "book" is lacking in interesting details. Also, Olszewski's style is to write *at* us, not *to* us. "Look at me, I researched this obscure, long-forgotten actress" seems to be the between-the-lines message. Quoting whole articles verbatim is always unnecessary, and all too often it leads to repeating information or including false information.

Even at 90-odd (very odd) pages, he wastes a lot of space on people connected to Marjorie. There are chapters on Fred Stone, Eddie Tierney, Winfield R. Sheehan ("biographical information on him is scarce, if not semi-nonexistent," so his chapter is "culled" from Wikipedia), and her sister, Belva Harmony Guthrie. After two blank pages, we have a chapter on the Duncan Sisters. Why? He admits the only reason they are here is because the White Sisters took over roles the Duncans originated in *Tip Top* and *Topsy and Eva*. Oh, and "Another connection is a bit more personal: My mother remembers seeing the Duncans on stage in Chicago as a young girl in the 1930s." Oh, now I understand. Presumably, if his mom had seen the Hans Kasemann Midgets or Daisy and Violet Hilton, he would have included chapters on them, too.

I was also confused by this: "Evelyn, the older sister of Rosetta and Vivian [Duncan], did more behind-the-scenes work, such as writing and producing their acts, and rarely actually played on stage with them. She was to them, workwise and business-wise, what Moe Howard was to the Three Stooges (no pun intended)."

Pun? What pun? The writer probably had second thoughts about comparing the lady to Moe, who always played a violent halfwit, and wanted to convey "no offense intended" or "no harm meant" or something like that.

One of the book's better points is that it does have some interesting information on Marjorie's husband Eddie Tierney, especially in regards to his life after her death. However, this is an unconventional "biography," to say the least, and the author puts himself into the narrative way too much.

About *Just Imagine*: "I'll capsulize this by stating that I'm a biographer, not a film critic, so I'll try not to go into too much detail describing this Z-grade atrocity of 1930 sci-fi fantasy that even Marjorie White couldn't save, through her character 'D-6.'"

Then there is the weird comment at the end of his short paragraph about *Her Bodyguard* (1933), in which he wastes time saying it's a lost film, but then he ends it with "IT'S ALIVE! IT'S ALIVE! I'VE FOUND IT! AND IT SUCKS!!" Ai yi yi.

The March of Time (1930) and *Broadway to Hollywood* (1933): "Even though both films are truly gone, rumor persists that a copy of *Broadway to Hollywood* is out there somewhere." Too bad he never heard the rumor that Turner Classic Movies broadcast it around the world and it was seen by every Marjorie White fan, minus one.

Often, he doesn't tell us what Marjorie does in her movies. About *Possessed* (1931), he writes, "Her scene is vital to the storyline, and her character (in Marjorie's first try at serious semi-dramatic acting) comes across quite well as the perfect antithesis to the stuffed-shirt 'hoi polloi' who fill out the story." Clear as mud. You'll notice that the author's use of "hoi polloi" was nonsensical. He was probably thinking of "hoity toity."

Once again demonstrating a weakness in describing things accurately, he claims that RKO is the "poverty row" cousin of Fox.

"*Woman Haters* is probably the best known and most thoroughly documented of all Marjorie White films, so there is no need to cover its description here. ...The complete story of how this one was put together can be found on page 78 of Moe Howard's book, *Moe Howard and the Three Stooges*." Okay, that was lazy. An author shouldn't encourage readers to set his book aside to look at another book. Because, believe me, this book is the perfect example of the old zinger, "Once you put it down, you can't pick it up."

"A son was born April 1930 to her brother Orville and his wife in Toronto. I find this very interesting for the following reason: with that child born in 1930, in his adult years he would have a family of his own, and his children would today be roughly aged 60 (the age of your author at this writing). If their offspring have children and grandchildren, as I do, this means I've opened the doors on six generations (to date 2008) of Marjorie White's family. I find this simply astounding, and emotionally rewarding." Good for you! And this is important to note … because…?

The author says that Marjorie and Thelma White were close friends, but then later quotes Thelma's book saying they were not close. Indeed, if you read Thelma's book, they had some issues that are left unmentioned here.

"Studying the period pictures, and using my knowledge of urban development of most major cities, I've determined that Winnipeg was no different in its development from most others in North America in that period." His Google Map search image "shows" us Marjorie's birthplace and the area in which the family lived. Well, not really. It's just a line drawing with no details—which could sum up this book nicely. I also can't help but wonder: If it took him seven years to do the small amount of research seen here, how long did it take him to become an expert on the urban development of most major cities?

"Though long ago, the story of Marjorie White truly embodies the joys and sorrows, hopes and dreams of our lives today." It's too bad he did not actually manage to convey this. This book is a patchwork of ideas, personal meanderings and incomplete information. The author could have described Marjorie's film roles, talked more about the Winnipeg Kiddies and her stint with them, and presented her life in a more coherent manner. For an excellent write-up about Marjorie, I direct you to Eve Golden's 2012 "Queen of the Dead" appreciation available at https://ladailymir-ror.com/2012/11/06/eve-golden-queen-of-the-dead-marjorie-white/. It makes me wish that Eve had written a book on Marjorie White. This "book" is awful, no pun intended.

When Dracula Met Frankenstein: My Years Making Drive-In Movies with Al Adamson
by Sam Sherman

Producer-writer Sam Sherman is one of the great exploitation filmmakers, so I was thrilled when I learned that he had written a book about his film experiences, **When Dracula Met Franken-stein: My Years Making Drive-In Movies with Al Adamson**, with a foreword by writer-director John A. Russo and an after-word by Tom Weaver (Murania Press). In 1968, with Al Adamson and Dan Kennis, Sherman co-founded Independent-Internation-al Pictures, a production and distribution company. In addition to making movies, they took existing films and shot additional footage, in order to create a "new" movie.

The volume is in two parts; the first deals with the produc-tion side (financing, casting, marketing, distribution), the second a film-by-film listing with Sherman's well-written comments: *Angel's Wild Women* (1972), *Black Heat* (1976), *Blazing Steward-esses* (1975), *The Bloody Dead* (aka *The Blue Hand*, 1967), *Brain of Blood* (1971), *Cinderella 2000* (1977), *Doctor Dracula* (aka *Luci-fer's Women*, 1978), *Dracula vs. Frankenstein* (1971), *The Dynamite Brothers* (aka *Stud Brown*, 1974), *Exorcism at Midnight* (aka *Naked Evil*, 1966), *Five Bloody Graves* (1969), *Frankenstein's Bloody Terror* (1971), *Girls for Rent* (1974), *Horror of the Blood Monsters* (1970), *In Search of Dracula* (1975), *Mean Mother* (1973), *The Naughty Stewardesses* (1973), *Nurse Sherri* (1978), *Psycho a Go-Go* (aka *Man with the Synthetic Brain* and *Blood of Ghastly Horror*, 1965), *Raid-*

ers of the Living Dead (1986), *Satan's Sadists* (1969), *Team-Mates* (1978), and *Uncle Tom's Cabin* (1965/1977). As you can see by this list, the movies are in alphabetical order, not by release date. In my opinion, this is the book's only fault; it would have made more sense to put them in production order.

An old-movie fan from way back, Sherman cast actors Lawrence Tierney, Kent Taylor, Scott Brady, Russ Tamblyn, Paul Naschy, Harry and Jimmy Ritz, John Carradine, Donald Barry, Yvonne De Carlo, Reed Hadley, Grant Williams, Jim Davis, J. Carrol Naish, Lon Chaney, Jr., Angelo Rossitto, Aldo Ray, Bob Allen, Paula Raymond, Zita Johann, Robert Livingston (and others) in their movies. In fact, Sherman considers Livingston his all-time favorite!

There are many nice scene stills and behind-the-scenes photos. I especially like the caption for a screen grab from the Philippine-made *Tagani* (which Sherman transformed into *Horror of the Blood Monsters*). My favorite, though, is a *Blazing Stewardesses* candid of Donald Barry and Robert Livingston conversing on the set. The chapter on the latter is also my favorite, as Sherman recounts that Tex Ritter's *The Mystery of the Hooded Horsemen* (1937) was an inspiration and that he tried unsuccessfully to get Rita Hayworth for the part ultimately played by Yvonne De Carlo.

Sherman doesn't just tell us his memories of working with the actors. He relates how the films were made, what problems they faced during production, what happened when they ran out of money or when the film lab went out of business. When it came to the movies he and his company reissued, he lets us in on the process of editing, filming new scenes and retitling. Movie fans will absolutely love this book!

Why I Failed Charm School: A Memoir
by Tisha Sterling

Barbara Feldon's keen writing (with no typos!) in her book (see above) spoiled me. Tisha Sterling, the daughter of Ann Sothern and Robert Sterling, started acting in the 1960s on television (she was even on an episode of *Get Smart*) but she's best known for the movies *Village of the Giants* (1965), *Coogan's Bluff* (1968) and *The Whales of August* (1987), in the latter playing a younger version of her mother. Her book, **Why I Failed Charm School: A Memoir**, is one wild ride—and I don't mean just the typographical errors, misplaced apostrophes, and the fact that she failed English class, too.

If you are an Ann Sothern fan, proceed with caution. The picture it presents of Ann is not flattering; she was a complicated lady, unhappy, wanting to be in control, addicted to food, and suffering from back pain. Her relationship with her daughter was not an easy one. This came mainly from Tisha's drug and alcohol addictions and her ability to attract the wrong men. One of those men: Arthur Lake's son! That was pretty shocking, as was the photo of him: He looked like a hot, buff Dagwood Bumstead, if you can picture that and not be scarred by the image. The little interlude about the Lakes, father, son and mother Patricia Van Cleve, was a bit disturbing, but probably typical, as they were all alcoholics. Tisha was at the house when Senior died. Pat, as many of you know, was secretly the daughter of Marion Davies and William Randolph Hearst but was passed off as the child of Davies' sister Rose. The story of Pat's behavior at her husband's funeral is koo-koo!

Speaking of alcoholics, we learn that Tisha's father Robert Sterling was one and he was a cold, distant man. I believe the only people who came off well and not dysfunctional are Anne Jeffreys (Sterling's second wife) and Roger Pryor (Sothern's first husband). Tisha comes across as a real whiner—and winer—but she has the right to complain about every little thing her mother ever did or didn't do for her. The negativity is a little wearing, and her rambling, redundant narrative shifts haphazardly through time and space. Organization and editing would have made this better. Also, I wish she knew more about her parents' careers, and that she had written more about her own work. Tisha was a good actress before she got derailed by her "demons."

Wild Wild Westerners: A Roundup of Interviews with Western Movie and TV Veterans
by Tom Weaver

Classic Images readers know Tom Weaver has done many books talking with actors, writers, directors and the like about horror and science fiction films. **Wild Wild Westerners: A Roundup of Interviews with Western Movie and TV Veterans** (BearManor) is a big U-turn in subject matter but everything that made Weaver the leading interviewer chatting with horror/sci-fi people is here. By the way, all the interviews appeared originally in the print publication *Western Clippings*. Boyd Magers, who publishes it, wrote the book's foreword.

It's a slim volume, but packs a roundhouse punch. Here are the interviewees: Charlotte Austin, Kenneth Chase (makeup man on TV's *The Wild Wild West*), Gary Clarke, Robert Clarke, Robert Colbert, Lisa Davis, Maury Dexter (director), Ed Faulkner, Andrew J. Fenady (producer of *The Rebel*), Pat Fielder (*Rifleman* writer), Beryl Braithwaite Hart (actor John Hart's widow, here talking about Hart, TV's *Hawkeye and the Last of the Mohicans* and Lon Chaney), Richard Kline (cinematographer, talking about Charles Starrett), June Lockhart, Fess Parker, Bill Phipps, Paul Picerni, Ann Robinson, Jo Ann Sayers and Paul Wurtzel.

Weaver, as always, gets the goods. I was particularly interested in Robert Clarke's memories of working at RKO and Andrew J. Fenady recalling Nick Adams and the TV series *The Rebel*. I believe this is the first I ever read about a made-for-television movie Ann Robinson did with Johnny Carpenter, *The Rimrocker* (1949). Try to look it up elsewhere and you'll find nothing; here, the delightful Robinson tells the behind-the-scenes story (and provides photos which just barely escaped destruction in a house fire a few years ago). Something that really intrigued me was Lisa Davis' memory of *Fury at Gunsight Pass* (1956). The accepted version of how her co-star Richard Long found out about his wife Suzan Ball's death was at her deathbed where, dramatically, she said the word "Tony"—referring to her "great love" Anthony Quinn. The moment supposedly tormented Long for the rest of his life. Here, Davis says that Long was with her, on the set of *Fury*, when he was told the news of her death by his brother-in-law, Marshall Thompson (and no mention of "Tony").

I like that Weaver's books often debunk longstanding myths. He is a good writer, asks the right questions (harder than it seems) and gets more out of his subjects than anyone else. Sad to say, even though the book is only a few years old, half (or more) of these people have already passed away.

I could have done without Chuck Connors on the cover, though. Yes, Connors is talked about within, but he is not a subject of an interview and it gives out the wrong message. Fess Parker should have been the cover boy.

Wings and Other Recollections of Early Hollywood: Narrated by Richard Arlen to Maxine Koolish and Edited by Judy Watson

I have long been tormented by Hollywood memoirs we will never see. George Marshall, Bruce Cabot, Robert Cummings, Don DeFore, Robert Hutton, Johnnie Johnston, Edmund Purdom, John Ireland and others have all written autobiographies that have never been published. Imagine my delight when I found that one of my favorite actors, Richard Arlen, had written one...and it has been published, quite under the radar, through Amazon's Cre-ateSpace.

For the last 13 years of his life, Arlen (1899-1976) was separated from his third wife, Margaret Kinsella, and in a relationship with his secretary, Maxine Koolish. (Unlike other books of this type, this one features photos of the two together.) Maxine's daughter, Judy Watson, found amongst her late mother's things a collection of photographs, books, letters, manuscripts, tapes and diaries per-taining to Arlen. Maxine had been helping Arlen with his autobi-ography. After he died, the book was never completed.

The title Miss Watson decided to go with was the ill-advised **Wings and Other Recollections of Early Hollywood: Narrated by Richard Arlen to Maxine Koolish and Edited by Judy Wat-son.** When I first noticed this, I thought it was a DVD about Arlen's most famous movie, the silent classic and Oscar-winner *Wings* (1927). They probably felt *Wings* was the main selling point, but it's just confusing. The grainy cover photo of Arlen in an air-plane from *Wings* is really not an eye-catching image.

I truly wanted to love this book. I was interested in Arlen's life and career and curious as to what he had to say about the people he worked with.

It starts off with Watson giving us a brief history of her mother and how she came to meet Arlen. There are some revealing passages about Arlen's alcoholism: "Down on his luck, his money gone, and drinking heavily, Richard was in a place he could no longer under-stand when he met Mother. Maxine rescued him from lost, drunken binges." I wish Maxine had chronicled her years with Arlen.

The first chapters are charming and appealing, with Arlen talk-ing about his childhood in Minnesota ("one glorious adventure for a boy of my era") and the odd jobs he took to earn a living. Espe-cially enjoyable are his recollections of his stage work, wearing a "small black Dutch bob wig"; his bumbling attempts at being an actor included getting lost in the folds of the curtain and goosing the leading man with a sword and knocking him into the orchestra pit. His description of actor Arthur Edmund Carewe is hilarious.

In the early 1920s, Arlen arrived in Los Angeles, did extra work in movies and had jobs in a film lab and as a camera assistant. These memories are blessed with Arlen's self-deprecating humor, and they flow nicely. Especially amusing is his recall of the indie *Vengeance of the Deep* (1923), in which he played his first featured role. There are also special chapters about his friendships with Gary Cooper, Walter Huston, Laurel & Hardy and the Gabor Sisters, and his memories of the first Academy Awards. A few other tidbits are devoted to Harry Cohn and Charles Laughton.

The book pretty much takes a nosedive when we get to *Wings*. In 1976, Koolish wrote Lonnie Raidor of the Society of World War I Aero Historians to obtain a program from their 1968 showing of *Wings*. She told him she was helping Arlen write a book about his life and she needed information about the movie. After supplying the brochure, Raidor replied, "A hint to the wise: Arlen was a World War I pilot—get him to detail some of his flying experiences during 1918. This will add zest to his biography." Well, there are no such flying experiences in this book—if he indeed had flying experiences in the Great War. About that *Wings* program: All the info is transcribed verbatim here (attributed, of course), and it seems Koolish and Watson did no other research on the movie.

There are a bunch of random chapters detailing Arlen's opinion on nightclubs, red cars, baseball at the beach, etc. There's absolutely no reason for a lengthy section called "History of Five Studios." Arlen is not a film historian and neither is Watson; she doesn't even attempt to correct his many, many mistakes. For my sanity, I am only including a few:

The Big Parade (1925) was MGM, not Fox.

The history of Fox here is wacky—Zanuck made stars of John Barrymore and Irene Rich?? There's also something about Al Jolson making his first talking picture for Fox in 1925, before *The Jazz Singer.* No idea.

Contrary to this book, Samuel Goldwyn was not ever a partner at MGM and had no role in decision-making there, despite the fact that the studio bore his name.

It is not true that, in 1934, William Powell, Kay Francis and Ruth Chatterton "didn't fare too well under Warner Brothers."

Min and Bill was not a series in the way of Andy Hardy. Marie Dressler and Wallace Beery were a popular team, but they did not play the same characters from film to film.

A lot of spelling mistakes: Wallace Berry (multiple times); Margaret Herrick Library not Martha Herrick Library; Louise Dresser not Louise Dressler; Merian C. Cooper not Marion Cooper; Thomas Meighan not Thomas Eighan (elsewhere it is spelled Meehan), etc.

There are numerous footnotes scattered about, describing people whom anyone reading a book about Richard Arlen would know. Yet when Arlen writes that he made two movies in England in the 1950s, he mentions *Devil's Harbor* (its U.S. title; it's actually *Devil's Point*) but then says, "Unfortunately, the other one escapes me." Watson doesn't even bother to look it up and include the name: *Stolen Time* (1955) aka *Blonde Blackmailer*.

What's here is sketchy, at best. Watson could have written a substantial biography about Arlen, utilizing all the material here and adding so much more. Koolish's voice is nowhere. Her relationship with Arlen should have been the focal point of this volume. The publicity says Koolish was a "born chronicler and storyteller," but this book fails to prove it.

If you are a fan of Arlen, however, you will enjoy some of what's here. Just don't expect him to be talking about many of his co-workers or the bulk of his movies.

Winnie Lightner: Tomboy of the Talkies
by David L. Lightner

Recently, I was watching an entertaining B called *I'll Fix It* (1934), starring Jack Holt and Mona Barrie. The secondary couple was played by Edward Brophy and Winnie Lightner, and they were so funny together. I got to thinking of Lightner and how I felt she ranked up there with Una Merkel and Iris Adrian as one of Hollywood's best female comics. I guess it didn't help that she did most of her work on stage and made very few movies. She could wisecrack with the best of 'em and was also a helluva singer.

Winnie Lightner: Tomboy of the Talkies by David L. Lightner (University Press of Mississippi) is a good biography of this neglected performer. Lightner starred in movies during the pre-Code era: *She Couldn't Say No, Hold Everything, The Life of the Party* (all 1930), *Sit Tight, Gold Dust Gertie, Side Show, Manhattan Parade* (all 1931), and *Play Girl* (1932). "In the best of them, she was the comic epitome of a strident feminist, dominating men and gleefully spurning conventional gender norms and moral values," writes the author (who is no relation to Winnie). Because many of her movies are either lost or rarely shown today, she is someone movie fans seldom discuss.

The author does a good job chronicling her stage and film work and her life before and after showbiz. There was too much plot related from *The Life of the Party*, but I loved the way the author described *Gold Diggers of Broadway* (1929), her first film, and her other movies.

This one should prove particularly interesting to musical fans. Lightner was a popular entertainer who has gotten lost in the shuffle. Excellent photos.

The Worldwide Film Noir Tradition: The Complete Reference to Classic Dark Cinema from America, Britain, France and Other Countries Across the Globe
by Spencer Selby

I make a point of reading every page of every book I review here. Since I began reviewing in 2001, there have been only a few instances where I could not finish reading something. The first was *Up from the Vault: Rare Thrillers of the 1920s and 1930s* by John T. Soister. And now it has happened again with **The Worldwide Film Noir Tradition: The Complete Reference to Classic Dark Cinema from America, Britain, France and Other Countries Across the Globe** by Spencer Selby (Sink Press).

Let me start by saying that Selby is a highly regarded authority on *film noir*. I like his *Dark City: The Film Noir* (McFarland) and consult it often. That book contains a list of 500 *noirs* with credits and short plot descriptions. This new book promised to be even better, a more comprehensive list of classic and proto-*noirs*: 796 films from the classic "American *Film Noir* Cycle," 177 "Classical French *Film Noir*," 338 examples of "Classical British *Film Noir*" and 257 *noirs* from such countries as Argentina, Austria, Belgium, Brazil, Canada, Chile, Czechoslovakia, Denmark, Egypt, Finland, East and West Germany, Greece, Hong Kong, Hungary, India, Italy, Japan, Lithuania, Mexico, Norway, Poland, South Korea, Spain, Switzerland and Turkey.

Sounds amazing, doesn't it? And it should have been, if only Selby had had an editor along for the ride. I got up to page 92 and finally had to stop—my head was throbbing. The number of errors and awkward sentences were mind-boggling and too much for this poor little girl to handle. Where do I even start?

Name misspellings: June Truesdale (instead of the correct Truesdell); David S. Horsely (instead of Horsley); Frederic March (instead of Fredric); Robert I. Richards (instead of Robert L. Richards); Berne Gilier (instead of Giler); Harvey Glass (instead of Gates); Garret Fort (instead of Garrett); Leonardo Barboni (instead of Leonida); Lewis W. Oconell (instead of O'Connell); Edward Albert (instead of Eddie; his son's name was Edward); Gordon Macrae (instead of MacRae); John Eldridge (instead of Eldredge); Joseph Cotton (instead of Cotten); Pedro Armandariz (instead of Armendáriz); Brian Donleavy (instead of Donlevy); Everette Sloane (instead of Everett); Roy William Neil (instead of Neill); Fred Zinneman (instead of Zinnemann); Rhue McClanahan (instead of Rue); Sylvia Sydney (instead of Sidney); Jane Mansfield (instead of Jayne); Edmund O'Brien (instead of Edmond); Edward Franz (instead of Eduard); J. Carroll Nash (instead of J. Carrol Naish); Chuck Conners (instead of Connors); Hugh Marlow (instead of Marlowe); Bordon Chase (instead of Borden); Nona Foch (instead of Nina); Katherine Hepburn (instead of Katharine); Richard Wharf (instead of Whorf); Douglas Dumbrille (instead of Douglass); Barbara Fuller (instead of Barbra); Phillip Tierney (instead of Philip Terry); De Forest Kelley (instead of DeForest); John Carrolll (instead of Carroll); Shelly Winters (instead of Shelley); Bill Williama (instead of Williams); Fay Emerson (instead of Faye); Joseph La Shelle (instead of LaShelle); Don Defore (instead of DeFore); Olivia De Havilland (instead of de Havilland); John Harrison (instead of Joan); Cornell Woolwich (instead of Woolrich); Edmond Lowe (instead of Edmund); Ronald Coleman (instead of Colman); Mervyn Le Roy (instead of LeRoy); Adolph Menjou (instead of Adolphe); Tomas Gomez (instead of Thomas); Lynn Roberts (instead of Lynne); Lawrence Olivier (instead of Laurence); Lenore Albert (instead of Aubert); Hugh Beamont (instead of Beaumont); Lowell Gillmore (instead of Gilmore); Jody Lawrence (instead of Lawrance); Roddy MacDowell (instead of McDowall); Walter Mathau (instead of Matthau); Same Levene (instead of Sam); and the list goes on and on.

Ludicrous, isn't it? I can see if you have a couple of misspellings here and there—it happens to the best of us—but there was just a ridiculous number of errors in this book. Some names, such as Joseph Cotten's, were wrong numerous times. How can you possibly take a book seriously when there are so many errors?

The problems do not stop there. The short plot blurbs are often clumsily written, sometimes missing words or adding unnecessary ones, thereby rendering the sentences difficult to follow. Sometimes the plot descriptions sounded weird, or vague or trite, or just plain wrong; other times, he gives away the endings as with *Caged* and *The Maltese Falcon*).

Flesh and Fury: Deaf mute boxer gets an operation, doesn't like what he hears as a result.

Autumn Leaves: Lonely spinster is courted by a man half her age, but that's not the real problem.

Decoy: A dying femme fatale tells police what she's been through trying to get loot hidden by her partner before he was captured and executed.

Don't Bother to Knock: Airline pilot romances a girl who's taken a job babysitting in hotel room across the hall, soon realizes she's totally deranged.

Lure of the Swamp: Bayou boat guide accepts job dropping off man in swamp that is turns out to be bank robber and is discovered dead. The guide must decide whether to capitalize, do nothing or go to police.

The Mugger: Police psychiatrist works to catch mugger who that leaves scars on victims' faces.

Naked Alibi: Police detective loses his job for roughing up suspect in murder case, travels to Mexico to prove he was right.

High Sierra: Aging criminal is released from prison so he can pull casino heist. [Not much of a reason to release a man from prison!] Most of the gang is killed, he is betrayed and dashes for freedom with sad girl by his side.

Dial Red O: War-torn vet escapes from mental ward looking for his wife. She is killed and is jailed but escapes again.

And, for some reason, I laughed at his "pithy" recap of *I Want to Live!*: "Sordid life of life of woman on death row, who was a prostitute, thief, drug addict, but maybe not guilty of murder." It doesn't help that he repeats "life of."

The author doesn't seem to know the difference between "fiancée" and "fiancé" or the proper usage of "that" and "who." Also, the word "beau" applies to men only, you do not call a woman that—except in this book. Unless one has body odor, the correct phrase is not "reek havoc," but "wreak havoc."

Some wrong movie info: The photography for *Abandoned* (1949) was by William H. Daniels, not David S. Horsley. Just as Gert Anderson was the camera operator for *All the King's Men* (1949), he was not the photographer—that was Burnett Guffey.

You get the idea, and it's not pretty. I truly wanted to like this book, and had high hopes for it, but there were just too many mistakes. The list of *film noirs* is still viable and it's the most comprehensive yet and can certainly serve as a checklist...but are you willing to pay $80 for a checklist? Selby needs to get an editor to go over this carefully and fix all the errors, and then maybe this will be worth the price. Photos are pretty dreadful, too, a lot of smallish screen grabs reproduced poorly. As hard as it is to believe, this book on *film noir* has a pink cover—that's right, PINK. Ugh.

Afterword

September 2024 will mark my 29th year writing for *Classic Images*. The way it all came about was a strange twist of fate: A friend was in a Washington State mall looking through movie memorabilia when she met a lady named Peggy Biller. They got to talking about their favorite actors. When Peggy mentioned Van Johnson, my friend said she knew another Van Fan, and gave Peggy my address. Peggy and I started to correspond and then began talking on the phone. It was Peggy who phoned editor Bob King and requested a Van Johnson article. Bob said that if someone would write one, he would print it—and Peggy suggested me. Bob took a chance those many years ago. My Van Johnson article was less than stellar, but he printed it and encouraged me to continue writing. I will always be indebted to Peggy for helping me and to Bob for following through. Another one of my early articles was on Phil Harris, who had just died. His widow Alice Faye called me to tell me how much she enjoyed it. That was quite a moment for me!

It seems I have always loved movies. My mom was a big reason for that: As I was growing up, she always had an old movie on TV. Back in the 1940s, long before my time, she used to frequent a movie theater in Yonkers, New York, where they showed mostly B movies, and she remembered seeing a lot of Monograms. For the time, she had "odd" taste for a teenager: Her favorites included Mickey Rooney, Jimmy Lydon, Claudette Colbert, Ginny Simms,

Jack Smith, Forrest Tucker, Phil Harris, Irene Dunne, etc. She was into musicals and war movies (*Objective, Burma!* was her favorite).

I watched a wide variety of movies and old TV series even before I was a teenager. I loved *The Lone Ranger*, Popeye, the Bowery Boys, Charlie Chan, *The Outer Limits*, the Marx Brothers, *I Love Lucy*, Godzilla, kung fu movies, etc. *Flash Gordon* (1936) started my love of serials. *Don Winslow of the Navy* (1942), *Zorro's Fighting Legion* (1939) and *The Lost City* (1935) followed—and I was hooked! *Matinee at the Bijou* premiered when I was about ten years old, and I was able to watch more B movies and shorts.

Needless to say, my 1970s-80s childhood was not typical. In fourth grade, I wrote a book report on Max Fleischer. My teacher took one look at it and remarked, "You are a strange little girl." I guess I was! I read old comic books, pulps, mystery novels and the Dick Tracy and Little Orphan Annie comic strips, listened to big band music, and sought out more obscure movies on television. I had scrapbooks devoted to B movie actors.

Leonard Maltin was my first inspiration. His book *Movie Comedy Teams* started it all. It was through reading him and James Robert Parish that I decided that I wanted to be a film historian. I read every movie book in my school library, mostly during lunch. At 12, I began writing down the titles of every movie I watched, complete with date and cast. I continued that for many years.

Through it all, my mother remained my biggest booster (and the one I watched movies with). She would always ask who the secondary and bit players were, sparking my interest in the obscure actors. We wondered what *their* stories were. While I like the big stars, it was the actors who barely got noticed that interested me the most.

An influential book was Danny Peary's *Guide for the Film Fanatic*, which came out when I was 16. I was already into an eclectic mix of movies, but Peary's ideas broadened my taste considerably. He frowned upon fans who judged a movie by its status, or what other people thought of it. A two-star movie, he wrote, might be just as interesting, if not more so, than a three- or four-star one. I have never truly hated a movie because I always find something to enjoy.

After I started writing for *Classic Images*, I came in contact with writer Doug McClelland, who became my mentor. He constantly encouraged me and found something to praise even in my worst articles (and there were stinkers!). He taught me, among other things, to form my own opinions; don't rely on what other writers have already presented; don't be afraid to go against the popular consensus. He was always driven to write about lesser-known actors and actresses. When he did his two-part article on Maris Wrixon, he was asked, "Why Maris?" and not, say, Bette Davis? Ever the movie lover, Doug replied, "Maris needs it, Bette doesn't." That last sentence has stayed with me to this day.

It was Doug who literally yelled at me in 2001 to become book reviewer for *Classic Images*, even though I was unsure I could handle it. The first time I panned a book, I got a series of nasty letters from the author. Yes, a *series* of nasty letters. It made me a little uneasy, but Doug was ecstatic: "Don't worry about that guy! Write what you want; give your opinion, no matter how much it hurts 'em. Who are you trying to please? Why do you care? Who are they to you? Tell the truth!" With that, I let loose.

Doug was instrumental in helping me improve my writing, but there were others. Bob King, of course, has been a huge help in trying to fix my articles. Ray Hagen was another. We "met" through the now–sadly-defunct Movie-Entertainment Book Club due to our love of the same singers. Ray is probably the smartest person I've ever known and a really perceptive guy. At first, I found him a bit cynical but I came to see that his was a realistic view of life that I didn't yet understand. I am thankful that he took the time to brutally critique my writing and make me less of a wuss. He made me look at the films I love more sensibly and I am grateful for that. With Ray, I wrote the book *Killer Tomatoes: Fifteen Tough Film Dames* in 2004. It was the first of my seven books; *Hollywood's Hard-Luck Ladies: 23 Actresses Who Suffered Early Deaths, Accidents, Missteps, Illnesses and Tragedies* is my latest.

These almost-30 years with *Classic Images* (and *Films of the Golden Age*) have been wonderful, and I am now a contributing editor. I interviewed numerous actors for articles I've done (e.g., Felix Knight, Joan Leslie, Virginia Mayo, Tony Martin, etc.) and have read good and awful books. Bob King has given me an outlet to write about obscure actors. What other magazine would okay articles on Victoria Faust and Leni Lynn?

I am happy to note that I have improved much after all these years. Again, I could not have done it without the people I've mentioned. I hope to continue here for a few more years. I have a lot more actors to write about, and many more books to review.

Just a note: *Classic Images* and *Films of the Golden Age* are both print publications, they are not available online. Please support these magazines by subscribing. Call editor Bob King at 563-383-2343, or email him at bob.king@lee.net. These are the last two magazines dealing with all kinds of movies, from the silent era to the 1960s.

And, remember, tell 'em you read about it in *Classic Images*!

List of Publishers and Writer Websites:

https://alankrode.com/
Allen & Unwin: https://www.allenandunwin.com/
https://www.amazon.com/
www.anndvorak.com
Applause: https://www.applause.com/
https://www.barbarafeldon.com
BearManor Media: https://www.bearmanormedia.com/
Belle Publishing: https://www.ipgbook.com/belle-publishing-llc-publisher-BLE.php
https://candacehilligoss.com/
http://www.caroljonesbooks.com/.
Chicago Review Press: https://www.chicagoreviewpress.com/; 814 North Franklin Street Chicago, Illinois 60610; (800) 888-4741.
Covenant Books: https://covenantbooks.com/; 800-452-3515.
Counterpoint Press: 2560 Ninth Street, Suite 318 Berkeley, CA 94710; https://www.counterpointpress.com/, 510-704-0230.
CreateSpace: www.createspace.com
https://davidctucker.blogspot.com/
https://www.davidnschecter.com/
https://www.deborahgracewiner.com/
Dey Street Books/HarperCollins: https://www.harpercollins.com/pages/deystreetbooks.
http://evegolden.com/
Farrar, Straus and Giroux: https://us.macmillan.com/
http://www.gregorymank.com/
Grove Press: https://groveatlantic.com/; 212-614-7850.
Hachette Australia https://www.hachette.com.au/.

HarperCollins: www.harperdesignbooks.com; 195 Broadway, New York, NY 10007; 212-207-7000.

Jacaranda https://www.jacarandabooksartmusic.co.uk/.

http://www.john-odowd.com/

https://leonardmaltin.com/

https://lesliezemeckis.com/

https://mayomethot.com/.

McFarland & Company: https://mcfarlandbooks.com/.

Midnight Marquee Press: http://www.midmar.com; 9721 Britinay Lane, Baltimore, MD 21234; 410-665-1198.

Murania Press: https://muraniapress.com.

New Texture: www.newtexture.com; NewTextureMail@gmail.com; http://www.menspulpmags.com/.

Northeastern University Press: https://www.hfsbooks.com/.

Penguin Books: https://www.penguin.com/.

Pinnacle Books, Kensington Publishing Corp.: https://www.kensingtonbooks.com/.

Running Press: https://www.hachettebookgroup.com/imprint/running-press/.

http://www.rutalee.com/

Schirmer Trade Books: https://www.musicarts.com/books-sheet-music-media?terms=BrandName:SCHIRMER%20TRADE.

Simon & Schuster: https://www.simonandschuster.com/.

https://stephenbourne.co.uk/

University Press of Kentucky: http://www.kentuckypress.com; Hopkins Fulfillment Service, PO Box 50370, Baltimore, MD 21211-4370; 800-537-5487 or 410-516-6956.

University Press of Mississippi: https://www.upress.state.ms.us/.

https://www.wrwilkerson.net/

Xlibris: https://www.xlibris.com/en/; 844-714-8691.

Made in United States
Orlando, FL
20 September 2024

51758271R00143